MW00884908

THE DECIBEL DOCTRINE

A TWENTY-YEAR COLLECTION OF ARTICLES

FINALLY! A Book that
Reveals WHY Church Music has
Become So Loud in the Sanctuary.

by David Clark

Decibel Doctrine

By: David Clark

ISBN: 9798833943625

Copyright © 2022 by David Clark

ALL RIGHTS RESERVED. No part of this publication may be reproduced or transmitted in any form or by any means, electronic or mechanical, including photocopying, recording, or by any information storage and retrieval system without prior permission of the author, with the exception of short quotes that are properly credited.

For Information, Contact:

Decibeldoctrine@gmail.com

Dedication

Dedicated to Elder Murray E. Burr, the man who taught me RIGHT and warned me against NOT-RIGHT. And prepared my heart for the war against the **Decibel Doctrine**.

Table of Contents

SECTION ONE

Principal Articles

Foreword

Twenty-First Century worship of the one true God has deserted, diverged, and departed, from worship that is Biblically certified/validated by the inspired Holy Scripture. The deceptively deadly **Decibel Doctrine** has chronically divorced some Christian religions from the worthiness intended in Biblical Worship.

The enemy-of-all-righteousness has consumed/devoured the insinuated worth of worship exemplified in Holy, God-inspired Scriptures, AND regurgitated an obnoxious substitute. The master-of-deception has somehow convinced us to offer the **Decibel Doctrine** and its fruit to our Creator as Worthy Worship.

This publication is not a typical book of chronological themes and chapters, but rather, it is a collection of individual articles. Articles describing the **Decibel Doctrine** and its fruit. Articles describing my personal experiences. Articles that convey other saints' experiences that were shared with me. Articles concerning Biblical worship and praise. And articles of allegories, parables, satire, and mockery.

The reader of this collection of articles will discover answers to the question most frequently asked by the sheep; **"Why is the music getting so loud in our church?"**

****

My life was blessed to have what many considered a spiritual giant for a Pastor. I have earnestly contended to keep his teachings and apply them to my life. While he was alive, I shared with him my desire to be a formidable enemy of *Not-Right* worship. While staring at me with those piercing black eyes that seemed to read the end from the beginning, his immediate response was approval, followed by a warning;

"Brother Clark, when I wrote *The Music of the Golden Calves*, I touched the raw nerve of hell itself."

On another occasion, I felt the weight of my Pastor's burden fall upon me as he asked me this very sobering question: "Bro. Clark, can you tell the real from the not real?" I still feel the gravity of that moment even today.

These face to face encounters with Pastor Murray E. Burr, allowed me to experience his no-nonsense mode that left no room for jesting.

When he wrote, his pen was a double-edged sword of truth. Men of renown and wisdom have described Elder Burr's pen as unable to "look the other way while church evils feed on silence and grow in secrecy." His pen fearlessly "unmasked the devices of the adversaries, whether they be in high places or low."

Elder Burr recognized that "many saints are destroyed for lack of knowledge," (Hosea 4:6) and his pen offered a remedy called Truth. All of his writings rested upon the foundation of this favored principle: "**When Truth No Longer Means Everything, Truth No Longer Means Anything.**"

Yet there were times of weakness in this old giant, and his pen would hesitate until the Lord would encourage him with **Jeremiah 1:17**:

Thou therefore gird up thy loins, and arise, and speak unto them all that I command thee: be not dismayed at their faces, lest I confound thee before them.

And his pen would re-ignite and begin to stroke as an unsheathed sword in the presence of an enemy.

Elder Burr privately spoke of thrice throwing to the floor his unfinished manuscript of *The Music of the Golden Calves*. Each time he told God: "If I write this, my peers will hate me, including my own grandson and family." And all three times God said, "How will they ever know?"

[I include the man Murray E. Burr in this Foreword because he is the one who spiritually molded me.]

A collective series under the title of *The Music of the Golden Calves* by Murray E. Burr is available on Amazon.com or **Decibel Doctrine**, P.O. Box 374; Hillister, Texas 77624. This reprint includes four articles authored by Murray E. Burr: *The Music of the Golden Calves, Serpent Seed Music, Satire in Slang*, and *Burial of a Prophet*.

I have made my feeble but honest effort to follow Elder Burr's pattern of exposing church evils that feed on the silencing of the sheep while growing in secrecy. But in part, I have failed a generation by waiting too long to write. The sickening reality of sin in high places of religion has caused me to flinch with nausea. I have flinched for over twenty years. Not in fear of man, but in guarded refrain, continually compiling facts and assuring this agenda to be called of God.

The only request that Pastor Burr asked of me concerning my writing and warnings against the **Decibel Doctrine**, was to "*not withhold my sword from blood.*" I am not sure that I have fulfilled that request. But I pray that I have said enough to help the innocent and unaware Christian, while exposing the intentionally deceptive pseudo-ministry.

In honor of Elder Murray E. Burr and all that he taught in Faith Tabernacle of Port Arthur, Texas.

David Clark

Decibel Doctrine Definitions

Decibel (n.) *Physics* - One tenth of a bel, the common unit of power ratio: a measure of sound intensity.

Bel (n.) *Physics* - A unit expressing the ratio of the values of two amounts of power, being the logarithm to the base 10 of their ratio: a measure of sound intensity. [after A. G. Bell]

Doctrine (dok'trin) (n.) 1. That which is presented for acceptance or belief; teachings, as of a religious or political group. 2. A particular principle or tenet that is taught, or a body of such principles or tenets.

Decibel Doctrine (des'e-bel, dok'trin) (n.)

1. A principle or tenet presented for acceptance or belief that relates and associates the power and intensity of God's presence, in a given place and time, as equivalent to the power and intensity of sound produced by electronic technology in that same place and time.

2. The belief that intense volumes of music, facilitated by electronic technology that evolved in late 20th century physics, attracts the presence of God, orchestrating the power of God falling, with favor and demonstration, upon any human subjected to the intense sound volumes of music.

3. A practice that affirms the power of volume in a church setting to be of God; employing that related power of extreme decibels of music to instigate worship of God, and propagate praise of God, and even facilitate repentance unto God, in that particular church setting.

4. The belief attributing the physiological effect of extreme decibels of music upon the human body in a church setting, to be the approval and the touch of God Himself upon that individual human.

5. The belief that extreme decibels of music in a church setting will help save the eternal soul of young people who are subjected to the extreme decibels of music in that same church setting.

6. A teaching and belief that the physiological response of the human body to extreme volumes of music and beat is Biblical worship.

7. The teaching and belief that the power of the volume of music and the intensity of the beat in a church setting, pleases the God of creation and can ignite the soul of the church body to "come alive and have church."

Disciple (di-si'pal) (n.) One who accepts and follows a teacher or a doctrine.

Decibel Disciple (des'e-bel, di-si'pal) (n.) 1. One who has sit at the feet of a teacher of the Decibel Doctrine and received teaching concerning the functional specifics of the Decibel Doctrine.

2. One who is indoctrinated to believe that the core beliefs within the Decibel Doctrine are Biblical and that the Decibel Doctrine is a viable alternative for Christian worship.

3. One who practices, propagates, embraces, follows, adheres to, has faith in, and trusts in… the principal tenets and foundational ideology of the Decibel Doctrine.

Introduction

The Decibel Doctrine

A Collection of Articles

It was 1995, and all was going well. I was blessed with the best wife and daughter, Theresa and Bridgette, in the whole world. And I attended the best church in the whole world. I loved my family, I loved my church, and I loved my Pastor. I just loved life. I was the "Happy Camper," enjoying that more abundant life that only God can give.

God had miraculously blessed me with a beautiful house and acreage that bordered the marsh just south of Bridge City, Texas. A peaceful pond at the back of the property was complemented with a picnic table which we and friends used often. Our picnics at the pond were shared with wood ducks, a beautiful grey and black Brahma bull, and an alligator named Fred. Fred loved picnic scraps and anything else that was edible. If Fred did not show up for the picnic, we would stand on the bank of the pond and yell his name "Fred." Soon Fred would swim out of the marsh and across the pond to glean picnic leftovers.

In 1995, I had been self-employed for six years, enjoying the blessings of God. I had the very best of families, both the blood kin and the church family. And.., the best of duck hunting (which I often joke as being the love of my life) in Johnson Bayou, Louisiana. 1995 was a landmark year in my life. Every day was a happy day.

This was the year that my Pastor, Murray E. Burr, retired from his forty-two-year pastorate of Faith Tabernacle, in Port Arthur, Texas. I was completely unaware of the devastating change about to take place in every facet of my life. Little did I know that life would soon lose its luster, and I would engage in a battle for my very own soul. New Pastoral leadership, new paths, a new doctrine of "worship," and much more; wrought Spiritual carnage to the core beliefs that had always supported my Biblical foundation. My happy days waned away.

The love of life became a vague memory. The zeal of the business that God afforded me began to dissipate. I dropped the duck lease that I had hunted for 23 years. The sparkle that had left my eyes was noticed and questioned by many friends and acquaintances. Above all, the joy of attending church was wrested from me. Instead of a day of rest, peace, and joy, Sundays became a dreaded day. Twice on Sunday a man had to "face the music," literally. The new paths of "worship" replaced the Word of God, especially on Sunday nights which became referred to from the pulpit as "Jubilee" nights. It all began in 1995, when the man of God in my life was substituted with a **Decibel Disciple,** and I was abruptly introduced to the **Decibel Doctrine**.

Now I am fully aware that very few of my readers will have even heard of Port Arthur, Texas. Most readers of this collection of articles will have never known of my Pastor Murray E. Burr, nor ever known of my home church, Faith Tabernacle. But many readers will understand what it means to have a Pastor in whom you trust and a church that you love. I use real names of people and places in this collection of articles because these people and places are real; and real names are often used to protect the innocent.

Most every Christian church-attender of today will already be somewhat familiar with the **Decibel Doctrine** in some form or fashion. The practice of using extreme volumes of music and audio for special effects has become more and more prevalent through the years in church settings. Many Christians in America will have by now tasted of its intoxicating wine, some to favor and some to disfavor; giving no thought to assign a name to identify this new path. Yet every wine has a date and a name and a manufacturer. And every wine is intoxicating; dulling the senses of reality.

The beginning date of this repugnant practice has to be within the twentieth century, since man's technology that enables this New Age practice is fairly new to the world; *and to God.* When the effect of the special effects created by extreme decibels of music is promoted as of God, for God, from God, by God, or even Biblical, it becomes a doctrine. The name of this intoxicating wine is The **Decibel Doctrine**. Its date is "New Age." The manufacturer of this New Age intoxicating wine called the **Decibel Doctrine** is a beautiful creation of God named Lucifer, a fallen angel, who delights in deceiving nations.

A long time before medical advancement discovered the physiological and psychological effects of extreme volumes of music upon the human body, simple men were witnessing these visible manifestations in dance halls, bars, and rock concerts. Advanced science has since then proven *Why* the effects manifest, but a carnally minded ministry cares not *Why*. They just care that "it works."

Worldly users of extreme decibels of music know that it will work wherever humans are gathered, even within church assemblies. And the desired results, the desired effect, is ecstatic emotional motion of the human body. When extreme volumes of music are used in church settings for desired effect (often physical commotion), it is the practice of the **Decibel Doctrine**. The **Decibel Doctrine** is very popular today because "it works," in fact, **it works like magic.**

The charismatic church world has been very excited about the **Decibel Doctrine** for years, and the denominational church world is currently discovering that "it works."

Many of today's denominational churches are having two worship services; one is called "Traditional Worship" and the other is referred to as "Contemporary Worship." In these "Contemporary Worship" services, the music is thunderous and at such electronic volumes that the human body is overwhelmed with awe and the produced adrenaline is invigorating and often uncontrollable. The "Contemporary Worship" is designed to appeal to the carnality of youth, and they have discovered that "it works."

The denominational church world got this practice from the Charismatics; the Charismatics got it from the Pentecostals, and we Pentecostals got it from the world of Rock-N-Roll.

Most of the Pentecostal Churches in my circle of fellowship now have only one type of worship service. And sadly, as documented by current History, the footsteps of the **Decibel Doctrine** have led Pentecostal "worship" to bypass Traditional Worship (Biblical Worship) and consolidate all "worship" into one and only one "worship" service. And that is the worldly popular Contemporary Worship.

Today, a Biblical Worship service where the music is not thunderous and the praises of redeemed voices can be heard over the music is considered: Dead Dead – Dead!

The **Decibel Doctrine** produces New-Age cutting-edge man-made "worship" in the sanctuary.

And it is as loud as money can buy…. And…, "it works." So-they-say.

As the author of this collection of articles, I want all to know that my pen mocks and deeply exposes the practice of the **Decibel Doctrine** among the Pentecostals. The reasonable reason being that I am Pentecostal and my experiences come from my small world as I have lived among the Pentecostal Church culture.

I am Pentecostal – meaning I have received the same Holy Ghost as described in the Bible in the second chapter of Acts on the Day of Pentecost. I am Apostolic because I obey the teachings of the Apostles – such as repentance, water baptism in the name of Jesus, and clean living to the best of my ability. So, when my pen says SHAME-SHAME-SHAME; I am speaking to my own among whom I live.

I am blessed with much fellowship with Pentecostal Pastors. I have found the best of the best of clean-living Christians among the Pentecostal ranks. Yet, I must needs follow my calling and speak truth with my pen without fear or favor.

My heartbeat is to avoid *fruitless offense* of those whom I love; I cannot be dismayed at their faces.

We Pentecostals practice water baptism as taught in the Bible. We receive the Holy Ghost just as taught in the Bible. We live and teach the Apostles Doctrine referred to in Acts 2:42 as taught in the Bible.

For the sake of the Living God our Creator; WHY can't we honor and practice Worship as taught in the Bible?

GOD HELP US ALL.

David Clark

The Intended Audience

As I write, there is an *intended audience* that I hope to reach. That audience is the church member, or potential church member, who is still confused as to why music has become so loud in church settings. If you find yourself questioning the purpose of the intense volumes of music that has pervaded the 21st Century Church world, you are the *intended audience* of my efforts in writing this collection of articles titled: **The Decibel Doctrine**.

If you have questioned "why is the music getting so loud in our Church Sanctuary?", and the answer that you received from the pastor or the sound-man had a hollow ring to it, and the credibility of that answer seems to do injustice to average common sense; you are my *intended audience*. Or if you diagnose the entire loud-music-scenario-in-the-Sanctuary as asinine, then you are the purpose of my labor in writing. If you are the timid type that avoids confrontational issues and avoids being falsely labeled as a "trouble maker," yet you cannot escape the reality that the practice of the **Decibel Doctrine** is quackery enjoyed by the quirky, then you are the audience that compels me to expose this spirit by writing.

If you even remotely suspect that the new trends of rock-concert volumes of music in the Sanctuary are diametrically diverse from Biblical principles and all sane reasoning, then you are the *intended audience* that I want to reach for and help.

If the pulpit before which you assemble is used to discredit your spirituality, belittle your dedication to God, embarrass you, or intimidate you because you cannot grasp the spiritual value of extreme volumes of music in the Sanctuary, then the revealing and exposure of man-made "worship" within this collection of articles titled **The Decibel Doctrine** will educate you.

But on the other hand, if you have embraced the empty promises and carnal fruit of **The Decibel Doctrine** as the demonstrated power of God, this collection of articles titled **The Decibel Doctrine** cannot help you.

Your decision is without remedy.

David Clark
7-19-17

The Decibel Doctrine Question
The Number One Complaint Among Church Members

There is a question repeatedly asked in today's Christian Church culture. This question has lived in the minds of untold numbers of Christians for a long time. In fact, this question stems from the most common complaint in churches today.

[Search any internet website or forum – "The Number One Complaint in Churches"]

Some ask this subject question among their friends. Some ask behind closed doors. And some silently ask over and over in the recesses of their own mind. But all are puzzled, all are perplexed, and all want to know the answer to this viral question that seems to have no logical reasoning for even existing.

THE MOST FREQUENTLY ASKED QUESTION IN CHURCHES

WHY HAS THE MUSIC VOLUME BECOME SO LOUD IN MY CHURCH??

This question is answered verbosely, inside and out, in this Collection of Articles

Question: Why is the volume of the music getting so loud in my church? Loud enough to damage my family's ears. Loud enough that my head and chest feel the beat. So loud that I can no longer sing the songs of Zion. So loud that I struggle to talk to my God in the Sanctuary. So loud that I leave church with a headache. So loud that I am embarrassed to bring visitors So loud that I don't want my grandchildren exposed to such ear-damaging volumes.

Answer: This easy answer in country-boy vernacular is "a no-brainer." The reason the music is so loud in your church is because your Pastor likes it loud because he is a Decibel Disciple. He understands the awe and magic that loud music and thumping beats usher into the Sanctuary.

As proven over and over in this collection of articles;
practice of the **Decibel Doctrine -**
CREATES AND PROMOTES EPIC DECEPTION.

There are God-made things, and there are Man-made things.

The **Decibel Doctrine** is not a God-made thing.

And trust me and my experiences; there is nothing that you as a Saint can do about it.

The delusion is much too dark.

David Clark
7-17-2017

Natural Response of Sincere Christians to the Decibel Doctrine

Pictured, is the natural reaction of sincere people as they experience the **Decibel Doctrine** for the first time. The Decibel Disciple will teach the people that what they feel is the power of God. The simple and shallow will be impressed at such "supernatural" power.

The majority will walk away wagging their heads in disdain. Then the Decibel Disciple will preach to the simple and shallow;

> *Make a joyful noise unto the LORD, all the earth:*
> *make a loud noise, and rejoice, and sing praise.*
> **Psalm 98:4**

The Decibel Disciple will convince the simple and shallow that the psalmist was referring to 21st Century technology and electronic sound systems.

The simple and shallow will continue to be impressed with such pseudo power, while the majority continue seeking the real.

The hand-over-ears is a sign that follows a crowd of people blessed with an IQ of at least average or mediocre, accompanied with a small handful of God-given common sense, as they are introduced to the power of a Decibel Disciple's god.

Can you imagine convincing intelligent people that the power of the sound system is the power of the One True God? Plainly, as evident in the 21st Century, this requires spiritual assistance. Assistance in deception from the Dark Side. From the Master of Deception.

David Clark
8-27-17

Intimidation Cartoon

This is one of the many intimidation efforts devised by the New-Age Christian to hopefully shut the mouths of non-believers. (Non-Believers of the **Decibel Doctrine**)

I confess – I am old. Old in years, Old in Wisdom, Old in Doctrine established in Old Scriptures. And I still ask for the Old Paths written and inspired by an Ancient God, long ago. Yes, hopefully, my ways are even older than I am.

In Fact, my God that I serve is referred to as the Ancient of Days. So maybe I am also Antique in my walk with an Ancient God.

And, as indicated by this cartoon, the **Decibel Doctrine** is a **New Thang**, offered as **New Worship**, to a **New God**.

I hope that in my Old Ways, I can please my Ancient God and make it to Heaven, where the Old Ways of Biblical Worship exist forever and forever and never grow old.

David Clark
Old Non-Believer of the **Young and New Decibel Doctrine.**

A Professional Diagnosis of the Decibel Doctrine

Of all the signs of *Not Right* worship that continue to find me, my introduction to Doctor Don Hodges has been the most intriguing. Doctor Hodges is the director of the Institute for Music Research of the University of Texas. The following excerpts are from one of the Institute's many studies of the effects of music upon the human brain.

Their studies show "music has profound effects on the brain." "*Music is proven to increase the activity of the brain.*" "*The only part of the brain that didn't record increased activity was the frontal lobe, which controls reasoning. There was actually less activity when performing (music) than there was while doing nothing.*"

In plain vernacular, sound waves in the form of music enter the brain in the form of vibrations via the ear. These vibrations decrease the activity of reasoning in the brain. The words of Elder M.E. Burr, as a formidable enemy of the "Spirit of Serpent Seed Music," make more sense now: "Mindlessly reacting to the volume and beat of the music, with the brain turned off." And; "Mindlessly taking orders from the drum beat."

God revealed to Elder Burr what extensive physiological studies revealed to Doctor Hodges; the increased activity of the brain resulting from excessive vibrations of music is shy on reasoning. Decibel Disciples take advantage of this fact and increase the volume of music to a level that most of the brain tells the body; "get crazy and wild for Jesus," overriding the frontal lobe that controls reasoning.

While explaining the **Decibel Doctrine** in conversation with Doctor Hodges, I was surprised to find out that he was familiar with the doctrine. His denominal church Pastor believes like many of my Pastor friends, that the volume of music will bring in the youth as well as "keep" them. It would be interesting to know who was deceived first; did the denominal church world receive the **Decibel Doctrine** from us Pentecostals or vice versa?

Because of the ear-splitting decibels of music necessary to draw and "keep" youth, the church attended by Doctor Hodges now divides their worship services. The youth "worship" in a room power-packed with extreme decibels of music. The mature members worship in the sanctuary, presuming that God is not impressed with electronic volumes.

When I questioned the physiology that drives this trend of ever-increasing decibels of music, Doctor Hodges compared it to drug addiction. He explained that "**the rush caused by extreme decibels of music establishes a dependency**

that can only be satisfied by a little more volume."

Insatiable thirst for adrenalin; catered to and enabled by church leaders that say "give the youth what their flesh wants." Insatiable desire of the flesh for rock-volume music is the moral of the banner: "GIVE ME MORE VOLUME OR GIVE ME DEATH."

It is easy to understand why Pastors cheerlead from the pulpit with thumbs up to the sound-man.

The relentless TRUTH is that Adam and Eve were created for God's pleasure. And until sin entered the picture, they did accomplish the purpose of their creation, without manmade paraphernalia.

Decibel Disciples have perverted Biblical worship; but they say, "NAY, we are True Worshippers." They have perverted a precious pleasure that belongs to God, but, "Nay," they say, "we are God-Pleasers."

It is inevitable that they face TRUTH one day. The Hound Dog Tenacity of Truth will bay them.

It is their destiny.

But until then I say, "Poor God!"

David Clark

Scientific Intellectual Studies and Research on Loud Music

At the end of the absolutes documented in this article question yourself again; is the **Decibel Doctrine** a godly practice that has scriptural permission to dominate the Sanctuary???

Are the demands and agenda of a Decibel Disciple forced upon Saints in a church assembly God-ordained???

Are the physical demonstrations demanded by extreme decibels of music God-pleasing???

Do those demonstrations even remotely reflect Biblical Worship???

Suppose the reader thinks: "very interesting, but so what?"

The following absolutes are forever established many-times-over by science, but "So What?"

I agree, until we know that Decibel Disciples use these absolutes for special effects in religion to lead sincere Christians to pasture where they themselves feed on foreign fodder. When a Decibel Disciple convinces Christians that the science-proven special effects of loud music are the true power of God, then I cannot allow myself to say, "So What?"

Most unfortunately, the **Decibel Doctrine** is very attractive to the flesh

Spiritually enabled, the **Decibel Doctrine** is dangerously persuasive and consumingly convincing and overwhelmingly powerful - to the flesh.

It is a very present power that requires no faith to embrace, for it is physically tangible.

Sadly, these absolutes diagnose the **Decibel Doctrine** as a carrier of the invisible Death-Seal of Deception.

David Clark

****

These selected excerpts of factual truths are included in their original form as study notes.

The following excerpts of Science and Research are Public Domain and are easily accessible.

****

Excerpts of Absolute Facts

Discovered – Identified - Summarized

Unlike vision, which has *voluntary control* to select what is being seen, hearing is tightly coupled to our sense of the environment *without control*.

Advertisers who present messages before movies know that loudness sells because you cannot focus on any other sonic event. You cannot escape physically or perceptually. They own your aural space, and they know it. (It is obvious to us all that the advertisements within any program are amplified to demand attention. Loud attracts, and Loud sells.)

An aural space with loud music is often experienced as "exciting" because *loudness represents intense activity*. Because sound is always associated with a dynamic event that requires energy, loud music is equivalent to intense energy.

In our pre-electronic world, creating a loud sound always required intense physical exertion. Loud drums require violent pounding. We respond to the implied physicality of loudness, even though electronic amplification only mimics physical exertion. From an evolutionary perspective, we still respond to loudness as if it represented a big event that was relevant to our survival. Loudness gets our attention. That is why advertisements are purposely louder than the program into which they are added. (Any listener to radio can attest to this absolute.)

Raising the loudness of music, like a double shot of whisky, elevates the intensity of the experience. Background music at 40 dB is very different from a pounding rhythm at 120 dB. Listeners respond differently. Loud music can enhance neurological attentiveness, which psychologists call arousal.

While much of the evidence is inferential and speculative, there is no question that loud music is complex stimuli that, under certain conditions, can significantly change the mind/body state. Neurobiologists are only now beginning to understand the complexity of our brain. Music interacts with brain substrates that are associated with rewards and emotions, (Levitin, 2006).

Music is a stimulant, like caffeine, sugar, alcohol, anger, vigorous exercise, sexual activity, and many others. **Loud music is simply a stronger stimulant.**

Fast and loud music has been shown to enhance exercise on a treadmill without changing the perceived effort, (Edworthy and Waring, 2006). Musicians exposed to loud music report intestinal distress, (Rapid, 1990) Loud music has been shown to extend the influence of the drug ecstasy in rats, (Iannone et al., 2006).

Loud music has also been implicated in: psychological disorientation, inability to focus on other tasks, increased heart rate, decreased vascular blood flow, increases in the body's core temperature, and distress in the immune system.

In one study, researchers found that loud music activated those brain regions that are associated with euphoria drugs, such as cocaine.

There is evidence that music elevates endorphins connected with pleasure centers in the brain.

Conversely, there is some evidence that when a person is exposed to high level sound, the brain contains chemicals that are also found in patients diagnosed with schizophrenia

Studies suggest that there is an increase in alcohol consumption in environments with loud music, (van de Goor, 1990). Perhaps because loud music overpowers the senses and cognitive judgments, people at parties often overeat.

In another study, some students who consistently listened to loud music exhibited maladaptive behavioral patterns consistent with substance abuse, (Florentine et al, 1998).

The American Academy of Pediatrics warns that loud music overstimulates children with attention deficit disorder.

Music has been around since recorded history just because it has such a strong influence on human mood and behavior. Religious and political leaders have used loud music to **stimulate strong emotions and to suppress rational thinking.**

The military uses marching bands, and the old Roman armies used mechanical noisemakers to stir passions and to frighten the enemy. In order to demoralize and disable their targets, the US used highly amplified music in the siege of Manuel Noriega at the Vatican Embassy in Panama, and at the siege of the Branch Davidian compound in Waco. Loud sound has been an effective weapon of torture.

As N'omi Orr once stated, "Military drums play music designed to make your feet take you where your head never would. Music is almost as dangerous as gunpowder." If we look at history, as far back as organized warfare can be seen, there have been attempts to engage soldiers into battle by beating drums first slowly (consistent with heart beat) and then more quickly as troops enter battle.

This protective old brain (neo cortex) response (survival response) causes the blood pressure to increase and heart to beat faster so blood (oxygen) can be pumped to the muscles to fight off the perceived saber-tooth tiger. The blood thickens so that if scratched or bitten in the battle, you won't bleed to death (cholesterol increases since it is a thickening agent to stop bleeding), we experience hyper brain wave activity to be more vigilant, the palms of our hands get sticky so we can hold the club to beat off the beast, and the bottoms of our feet get sticky, as well, so we can get traction to run away and escape the attack.

But today we aren't fighting a saber-tooth tiger; we are merely listening to loud music (the old brain only reacts to protect the body to survive). If we aren't physically fighting or fleeing, then what happens to our body when all of this physiology is occurring and we are sitting inside a car, or a concert, or a sanctuary? What is happening, to varying degrees, is that the body is responding in a way that may be averse to your physical health.

****

As the author of this collection of articles titled *The Decibel Doctrine*, I add my non-professional summation of these professional studies and research for the reader. When that physiological response discovered and documented by **Scientific Intellectual Studies and Research** is called "of God," then it is averse to your spiritual health. Making therefore, the **Decibel Doctrine** absolutely adverse to your spiritual wellbeing.

****

References

Branco, C., & Rodriguez E. (1999). The vibroacoustic disease-an emerging pathology. Aviation, Space, And Environmental Medicine; 70(3,Suppl.):A1-6. Alexandria, VA.

Buckley, J. P., & Smookler, H. H. (1970). Cardiovascular and biochemical effects of chronic intermittent neurogenic stimulation. In B. Welch & A. Welch, (eds.). Physiological Effects of Noise (pp. 67-82). New York: Plenum Press.

Cantrell, R. (1974). Prolonged exposure to intermittent noise: Audiometric, biochemical, motor, psychological and sleep effects. Laryngoscope, 84. 4-55. Fearn, R. (1972). Noise levels in youth clubs (correspondence). Journal of Sound and Vibration, 22, 127-1228.

Fearn, R. (1973). Pop-music and hearing damage. Journal of Sound and Vibration, 29, 396-397.

Glasser, W. (1976). Positive Addiction. New York: Harper & Row.

Glasser, W. (1996). Programs, policies, and procedures of the William Glasser Institute, California.

Jenny, H. (1974). Cymatics. Switzerland; Basilius Presse AG. Basel.

Medoff, H. S. & Bongiovanni, A. M. (1945). Blood pressure in rats subjected to audiogenic stimulation. American Journal of Physiology, 143, 300-305.

Orr, J. (1996). Rythm and intimacy in VR. Internet communication, based on article originally published in Computer Graphic World.

Peterson, E. A., Augenstein, J. S., Tanis, D. C., & Augenstein, D. C. (1981). Noise raises blood pressure without impairing auditory sensitivity. Science, 211, 1450-1452.

Racer, Paul (Nov. 17, 1996). Stress Puts Women At Risk, Study Says. The San Diego Union-Tribune, A-37.

Weightman, Cody D. 1996. Personal interview, San Diego, California, 2 December.

Professional Research / Power of Rhythm and Volume

This article is an abbreviated compilation of the research of professionals. The documentation of studies involving the effect of rhythm and volume upon the human body is vast and unlimited. These documentations are proven absolutes. They are not opinions.

These factually proven absolutes were found in Public Domain within websites easily accessible.

****

The Power of Volume

The science of physics explains volume as nothing more than an invisible source of energy, air pressure or air movement. But the effect of volume upon humans goes beyond the science of physics.

When music is too loud, it blocks out our other senses, and we lose touch with reality. Our thinking and actions are changed, and under a prolonged exposure to loud music, a moral apathy pervades.

Consider the following three types of damage that takes place in our bodies under exposure to loud volume.

First, loud volume slows down our ability to memorize and do other brain functions by constricting the flow of blood to the brain. In the words of Dr. Arnold Scheivel, professor of medicine at UCLA and an expert on brain growth, "If there is a bottom line, it is that no neuron is healthier than the capillary that supplies it. We have a very strong feeling that in the capillary supply system is the story of the maintenance or slow decline of the brain."

How does volume affect blood supply? The blood vessels undergo a narrowing of caliber in the presence of loud sound. This narrowing decreases the flow of blood to the different parts of the body, including the mind. A person studying under the influence of loud music has a decrease in the amount of blood flowing to the brain. This makes it more difficult to memorize and to understand their studies.

Second, loud music can cause a form of schizophrenia. When a person is exposed to high level sound, a chemical is formed in the brain that is normally found in schizophrenia patients in mental institutions. A music therapist, investigating the effects of loud music, gave an emotional stability test to 240 teenagers while they listened to music. A psychologist, who was unaware of how it was given, examined the results and determined that the test had been given in a mental institution.

Martin Polo, the director of Audio Visual Services at UCLA and noise consultant for the aerospace industry and related technologies writes,

> "Lastly, the presence of continued exposure to high level sound can trigger psychopathological impacts on individuals....These impacts can range from depressions noted among females during the menstrual period to actual presence in the brain of chemicals normally found in schizophrenia and psychosis. There are a number of other interesting reactions to the presence of high-level sound which involve the brain, including interference with vision."

Third, loud music can cause ulcers. When susceptible individuals are exposed to loud sound over a period of time, certain stomach functions are disrupted, and an increase of hydrochloric acid is released, causing ulceration of the stomach.

Martin Polo of UCLA writes,

> "The continuing exposure to high energy sound creates a stress reaction in the body that significantly involves the gastrointestinal system. Certain stomach functions are disrupted by abnormal contractions of the abdominal area, and increased infusion of hydrochloric acid causing dyspepsia. Recurring activation of this syndrome will lead to peptic ulceration in susceptible individuals."

The Power of Rhythm

Rhythm is a patterned measure of time. We sense it in music as stressed and unstressed beats in a pattern that repeats itself over and over again. This pattern of stressed and unstressed beats is used to either enhance or thwart the way we perceive things. Rhythm is also the glue that holds our very lives together. All of our systems, from the smallest to the largest, work under the influence of rhythm. Rhythm plays an important role in the ability of our mind to organize billions of electrical impulses into clear, understandable mental pictures. When there is movement of any kind or size, microscopic or gigantic, rhythm controls that movement. When you change the rhythm of a movement, you can also change the outcome of the movement. Rhythm then controls the way the message is sent along the neurological system, thereby controlling the way it is perceived. This means that rhythm can change our mental pictures or our perception of reality. A closer look at the way a message travels in the body will help us understand the use of rhythm.

Communication within the body is electrochemical. For example, when the ear picks up sound waves, it changes them to electrical impulses or messages. These electrical impulses then move from the neurons (in the ear) along an axon to a dendrite or dendrite spine to a synapse. This impulse or message crosses over the space to the synapse by a chemical movement to the next dendrite and continues moving electrically to the next neuron. This process is repeated over and over along the neurological system until the message reaches its destination. This process is repeated billions of times throughout our body in every minute of the day. The very fact that impulses move, places them under the control of rhythm. Research is beginning to show that this is the case.

On pages 90, and 131, of his book, Battle for the Mind, Dr. William Sargent, a leading scientific authority on the human nervous system, writes,

> "Electrical recordings of the human brain show that it is particularly sensitive to the rhythmic stimulation by percussion and bright light among other things, and certain rates of rhythm can build up recordable abnormalities of brain function and explosive states of tension sufficient enough to produce convulsive fits in predisposed subjects. Of the results caused by such disturbances, the most common one is temporarily impaired judgement and heightened suggestibility."

When the mind and body are subjected to rhythms that abide outside the law and are not in harmony with the body's natural rhythm, the mental picture is altered or not clear. The body is put under stress, and problems begin to appear.

Rhythm-induced stress shows up in many ways, including decreased performance, hyperactivity, increased errors in the work force, decreased decision-making ability, emotional pressures, depression, and lack of respect for authority. One doctor said, "In my practice, I have found that the academic records of many small children improve considerably after they stop listening to rock music while studying."

Unnatural rhythms, like many drugs, can become addictive. Repeated exposure to it causes one to seek it. It is as if a switch is thrown in the mind. After this switching takes place, the body begins to crave this unnatural beat or rhythm over a natural one.

It is as if the body can no longer distinguish between what is beneficial and what is harmful. In fact, the body actually chooses that which is destructive over that which is constructive.

Consider the following statements:

In Vancouver, during a 30-minute Beatles performance, 100 people were stomped upon, gouged and assaulted. (Satan's Music Exposed, L. Hart)

In Melbourne, nearly 1000 were injured at a rock concert. (Satan's Music Exposed, L. Hart)

"Our music is capable of causing emotional instability, disorganized behavior, rebellion and even revolution." (Beatles, 1960)

Here is what a person who attended a rock concert said, "After an hour or so, even I felt drugged. But 20,000 people, most of them high on marijuana, if nothing stronger, were rocking the whole building, swaying, standing on their seats, arms around each other…the crowd seemed hypnotized in thrall. It was part of a mass frenzy." (Readers Digest, July 1973, pg. 173.)

A popular rock singer said this about their music. "Rock n roll has always been sexual. Rock n roll has always been violent. It has teeth. It will scratch your face off. That's why I like it…..if you like having your brains blown out and pushed up against a wall, then it's for you." (Entertainment Tonight, January 9, 1982)

In "*Rock From the Beginning*," a 1969 book by Nik Cohn, Mick Jagger, lead singer for the Rolling Stones, described the heavy emphasis on rhythm in his group's music, saying,

> "It was nothing but beat, smashed and crunched and hammered like some amazing stampede. The words were lost, and the song was lost. You were only left with the chaos, beautiful anarchy. You drowned in noise. The sound destroyed you, raped you regardless, and you had no defense left."

"There must be a condition of harmony or perfect balance," wrote Boston psychologist Dr. James Girard in "*The Wanderer*," "between the mental, emotional, and physical operations of the organism if it is to function properly. It is precisely at this point that rock and roll, and much modern music, becomes potentially dangerous. This is because, to maintain a sense of well-being and integration, it is essential that man is not subjected too much to any rhythms not in accord with his natural body rhythms."

It would be impractical to explain through written word the difference between natural and unnatural rhythms. However, unnatural rhythms are almost always accompanied by other elements that are easily recognized. Following are some of the elements that accompany unnatural rhythms.

Lyrics: They promote drugs, sex, crime, and rebellion.

Style: The delivery of the singer or group is offensive to anyone who seeks a clean and fulfilling life. Their sound is **very heavy on the bass**, with a throbbing heavy beat. The vocals include **yelling**, and other primitive sounds. The "Music" is **repetitive**, using the **same chords over and over.**

Visual effects: The attire of the performers is trashy, scanty, or excessive in the style of costume. The performance is geared to grasp your senses and create a high, both physically and emotionally.

Body movement: The movement is vulgar and suggestive and **constant motion**.

Music video: The settings for the performers are often in back alleys, junk yards, abandoned buildings, or in places where **only the physical senses are excited**. Stages with **special effects lighting** is a favorite.

****

As the author of the collection of articles titled **The Decibel Doctrine**, I want to remind the reader; Rock n Roll music is simply a combination of volume and beat, with or without words. The effects of excessive volume and aggressive beat are the same; with or without words.

The effects of Rock n Roll music upon a human being are herein documented. These absolutes concerning rhythm hold true in Rock concert halls, in Rock rallies in the park, or in Christian-Rock-Worship services. Christian words do not exist that can be comingled with gospel-rock music to circumvent the undesirable effects on the human body as documented in these studies. All of these signs are manifested in our New-Age Pentecostal Churches. And we call it "worship" and offer it unto the one true God to show His Worth.

I beg of the sane; is it any wonder that I and other ministers of the Gospel are willing to pay the price of teaching and writing against the **Decibel Doctrine**??

David Clark

Bibliography

Bloom, A., *The Closing of the American MIND,"* New York: Simon & Schuster, 1987.

De Azevedo, Lex., *Pop Music and Morality*, California: Embryo Books, 1982.

Diamond, John M.D. *Behavioral Kinesiology*, New York: Harper & Row, 1979.

Hart, L., *Satan's Music Exposed*, Penn. Salem Kirban, Inc.1981.

Hutchinson, M., *Mega Brain*, New York: Ballantine Books, 1987.

Methvin, E., *The Riot Makers*, New York: Arlington House, 1970.

Oliphant, Bob., *Music and its Effects*, Essay, Professor at Ricks College: Rexburg, Idaho.

Restak, Richard M.D., *The Brain*, New York: Bantam Books, 1984.

Music Arousal and Torture

Subject excerpts from Professionally Proven Music Studies

Please note the fact that the following excerpts from scientific research are referring to the music volume and beat; with or without words.

Excerpt - *But in music, responses of the balance system affect musical arousal. The processing of sound information below the cortex greatly influences muscular and autonomic activity and allows a subconscious effect of wanting to "move to the beat." This unconscious powerful effect has been used to help Parkinson's patients improve walking with a beat.*

Excerpt – *Music can be used to torture a human being. Music, that is hopefully offensive to the victims and usually played very loudly, has been used as an assault technique (as used in Waco, Texas), and as an "enhanced interrogation technique," (see Guantanamo Bay). In "The Men Who Stare at Goats" by Jon Ronson, it is suggested that playing music as torture was either a test of subliminal effects of music on the victims, or, possibly more sinisterly, as a light-hearted anecdote to desensitize the population to the regular use of torture on terrorist subjects.*

After the U.S. invasion of Panama, the target of the invasion, strongman Manuel Noriega, sought asylum in the Vatican diplomatic mission represented by Monsignor Jose S. Laboa. To induce Noriega's surrender, U.S. forces played loud music outside the embassy[4] by cranking up the rock & roll from the armed forces' Southern Command Network radio station (which took requests and played such things as Van Halen's "Hang Em High" and Iron Maiden's "Run to the Hills"), and sometimes switching to shortwave station KUSW out of Salt Lake City for a change of pace.

My opinion – If they would have played the favorite Sunday night song of New Age Pentecostals: "I'm gonna dance, dance, dance, dance-dance-dance-dance, all night…….. all night…. all night," Noriega would have surrendered sooner. Especially if the volume and beat could have been made equal to a 21st Century special-effects-Sunday-night American church service.

It is torture to normal people…., but to Decibel Disciples, it is the sweet presence of their god.

On February 29th,1993, Loud "music," so-called by the world, was forced upon the compound of David Koresh and his followers in Waco, Texas to force the surrender of the occupants. Apparently, this torture was not sufficient, and more aggressive measures were employed.

<u>My opinion</u> - If the ATF would have known about the Decibel Disciple who introduced me and my family to the **Decibel Doctrine** in Port Arthur, Texas, in 1995, they would have hired him and his disciples to "have church" with their sound system in the front yard of the Davidian compound. Surely, the surrender of David Koresh and his followers would have been quick and complete, without the violent shedding of blood. A-N-D to put "icing on the cake," maybe the faith that Decibel Disciples have in their sound systems could have brought salvation to the whole bunch.

David Clark

Ask Marilyn

Marilyn vos Savant

Marilyn vos Savant (/ˌvɒs səˈvɑːnt/; born **Marilyn** Mach; 1946) is an American magazine columnist, author, lecturer, and playwright. **She was listed as having the highest recorded intelligence quotient (IQ) in the Guinness Book of Records**, a competitive category the publication has since retired.

Marilyn vos Savant wrote as a columnist in the periodical *Parade*. Her column was known as <u>Ask **Marilyn.**</u> In her column, she responded to questions on all subjects. Below is an article that she authored when responding to a written question on March 5, 2006.

****

<u>Article Title</u>: **Loud Music at Concerts Affects More Than Our Hearing**

<u>The Public question</u>: "Why do entertainers play their music at such high volume in concerts? I've been blown out of buildings by the noise."

The answer of an extremely intelligent person: "They're trying to generate excitement, and a high level of decibels accomplishes their goal. Subjected to such intense sound, listeners' bodies produce adrenaline, noradrenaline and more. These substances make the heart pound and give an impression of increased muscle strength. Not surprisingly, some people become psychologically addicted to this hormone rush, which is implicated in thrill-seeking behavior. What a way to get – and keep – fans."

****

Marilyn vos Savant understood how loud music affected humans long before man began to practice the same special-effects in Christian churches in the form of the **Decibel Doctrine**.

Most of the 21st Century Decibel Disciples that I know don't have record-breaking IQ's. BUT they do have an inside track from the prince of the air. They do receive insider information from the one they serve with their sound system.

Decibel Disciples just know. They know that IT WORKS.

In a Church Sanctuary where Rock-n-Roll volumes of music are introduced, they know that in time, ear pain will diminish away to numbness. **But the special physiological effect of loud music upon the flesh NEVER goes away.** All Decibel Disciples know this.

So, they force the sheep into submission until finally their ears become calloused to the assault. And as the Feeder of the Flock continues to feed "adrenaline and noradrenaline and more" with his sound system, the Flesh of the Flock continues to feed on the Magic-of-Loud-Music.

All Decibel Disciples know this Magic.

And God knows.

David Clark

Legal Liability Created by the Decibel Doctrine

I have discovered by perusing Public Domain information that the spiritually wacky virus called the **Decibel Doctrine** is a nationwide pandemic. I have also discovered that the **Decibel Doctrine** is evolving into a secular legal problem as indicated by this article from *"Sound Advice."* It is a self-inflicted problem, even to the Pseudo-Christians who embrace it as Biblical.

Please note that the amplified music is referred to as "worship"; an incessant sign that follows the **Decibel Doctrine**. I beg the reader to study the word "worship" in the Old and New Testament.

****

Sound Advice: Is Your Worship Too Loud?[1]

Article summary. *The music performed in some churches is of sufficient intensity and duration to cause permanent hearing loss in both musicians and members of the congregation. This article will review the effects of loud music, explore ways to reduce this hazard, and address a church's possible liability for ignoring the problem.*

The music performed in some churches during worship services and special events can become loud and intense. When electric guitars and drums are involved, the noise can become deafening. Consider a few examples.

•**Example**. A church uses a small band during worship services consisting of electric guitars, drums, and five singers. Some church members complain that the music is too loud.

•**Example**. A church uses a small band during worship services. A church member brings an audiometer to a worship service and measures peaks of 105 decibels on the front row with a sustained reading of 95 decibels. Is this level of intensity harmful to the hearing of persons sitting in the front of the church?

•**Example**. A church conducts youth services one night each week. These services include a prolonged period of singing, led by a worship band using electric guitars and drums. The noise is so loud that some of the youth experience ringing in their ears for hours after each service.

•**Example**. A church has a small orchestra that frequently performs during worship services. The orchestra includes several percussion and brass instruments.

---

[1] Internet/ Richard R. Hammar.

•**Example**. A church uses a small band during worship services. One of the band members is the church's music minister. After being in the band for four years, the music minister begins to notice a permanent hearing loss. She wonders if this is a possible workers compensation claim.

The Beginning of *Not-Right* Worship

And the Signs That Follow

Note: From this point forward, the reader must grasp the seriousness of the foundational truth within this single article which details **The Beginning of *Not-Right* Worship and The Signs That Follow.**

To fully comprehend the urgency and necessity of this entire collection of articles titled, ***The Decibel Doctrine***, you as the reader, must digest the consequences of offering *Not-Right* Worship to your God.

The authenticity of the principles found in this single article must be settled in your mind from this point forward in reading this collection of articles titled **The Decibel Doctrine**. As the author, I urge you to certify the entirety of this single article with your Bible.

****

When sin was committed by both Adam and Eve, they lost their relationship with God. And God lost the pleasure of walking and talking with His creations. The first created couple lost something precious that day, and their Creator also lost something precious. The subtle serpent robbed God that day of the pleasure He found in communing with Adam and Eve. And the perpetual agenda of the subtle serpent was revealed that day in Genesis; Lucifer knows the value of a conversant relationship between man and God, and will do everything within his power to prevent it or pervert it.

Lucifer's goal today is still to rob God of the pleasure He finds in man. And the **Decibel Doctrine** of the late twentieth century is a subtle ingenious thief that robs God of the precious pleasure that He receives when man shares his voice with his Creator. The **Decibel Doctrine** is the epitome of the works-of-man's-hands and has replaced the peaceful conversant relationship established in the Garden of Eden that God found precious.

In Genesis, we discover what happened when man sinned. Also in Genesis, we discover the first documented response of God to *Not-Right* worship.

And Adam knew Eve his wife; and she conceived, and bare Cain, and said, I have gotten a man from the LORD. 2 And she again bare his brother Abel. And Abel was a keeper of sheep, but Cain was a tiller of the ground. 3 And in process of time it came to pass, that Cain brought of the fruit of the ground an offering unto the LORD. 4 And Abel, he also brought of the firstlings of his flock and of the fat thereof. And the LORD had respect unto Abel and to his offering: **5** *But unto Cain and to his offering he had not respect. And Cain was very wroth, and his countenance fell.*

Genesis 4:1-5

The offerings of Cain and Abel were not law-prescribed offerings, for the law of sacrifices had not been written nor given. But rather, they were offerings to show honor, reverence, and respect for their Creator. Both Cain's and Abel's offerings exemplified oblation, obeisance, and homage. Very likely the offerings were attempts to regain the favor of God.

Thus, if I may say so, it was efforts of Cain and Abel to worship God; showing His worth as Deity. Allow me to call them *offerings of worship* to the God that their parents had often spoken of.

It could be that the cherubim and the flaming sword that God placed East of Eden to *"keep the way of the tree of life"* were visible to Cain and Abel. Even if not visible, still there was a respectable fear of God, their Creator. I want to believe that Adam and Eve often reminisced with their young sons, Cain and Abel, about the magnificent act of creation, and bringing pleasure to God by simply walking and talking with Him, and then being expelled from Eden for disobedience. This makes me consider that there was a compelling desire in Cain and Abel to bring offerings to appease and please their Creator. Allow me to refer to their offerings as WORSHIP.

So *"in the process of time, it came to pass"* that Cain and Abel worshipped; they worshipped the one true God. Having no Biblical instructions in offerings of worship, they made efforts to please God with what they found at hand. Cain brought fruits of his crop, and Abel brought fruits of his livestock. Both brought their own individual offerings of worship unto God.

The one true God responded to their worship that day; God had respect unto one and his worship, but unto the other and his worship, God showed no respect.

WHY?

The intent of this article is not to discover WHY; but to plainly point out that God does not respect all worship. Consequently, there were signs established in Genesis that day which follow unacceptable, *Not-Right* worship.

The cold hard facts dictate that God had no respect for one half of the worship that was offered that day. The unrelenting truth is that only one half of the worship offered by the second generation "walkers and talkers with God" received respect from God that day.

The Hebrew meaning of the word "respect" is "to gaze" (at or about). Two of the implied meanings according to Strong's Concordance is 1) consider, 2) compassionate. Therefore, when God had no respect for half the worship that day, in **reality He did not even look long at it, nor did He even consider it, nor did it stir God's compassion.**

There was no category of "almost right" worship. There was simply Yea and Nay. Simply Right and *Not-Right*. John 4:23 reveals that God seeks TRUE WORSHIP. It must be RIGHT. Cain's worship was not Satan-worship nor idol-worship. It was God-worship. It just wasn't RIGHT. And when worship unto God is not RIGHT, it is WRONG!

The Bible clearly states that God had no respect **unto Cain and his offering.** In other words, God showed no respect for Cain's offering of worship nor for Cain himself. So, **the clear message established from the beginning in this Book-of-Beginnings is: WHEN YOUR WORSHIP ISN'T RIGHT, YOU AREN'T RIGHT.**

The Core Principle that must be understood by the reader is, and I repeat, **WHEN YOUR WORSHIP ISN'T RIGHT, YOU AREN'T RIGHT.** Without this revelation and understanding, the reader will not adequately fear-for-his-soul the **Decibel Doctrine.**

God's deity allows Him the prerogative to accept or reject offerings made unto Him. And that day of offerings recorded in Genesis, found God rejecting the offering of Cain and respecting the offering of Abel.

God is not cruel or unjust. He was not quick to anger over the *Not-Right* worship offered by Cain that day. God patiently corrected Cain, assuring him that he and his offering would be accepted if he got it Right.

> *But unto Cain and to his offering he had not respect. And Cain was very wroth, and his countenance fell. And the Lord said to Cain, why art thou wroth? And why is thy countenance fallen? If thou doest well, shalt thou not be accepted? And if thou doest not well, sin lieth at the door. And unto thee shall be his desire, and thou shalt rule over him.*
> **Genesis 4:5-7**

Pleading with Cain, God was in essence saying: "There is no reason to anger. If you do it right, I will accept you and your offering." And then God warned him: "If you don't get it right, sin lieth at the door. It is just a matter of time before sin enters into your life." The "sin" referred to means "an offence" (against the Word of God) and "sometimes habitual sinfulness." Thus, declaring that when your worship is *Not-Right*, you are *Not-Right*, and there are signs and sins that habitually follow *Not-Right* worship.

So, in the pattern established in Genesis, we find the first two tell-tale signs that follow *Not-Right* worship: **ANGER** and **SINFULNESS**.

The first sign, **ANGER,** seems to remain hidden behind a cloak of *Christian niceties* until their *Not Right* worship is questioned or not accepted. But **ANGER** will manifest, vividly, in just a matter of time.

The second tell-tale sign established in the beginning is habitual **SINFULNESS**. This sign is a curse upon men who refuse to heed God's reasonable desires and instructions concerning worship.

The practice of the **Decibel Doctrine** is the practice of *Not-Right* worship. The euphoria produced by the **Decibel Doctrine** is the same for saints and sinners. This euphoria promotes a false feeling in the lukewarm sinner of "all is well with my soul," therefore leading the conscience to habitual sinfulness.

The third sign that follows *Not-Right* worship, established this same day in Genesis, is the **ABSENCE OF REPENTANCE**. God was not seeking tears of regret and remorse from Cain. God just wanted Cain to change his offering of worship. *If thou doest well,…* (just change your worship from *Not-Right* to *Right*). But there was no trace of repentance in Cain that day, nor the next day, nor the rest of the days of his life.

Today's Decibel Disciples offer worship according to what pleases them (literally what tingles their flesh and excites their heart rate). As Cain, they are incapable of repenting, or turning around from their *Not-Right* worship and embracing biblically mandated worship. Even if an angel of God should explain scriptural definitions and show valid examples of biblically ordained worship to a Decibel Disciple, the scene would remain void of even a hint of repentance.

The signs established in Genesis that follow *Not-Right* worship are alarmingly forever settled. The deception of the **Decibel Doctrine** appears to be final and complete in those who embrace it.

Of course, we all know that God-inspired prophecy always comes to pass. The prophecy that "sin lieth at the door if you don't get your worship right" continued to manifest in Cain's life. And it came to pass that Cain killed his brother Abel. It came to pass that the *Not-Right* worshiper rose up against the *Right* worshiper and the one who worshiped *Not-Right* slew the one who worshiped Right.

The murder of brother against brother, was all over worship. All over worship of God. Not worship of Satan, nor of idols, nor of man, but worship of the one true God. Worship with right intent, but not in the right way. So, the fourth sign that follows *Not-Right* worship is:

BROTHER WILL RISE UP AGAINST BROTHER AND COMMIT MURDER.

Murder of a brother seems too extreme to believe until one considers the spiritual realm and context of Genesis. John plainly described murderers as follows:

> **Whosoever hateth his brother is a murderer:** *and ye know that no murderer hath eternal life abiding in him.*
> **1 John 3:15**

Emotions like unto animosity and hate seethe from a Decibel Disciple when a brother dares to declare the **Decibel Doctrine** as non-biblical. A Decibel Disciple will "murder" a brother who vocalizes contempt toward the **Decibel Doctrine**. It is common today to assassinate the character and demean the name of any brother who challenges the scriptural authenticity of the **Decibel Doctrine**.

So, the establishment of the fourth sign, **MURDER**, came to pass that day and still persists with us unto today.

It is critical to note that the prophecy upon *Not-Right* worshippers is "sometimes habitual sinfulness." Multiple sins. Plurality of sins. And there was more sin added to Cain's life that day as one of the signs that follow *Not-Right* worship.

God knew that Cain had murdered Abel, but still He asked Cain, "Where is thy brother?"

Cain replied to his creator "I know not." On that very same day of *Not-Right* worship, Cain became a LIAR. His *Not-Right* worship sufficiently emboldened him to lie to God. (*Not-Right* worship in the form of the **Decibel Doctrine** creates a "holy boldness" mindset that cannot be hidden.) So, on this selfsame day in Genesis, the fifth sign that follows *Not-Right* worship, **LYING**, was forever established.

These two signs, murder and lying, begin to reveal the source of *Not-Right* worship.

> "the devil.… *he was a murderer from the beginning,… he is a liar, and the father of it.*"
> **John 8:44**

In choosing to be a *Not-Right* worshipper, Cain soon exemplified the very character of Satan himself.

So, if typology found in Genesis holds true, as I believe it does, all *Not-Right* worship carries the fingerprints of Satan. Tainted, distorted, covered, and perverted by the one that continually wars against God over worship. That is why when your worship is *Not-Right*, you are *Not-Right*.

Finally, Cain manifested the last and fatal sign that follows *Not-Right* worship; he went out from the presence of God, proudly and presumptuously carrying God's mark of protection on his life. Never, never, never to return. So, the sixth sign is **WALKING OUT OF THE PRESENCE OF GOD**, as well as **LIVING OUT OF THE PRESENCE OF GOD.**

> *15And the LORD said unto him, Therefore whosoever slayeth Cain, vengeance shall be taken on him sevenfold. And the LORD set a mark upon Cain, lest any finding him should kill him. 16And Cain went out from the presence of the LORD, and dwelt in the land of Nod, on the east of Eden.*
> **Genesis 4:15-16**

And Cain, the *Not-Right* worshipper, became the progenitor of the Canaanites, a blood line that hated the Lord Jehovah and His people. The Canaanites were and are a perpetual enemy of God's people forever and God's economy forever and God's pleasure forever. The Canaanites are, and were, the fruit of *Not-Right* worship.

Genesis establishes this irrevocable absolute: **there are far-reaching eternal consequences that stem from *Not-Right* worship.**

And now, thousands of years after Cain's *Not-Right* worship in Genesis, I have witnessed these same signs follow leaders of *Not-Right* worship in my lifetime. (My lifetime began on March 26, 1953)

The majority of my experiences with *Not-Right* worship is fruit of the **Decibel Doctrine**, a made-with-man's-hand doctrine that began to manifest itself in the early twentieth century. I will share these experiences and encounters with the reader in this collection of articles titled, *The Decibel Doctrine.*

It is only reasonable to consider the practice of the **Decibel Doctrine** as approaching blasphemy; **denying the ability of the Holy Ghost to change a man's heart without excessive volumes of music.**

Poor God, no wonder He still seeks True Worshippers.

> *But the hour cometh, and now is, when the true worshippers shall worship the Father in spirit and in truth: for **the Father seeketh such to worship him.***
> **John 4:23**

And again, I say "Poor God."

David Clark

Biblical Worship Defined

Biblical definitions - Biblical instructions - Biblical implications – Biblical illustrations, concerning Worship of the One True God - <u>**NEVER involve ecstatic motion**</u>.

But rather, the act of Biblical Worship, especially the physically manifested part witnessed and described in the Bible, is always indicative of a reverent respect and even awe to the Creator of all things. Assuredly, all Biblical Worship finds the creation (man) acknowledging the Worth of his Creator, as well as the humbling of the created (man) before his Creator.

The Worship that God seeks, is forever settled in the Word of God. God-ordained worship is so important and serious to God, that He plainly described it in His Word, so that all men would clearly understand.

Today we find various things offered unto God as worship. The most frequent offering of worship that dominates Christian Sanctuaries today is adrenalin-driven motion induced by extreme volumes of music and beat. It is a Manmade Fabrication found in the Twenty-first Century **Decibel Doctrine**.

Today's Christian Church World has completely comingled the word "Praise" with the word "Worship." Biblical "Praise" and Biblical "Worship" are two different words with different definitions, different instructions, different implications, different examples, and different illustrations.

This unjust co-mingling allows the convenience to "worship" **according to their personal preference.**

As evident today, the spirit of the **Decibel Doctrine** has been subtly successful in its usurpation of Biblical Worship.

God still seeks Worship.

*But the hour cometh, and now is, when the true worshippers shall worship the Father in spirit and in truth: for **the Father seeketh such to worship him**.*
John 4:23

David Clark

Biblical Definition
W-O-R-S-H-I-P

Old Testament

HEBREW - shachah

Pronounced - shaw-khaw'

A primitive root; to depress, i.e. prostrate (especially reflexive, in homage to royalty or God): bow (self) down, crouch, fall down (flat), humbly beseech, do (make) obeisance, do reverence, make to stoop, worship.

New Testament

GREEK - proskuneo

Pronounced - pros-koo-neh'-o

(meaning to kiss, like a dog licking his master's hand); to fawn or crouch to, i.e. (literally or figuratively) prostrate oneself in homage (do reverence to, adore): worship.

Strong's Exhaustive Concordance
Trusted Source of Bible Definitions

Sound Systems for Worship??

There is a popular Guide Manual by Yamaha, commonly used in churches to educate sound system operators that is very informative. The information shared in this guide manual is exhaustive and complete. Yamaha does an excellent job educating the reader with detailed physics and commonsense.

The front cover title of this Guide Manual is as below:

Guide To
Sound Systems For Worship

By Yamaha

This article is by no means slighting to Yamaha, which again I compliment their thoroughness within this guide manual. I am only using their title to make a generic point about a newly developed custom of worship within the Christian world.

****

It grieves me that we advocate and credit sound systems for worthy worship of our God.

I am an advocate of maintaining the original inspiration of God as it flowed through the pen held by the God-ordained writers of the infallible Word of God. I have lived long enough to witness sacred inspired words of God reduced to mere "catch phrases" that demean the original inspired intent. Specifically, the word "worship."

Cultural traditions have turned "Worship" into a socially accepted "catch phrase" that has lost its Biblical meaning and grossly diverged from God's original intended context.

For effect and emphasis, I have inserted below the TRUE meaning of Biblical Worship into the title: *Guide to Sound Systems for Worship.*

By doing so, I will replace the God-Inspired word, "WORSHIP," with its God-Inspired definition/intent.

I have comingled both the Hebrew and the Greek definitions for simplicity, which are concordant with each other.

GUITE TO

SOUND SYSTEMS

FOR…

Prostrating oneself in homage to God

Bowing down or falling down (flat)

Humbly beseeching God

Making obeisance to God

Showing reverence to God

Fawning or crouching before your Creator.

By Yamaha

Plainly, when the function of a Sound System is forced to associate with the God-Inspired word "WORSHIP," the blending just does not jive. ("Jive" is a slang word from off-the-street, but it fits well here.)

POINT – We have deserted the God-Inspired definition/intent/context of the God-Inspired word "WORSHIP." Consciously or unconsciously, I know not. But I do know that *New Age Worshippers* have been taught that Biblically-True definitions and illustrations are *boringly outdated*, and destined for the Fake-News trash can.

Decibel Disciples, as they honor the **Decibel Doctrine**, are the leading culprits of "catch phrases" that demean God-Inspirations, especially the noble act called WORSHIP in the Bible.

A closing question for Reality Check:

"When is the last time you heard music from your church's sound system that made you feel like humbly bowing before your Creator and Savior?"

Just wondering:

Do Decibel Disciples practice their version of worship when they are alone before their God in private time, or only in a crowd?

Think about it.

David Clark

Worship Should Exhibit Worthiness

All offerings of worship to our Savior and Creator-of-all-things should exhibit Worthiness.

21st century worship of the One True God has deserted, diverged and departed from worship that is biblically certified/validated by the inspired Holy Scripture. The deceptively deadly **Decibel Doctrine** has chronically divorced Sanctuary Worship from the worthiness intended to be manifested in Biblical worship.

The enemy-of-all-righteousness has consumed/devoured the insinuated worth exemplified in worship by the Holy Scriptures; AND that same enemy-of-all-righteousness has regurgitated an obnoxious substitute.

The subtle master of deception has somehow convinced us to offer the **Decibel Doctrine,** and its fruit, to our Creator as "worthy" worship.

What WORTH does your worship declare?

Bear with me in my redundancy in repeating this question: Do Decibel Disciples practice their version of worship when alone before God in private time, or **only in a crowd**?

Any Twenty-First Century Christian who is consciously aware will acknowledge the following criminal indictment against all **Decibel Doctrine Pastors** as valid:

The Crime: <u>Breaking the Law</u> of <u>Common Sense</u>

Lovers of the **Decibel Doctrine**

Boldly, Loudly, Boisterously, Repeatedly Demand:

Don't Rob Me of My Worship!

God silently thinks:

Don't Rob Me of My WORTH!

David Clark
A Lover of Biblical Worship

The Unexplained Mark of Protection

*And the LORD said unto him, Therefore whosoever slayeth Cain, vengeance shall be taken on him sevenfold. And **the LORD set a mark upon Cain**, lest any finding him should kill him.*

Genesis 4:15

If you have unanswered thoughts when you read the above verse and the story that it represents in the Bible, then you are normal. The underlying principle of this passage of scripture is more than intriguing. I cannot explain the "Mark of Protection" that God placed upon Cain. But in this article, I will make it relevant to today, knowing that the same God continues to be longsuffering with the carnality of His people.

As already established in this collection of articles, Cain's character is an established precedence of the signs that follow *Not-Right* worship. Anger, habitual sin, absence of repentance, murder of brothers, lying, and walking away from the presence of God; all actions of Cain when his *Not-Right* worship was refused by God.

The journey of the Hebrew nation toward the Promise Land was halted at Mount Sinai for one of the most awesome moments in History; the handing down of the Law to Moses. It is symbolic of today that the Israelites missed the awe of that moment in History involving the Law or Word of God

While Moses (the real man of God and True Pastor) was receiving Words of Life for the children of Israel, Aaron (the Priest) led the children of Israel in *Not-Right* worship of the Golden Calf. Aaron misled Moses and said, *"I cast it (gold) into the fire, and there came out this calf."* The truth is that he *"fashioned it with a graving tool, after he had made it a molten calf."* Aaron was a good man taught by an Elder who walked with God. Yet in the absence of his "Pastor," he *"turned aside quickly out of the way which I commanded them:"* God's words in Exodus 32:8.

We do not read where Aaron repented for *Not-Right* worship. I am uncomfortable presuming that Aaron manifested the Absence of Repentance, a sign that follows *Not-Right* worship. Scripture does not tell us yea or nay. But if Cain and today's leaders of *Not-Right* worship are our examples, there is no turning around (repentance). Once they turn quickly aside from TRUE PATHS of Biblical worship, there seems to be no turning around, no coming back, especially from the addicting power of extreme decibels of music.

Absence of repentance remains today as a sign that follows *Not-Right* worship.

Aaron's *Not-Right* worship caused about three thousand men to be slain in the day of the golden calf. Then later

> *"And the Lord plagued the people, because they made the calf, which Aaron made,"*
> Exodus 32:35.

Untold numbers paid the penalty for *Not-Right* worship – but not Aaron.

JUSTICE wants to scream - "UNFAIR!"

MANKIND wants to scream - "WHY?"

It seems that Aaron avoided the plague sent by God. And yet the story implies that he was guilty of leading God's chosen into idolatry. He seems to have unabashedly orchestrated *Not-Right* worship which caused the death of many of God's chosen people. <u>Clearly symbolic of the decimation of saints caused by Decibel Disciples of today.</u>

Never forget; **when your worship "Isn't Right," you "Aren't Right."**

Could it be that the Mark of Protection that God placed upon Cain was also placed upon Aaron? Aaron had been anointed for use in the ministry with Moses. Later to be used in the Tabernacle. There was a mark from God that protected Cain's life. It is very possible that a similar "mark" protected Aaron's life.

Our faith in God declares that He knows best. Maybe Moses needed Aaron? Whatever the reason, God did what was best overall.

However, Biblical principle declares that God does not "mark" away *Not-Right* Worship. When your worship "Isn't Right"- you "Aren't Right." Your destiny is written.

So, we question often: why does God allow today's Decibel Disciples to remain in pulpits and teach *Not-Right* worship? Possibly the same reason He allows many false prophets and many teachers of false religion to remain in their pulpit even unto today.

I have questioned this so many times that I am ashamed. I don't have the answer. I do trust God, and if I trust God, I have to trust His Word. And His Word repudiates the **Decibel Doctrine**. This **Decibel Doctrine** is a dangerous meme that has deceived our present Church Culture and led them into Non-biblical *Not-Right* worship. I do know that current leadership of the Decibel Disciple is to blame.

Of course, we cannot judge Aaron's eternity. Neither can we know the eternal destiny of Cain, nor the eternal destiny of his brotherhood of Decibel Disciples prevalent today. But my experience with this type suggests that it is easier to repent of transgression of all of the original 10 Commandments than it is to turn around from *Not-Right* worship. Especially *Not-Right* worship in the form of the **Decibel Doctrine**, because the power therein is extremely hard for the flesh to forsake.

The "MARK" placed upon a man by anointing from God into a position of ministry to help save a lost world, does not protect his soul from the penalty of unrepented sin.

The "MARK" protected Cain from other men. **It did not protect him from God.**

If a minister leads a people in *Not-Right* worship - his soul is plainly *Not-Right*.

His destiny is written.

David Clark

Thinking: Maybe it was the prayer of Moses that protected Aaron's life until Mount Hor.

> *And the LORD was very angry with Aaron to have destroyed him:*
> *and I prayed for Aaron also the same time.*
> **Deuteronomy 9:20**

Tell-Tale Signs That Follow *Not-Right* Worship

The signs of *Not-Right* worship have continued to find me. In particular, the signs that follow the **Decibel Doctrine**. This article covers a span of eighteen years of Tell-Tale Signs that I jotted down for records' sake as they found me.

There are tell-tale signs that follow *Not-Right* worship created by the **Decibel Doctrine**.

They are prevalent all the day long. Seemingly anywhere God seeks worship.

It is as though these last days have been the perfect incubator, and now the hatchlings are active.

****

Tell-Tale Signs

There is a common prelude that paves the way as the **Decibel Doctrine** lays its foundation in a Sanctuary. The prelude is a false statement declaring – "we cannot hear the music." This sign identifies their father who is the father of all lies. The truth is that "they" have always been able to hear the music. But somewhere in the gross darkness of deception, "they" have experienced a magical power in loud music that their flesh now covets. A power-driven lust that supersedes the fear of lying.

A workout partner of mine named Bryan invited me to his church, Triumph Church in Port Arthur, Texas. He was not normally adamant about church attendance, but this church rocked. He tried to describe what the thunderous volumes of music did to him, but he could not put it in words. He said that I would have to come experience it for myself. The ecstatic zeal on his face was highlighted by gold glitter dust that had fallen from the ceiling upon the crowd that Sunday morning for additional special effects during "worship." (Signs such as this began to push me to expose the delusive power in rock concert volume music when used in church settings.)

While in Memphis, Tennessee, I met a young evangelist and his wife. They had been attending the ACI / AMF conference for the first time. (ACI / AMF are initials for Apostolic Churches International / Apostolic Ministers Fellowship)

During our visit, he said that he asked the unpardonable question that is taboo in the ACI/AMF ranks: "why is the music so loud!?"

His wife piped in, still astonished: "the other night we sang in one of their churches, and the speaker on the floor kept moving my skirt!"

So, I explained the **Decibel Doctrine** to them as I had been experiencing it. Their encounter with the **Decibel Doctrine** had been distasteful. That was many years ago, and I often wonder about the long-term results of our meeting. Did they eventually embrace the **Decibel Doctrine** as Biblical, OR, did they run and hide themselves in the Word of God?

My secretary at work had Pentecostal friends from Virginia come to stay with her. Her friends expressed deep grief over the new paths of music that recently came (I say "slithered") into their home church. They grieved that their joy of church vanished along with their peace.

On 10-12-01, I heard this comment from my aunt's hairdresser: "I could hardly take the volume of music when I first started going there." (A Pentecostal Church in a small community of Louisiana called Whitehall) "I thought my ears would burst until they got used to it."

The numbing and deafening of the ears by detrimental decibels of music is a normal process of nature; it is not receiving a new revelation of Biblical Worship, as promoters of the **Decibel Doctrine** would have a Christian to believe.

Kevin, a close church friend of mine, was witnessing to the owner of a Ziebart Franchise in Beaumont, Texas. The mature and professional lady was open to his invitation to visit his church, Faith Tabernacle in Port Arthur, Texas. When she became aware of the location of his church, she recalled visiting the Triumph Church on Highway 69 very near my friend's church. She reminisced about regretting the visit because the volume of music hurt her ears. "Having no cotton," she said, "I stuffed a paper napkin into my ears, but it wasn't enough." My friend Kevin inconspicuously changed the subject for he knew the devastating electronic decibels that this spiritually hungry lady would experience in his own church. For his Pastor is a promoter of the **Decibel Doctrine**.

A friend of my wife visited an Assembly of God church as a favor to her niece who attended the church's drug rehab program. She told my wife that the young people jumped up and down the whole-time music was played. The music was so loud, she complained, that "it hurt my ears." "Why," she asked my wife, "is the music so loud?" My wife was too kind to call a spade a spade. The correct answer to the question "Why is the music so loud?" is that the one responsible for the volume (usually the Pastor) believes that the physical reaction caused by extreme decibels of rhythm and music honors God. They pathetically believe that the volume of music will "keep" the young people. Meaning, extreme electronic decibels will save those who struggle with drugs, or fornication, or any other transgression.

A young mother was heard to say, "I put cotton in my children's ears. I don't want their ears damaged." Humble and timid, this young mother would be scorned and ridiculed should she tell her Pastor the music is hurting her family's ears. Should she plead for mercy and the Pastor could control his anger, his words might be similar to this: "You poor thing, bless your heart, you just don't understand the power of God".

A young couple was seeking a Pentecostal church with conservative standards. After visiting an Apostolic Church in Vidor, Texas, they told a friend of mine: "The music was so loud it hurt our ears. We could never go there." I have personally visited the same church several times and only a few years ago, it was not so. But the Pastor, who is a good man, had recently begun to fellowship with Decibel Disciples. The **Decibel Doctrine** is a contagion of epidemic deception.

During this same year, 2001, a first cousin of mine experienced Pentecostal perversion of worship in the form of the **Decibel Doctrine**. This cousin is Baptist and attended an Easter play in a Pentecostal church in Alexandria, Louisiana. The music and song during invitation to pray hurt his ears. He told me that even putting his finger in his ear did not stop the pain. I wish that I could tell him that they did not know how loud it was – but I would lie. For the sake of his soul, I wish that I could call it an accidental oversight – but I would lie. I wish, for the sake of his soul, I could say that they do not believe that the electronically induced decibels he experienced was the power of God and had the ability to stir his soul from sin – but I would lie. This cousin may never know Biblical Pentecost. If he was to hunger for the Old Biblical Paths of Pentecost, where could he go?

Again in 2001. A second cousin of mine from Springfield, Missouri, recently told me that his church now has two worship services on Sunday. One service is referred to as old style where they sing songs such as "Amazing Grace." The other worship service is oriented to the youth. During this service, the music volume is increased to extreme decibel volumes that hurt the ears. Why? Because the **Decibel Doctrine** teaches that the volume of the music brings a move of God. No doubt, this denominal Pastor in Springfield, Missouri, has also discovered the "power" in extreme decibels of music. Power to "keep" the youth.

Around the year 2005, my wife and I attended a special event called *Times of Refreshing*. The annual event was sponsored by Reverend Poe and was held in the Airport Hilton Hotel in Houston, Texas. There were two enormous loud speakers on the floor next to the platform. Larger than I had ever seen. I took a picture of a person standing beside one of the macro speakers, and the comparison in size was like unto David before Goliath.

The service was Power-Packed. The loud music had bass tones so forceful that when standing near the back of the conference room, the sound waves vibrated one's bronchial tube in the chest. Several groups in the crowd complained that the volume of music actually vibrated and tingled their throat down into their chest. In humor, I demonstrated to my wife how I could make musical sounds by opening my mouth and allowing my bronchial tube to make tones from the vibrations.

Surely, Reverend Poe finds it reasonable that we have renamed his event - *Times of Enchantment*.

A Pastor friend of mine preached for us in Hillister, Texas on 6/30/06. He told me of a sound-man friend of his who boldly stated that he could control the spirit of his home church service. To demonstrate proof, as my Pastor friend stood beside him, the sound-man slid the sound volume controls forward during the song service on a Sunday night, toward more power, and instantly the people began to lift hands, clap hands, stand up and be more active.

It is no wonder that they say "See, it works." And it is no wonder that I say, "Poor God."

New Zealand Christians Find Confidence in the **Decibel Doctrine**.

Published Quote of a Music Director in New Zealand: "We have everything here, from gently amplified acoustic sounds to howling, head-banging rock for the all-electric youth service on Sunday nights. It (Sound System) can handle all of those sounds without batting an eyelid."

Brother Minson - Holy Trinity Music Director – New Zealand

August 24th 2006 - Sister Cruseturner, a lady in our church in Hillister, Texas, told me of her sister who attends a Baptist Church in Jasper, Texas. Her sister said the music is getting so loud that it is almost unbearable.

(Pity the innocent people as their Pastor seeks the power of God for his congregation.)

January 5th, 2009

I was walking for exercise in my neighborhood in Woodville, Texas. A neighbor named Riley stopped as he was driving by and told me of a Christian Singing Group that came to his church. Riley, who knows nothing of my spiritual challenge with the **Decibel Doctrine**, told me that the music was so loud that he almost had to leave. When he told the Christian Singing Group that their volume was almost unbearable, they made the excuse that they were used to playing in larger churches. I, of course, contested this excuse as a lie, and told Riley that the volume was intentional and for effect.

He then spoke of another Christian Singing Group that he and his dad went to see in another local Baptist Church. Riley said that his dad got up and left because the music was so loud.

(The Baptist and other Denominational churches received the **Decibel Doctrine** from us Pentecostals as a "GIFT." We Pentecostals received this "GIFT" from the world of Rock-N-Roll.)

(This "GIFT" that has been shared and given is nothing less than a Spiritual Trojan Horse.)

A sixty-year-old new convert in our church in Hillister, Texas, visited another Pentecostal church on a Sunday night. His comment to me later: "Brother Clark, the music got so loud, especially the drums, I was scared. Something about it scared me. I began to pray from fear."

(I had not yet taught him about the Spirit of Serpent Seed Music, so his reaction was of the Holy Ghost within him.)

It was mealtime at Men's Conference in Lufkin, Texas. The dining hall was full of brethren hungry for food and hungry for fellowship with each other. I saw two different ministers send a message to the soundman of the Dining Hall to "turn the music down so we can fellowship." Their requests were met with smiles and smirks.

(Satan despises fellowship between brethren. Have you ever noticed how hard it is to talk with friends after a church service, even if the music is turned down to Medium-Move-of-God volumes?)

I helped transport a youth group to a special AMF/ACI Youth Service in Ohio. The school auditorium was rented and had a raised stage for plays and performances. As I was praying down front before service began, I felt impressed by the Lord to raise my head and look around. As I observed my surroundings, I felt words of my Lord bringing to my attention; "the stage is packed with $200,000 of sound equipment, yet they brought no altars; not even homemade benches to kneel at and pray." (I later shared this experience with my wife.)

As the service began, a hosting minister by the name of Mead made this opening statement: "The rock concert down the road is worshipping their God with high decibels, why can't we?" The trained response of the present crowd of youth was applause and cheers. (Their trainers were Decibel Disciples).

My mental response to hosting-minister-Mead who challenged the crowd with "why can't we?" ....Because Their God is not our God..., or is He?

I scribbled the following two comments on a note pad on 2-2-09.

About two months ago, I overheard a Pastor answering a question concerning drums in the Sanctuary. His reply was that the drums were what "kept the service going."

This reply disappointed me because I highly esteem that Pastor as a Word preacher. I have reflected upon that statement many times, seeking a Biblical Principle that could give it support. I am still unable to justify such a statement pertaining to the Sanctuary of God.

Last Friday night I heard a member of another church saying that their Pastor amplified his bass guitar so loud that it vibrated the pew on which the member sat.

9-21-09 Monday night. Mom and I prayed for Uncle Al as he was slowly dying with emphysema. When Mom told him that he needed the Holy Ghost, Uncle Al replied "I'm just as saved as you are, I don't have to jump to prove I'm saved."

I suspect that somewhere in his life, a Decibel Disciple under the disguise of a Pastor, had tried to convince Uncle Al that the sign of spirituality was physical motion.

My mother is as sweet as honey and pure as gold. Her relationship with God is real. We siblings owe her much for raising us biblically. Only God knows the number of prayers she has prayed for me that He miraculously answered to my favor, precisely on time.

Mom is just real, no pretense. Almost naïve. Old-Path generation. Mature enough to know that nonbiblical New-Age-Paths are hazardous to one's soul. Yet, in her innocence, she has been duped by a Decibel Disciple who practices the **Decibel Doctrine** in the Sanctuary.

She recently told me of a song that a great vocalist sings in her home church in Orange, Texas. The entire song is sung/played at irritating volumes because the **Decibel Doctrine** dominates that Sanctuary; but the soundman is instructed to add even more special effects by really cranking up the volume for the ending few words: "Behold He Comes"!!!

My innocent mother told me that she and her friends agreed that the song would not have the same effect without the dramatic near-end increase of volume by the soundman. And she is absolutely correct about the word "effect."

It seems unfair to me that the unaware, the pure, the sincere, and the innocent, get duped by the magic of the **Decibel Doctrine** in the hands of a Decibel Disciple Pastor.

I participated in a Chapel service held in a Prison in Port Arthur, Texas. The preacher who preached to the inmates was a good and sincere man with a passion for Truth. When the Chapel service was finished, this preacher-of-truth turned to the female assistant Chaplain and spoke with a clenched fist: "when we get our equipment together, we are going to ROCK these walls!" I slowly turned to my close friend Kevin, questioning: "Did he really say what I heard him say?" With a sad-to-say grimace, Kevin replied: "Yep, I heard it also."

This godly Bible preacher had been duped and deceived by a Decibel Disciple whom he honored as his Pastor.

The **Decibel Doctrine** is Double-Deadly even to the Elect of Christ.

The **Decibel Doctrine** is not a Trivial Thing - It is to be Feared.

****

I fear that the Spirit of Serpent Seed Music is present in almost all Sanctuaries of the Christian Faith that have the money-means. The magic of the euphoria forced by the **Decibel Doctrine** has become an irresistible contagion of epidemic proportions among Christian Churches. Soon there may not be a Christian Church untainted by *Not-Right* worship induced by the **Decibel Doctrine**. Every day it appears easier for Pastors to jump on this Pied-Piper-Wagon because of the dark-truth-evidence that "It Works."

We cannot blame it all on the wolf-in-sheep's clothing that taught for 19 years in a Pentecostal School of Music in the State of Mississippi, and swore to change Pentecostal music. He was not the Leader, but only a Disciple of the Leader. No different than Decibel Disciples contemporary to today.

The active Leader today is still an anointed cherub of great beauty and was perfect in his created ways until he perverted the purpose of his abilities and sought to become the "Worshipped."

As I have edited and added and subtracted and re-edited this collection of articles again and again, the year 2021 has overtaken me.

I have many other documented experiences for another time. But I have to share the latest before closing this article.

A recent report came to me from a Pastor while he was attending a youth event in Oklahoma called PEAK. He sent me a text as he was experiencing PEAK "worship" from the safety of the balcony. These are the exact words of his text: "I'll tell you what… nobody can outdo their rock music! They have it perfected. I was in the balcony watching the show. That was the most awful mess I ever saw! A present and participating Decibel Doctrine Pastor called it a *party*."

The practice of the **Decibel Doctrine** is a run-away train of *Not-Right* worship.

In comparison, what are my feeble efforts to SCREAM…. STOP! - THAT'S NOT WORSHIP! - TURN AROUND! GO BACK!!??

Euphoria accelerates the addiction.

It is rampant.

**A complete metamorphosis at Hyper Sonic Speed;
from Biblical Pentecost into a Cult of Motion.**

David Clark

Not-Right Worship Continues To Find Me

In 2002, my family and I had escaped our beloved home church in Port Arthur, Texas, after it had become inundated with and controlled by the **Decibel Doctrine**. Not being sure of where to call home, we attended our family's home church in Orange, Texas. This change of environment allowed my family to find much spiritual healing.

For almost a year, the song service was actually pleasant. Soothing, soul washing, stirring, refreshing, and pleasing to God. Songs of praise that left one refreshed and peaceful, versus "beat-up" and flinching.

On a particular Sunday morning in Orange, Texas, my wife and I were enjoying the Evangelist who was proclaiming, "We can have Acts 2:38 revival this morning, today, right now." His faith was contagious, and I was anticipating Altar Call.

The phrase "Altar Call" literally means a call or invitation to come forward to the altars and pray. The phrase is still commonly used in some Christian churches today. Even though most churches have removed altars from the Sanctuary, the phrase "Altar Call" is still used to indicate a time for man to humble himself before the Lord and let God be God.

So, this particular Sunday morning in Orange, Texas, the Evangelist initiated the Altar Call with these words: "**Come on up musicians and play something fast.**" My faith dissipated into thin air. My hope was deflated like a punctured balloon. If my Faith had any human anatomy that morning, it ran out the door screaming, "Aaaahhhhh!" - With both hands over the ears.

"Come on up musicians, play something fast."

If average men were surveyed and asked to guess the source and setting of these words, their answers might be as follows:

1. A call of the emcee to bring life back to the party, following the rock band's intermission? ---NOPE! Wrong answer.

2. An effort to liven up a nursing home's bingo game? ---NOPE! Wrong answer.

3. Words to curb the chill of a winter time street dance? ---NOPE! Wrong answer.

Not even close!

To the extreme contrary, these were words spoken by a Pentecostal evangelist starting his altar call in my family's Pentecostal Church.

The powerful evangelist had just preached that "We can have Acts 2:38 revival today. If God did it for them, He will do it for us. The days of old time, old fashioned Holy Ghost outpouring are not over."

Thoughts of prayer and supplication in the Upper Room 2000 years ago filled my mind. I longed for the sounds of humble prayer described in similar stories of 1901 and 1906 Historic Holy Ghost outpourings. But my hungry soul grimaced when it heard "**Come on up musicians, and play something fast.**"

Fast music today always means loud also. Today's fast and furious music cannot achieve its desired effect without extreme electronic volumes. So, the grimace of my soul that Sunday morning was an involuntary reaction as my whetted appetite for Acts 2:38 revival was doused with ice water. I realized that the sheep would not be nourished. Neither would the ears of my soul be touched by the sound of prayer made during this altar call.

My-My-My, how 100 years can change the environment necessary for God to pour out His Spirit. Over 100 years ago, during the world renowned 1906 Azusa Street Revival, witnesses testified that they felt no need for music at all. That thought repels many of my friends, but it attracts me.

In the Jerusalem Upper Room described in the second chapter of Acts in our Bible, about 120 believers were obedient to God while tarrying, praying, and sitting. God filled them all with His Spirit without the assistance of loud, fast music.

I am remembering a Pentecostal Pastor friend from Moss Bluff, Louisiana who suggested to me that exciting music filled the Upper Room in Acts chapter two. And I presumed he believed that exciting music filled Cornelius' house in Acts 10. He was a Decibel Disciple, so "exciting music" in his world meant LOUD and FAST.

My-My-My, how 2000 years can change what man perceives as necessary for Holy Ghost Revival.

New Age Pentecost of today says: "Those are the old paths; we will not walk therein." "Those ways are ancient." "Rather than serve the Ancient of Days," we shall "Jam for Jesus."

Signs that follow *Not-Right* worship.

The safe haven I had found years ago in Orange, Texas suddenly was not. My soul became desperate to flee for safety as I realized that *Not-Right Worship* was continuing to find me.

David Clark
9/13/02

I Know A Secret

The third week of July, 2002 was a surprisingly interesting week.

Monday the 22nd of July, 2002, I was informed that others had discovered the secret. Tuesday night, the 23rd of July, I had a warning dream concerning my daughter. Wednesday, the 24th of July I had an unusual first-time visitor in my office.

Monday the 22nd of July, a mature Pentecostal saint relayed this following testimony. The six-year-old grandson said, "Granny, (with his fingers in his ears), the music hurts my ears, can we go up in the balcony?" (Now I know that the **Decibel Doctrine** teaches that extreme-volumes-of-music will "keep" the youth. I guess this 6-year-old didn't know that yet.) Of course, his Granny, suffering also while they were "having church," quickly obliged the young boy. She said that the balcony was tolerable, and they *endured* the church service.

The easy question that was not asked: could they hear the music from the balcony? Of course. They could have heard the music with understanding in the foyer, in the Sunday school rooms, in the restrooms, in the parking lot, even on the roof, for the pastor was "having church." The volume was just a little more tolerable in the balcony.

This Granny shared her experience with her husband, and it was his reply that informed me that **the secret is out**. Her husband told her that the church "sound man" acknowledged the extreme volumes of music; then had matter-of-factly informed him: "We have studied the decibels of music. While closely monitoring decibels, we have found that the people do not respond to the music except the decibels be set at a certain level." (Respond - meaning any physical demonstration of movement)

So, the secret is out – Anybody can "HAVE CHURCH" – IF…, POWERFUL SOUND EQUIPMENT IS AVAILABLE. (I am using Decibel Disciple lingo when I repeat the phrase "Have Church." The phrase "Have Church" is a New Age Christian misnomer alluding to physical stimulation by means of the **Decibel Doctrine.)**

In Elder M. E. Burr's writings against "*The Spirit of Serpent Seed Music*," he mentions that many rock-and-roll stars discovered their own **secrets** that would move the crowds.

For example, Elvis' secret was the Flex and Swing of his hips.

For another example, one of today's most popular rock bands is a Punk-Rock group called *Spinal Tap*. **Time** magazine interviewed this group, questioning the **secret** to their success. The reply of one of this era's most successful Punk-Rock bands: "you have to be louder than your competition."

What makes *Spinal Tap* audiences jump and scream? -- Extreme decibels of music and beat.

What causes their audience to fall in love with them, to follow them, to support them? -- Addiction to the adrenaline high caused by extreme decibels of music and beat.

I am sorry to tell you Elvis impersonators and *Spinal Tap*, but your **secret** is out. New Age Pentecost has discovered and stolen your **secret**.

There is a suppressed secret untold to the youth of my generation. *Spinal Tap* supporters long ago discovered that the airwaves activated by electronic vibrations in front of stage speakers would cook raw unshelled eggs. It was fun and trendy to place raw eggs up front of a *Spinal Tap* concert and have a snack of freshly boiled eggs when the show ended.

That secret, and others, are withheld from our youth by Pastors of the **Decibel Doctrine.**

A Secret Question: Have **Decibel Doctrine** Pastors lost their mind, or are their brains partially cooked?

July 23rd Tuesday night's dream was disturbing. I am not sure what time the dream occurred, but I got up to pray just before 1:15 a.m.

The dream was as follows:

I saw my daughter on a very large speedboat. The speedboat appeared to be the size of several, possibly many, large school buses. The seats were in rows, and she sat alone with her shades on, enjoying the sun in modest apparel. Her countenance was her normal innocent, peaceful, unaware, pleasant self that I have learned to love. The speedboat was traveling at seemingly supersonic speed, literally flying across the water at a frightening velocity.

As I observed the scene, I saw that no one was at the wheel. No one was steering the speed boat. With horror I realized that the boat was on a collision course with a solid embankment that would totally demolish it and take the life of my precious innocent daughter.

I am not sure just what the obstacle was, possibly a concrete wall. But I knew in my dream that my daughter would not survive the crash. With all my strength, I began to run to the front of the boat, toward the unattended steering wheel, hoping to take control of the boat's direction. I remember noticing that the rows of seats that I was swiftly running past seemed to turn into church pews. All too quickly I realized that I could not reach the steering wheel in time to divert the deadly direction that was on course for a catastrophe. I remember nothing else.

All I can relate this to, at the moment, is the countless Sunday night church services that my daughter has experienced in the last 7 years under the leadership of a Decibel Disciple. Where the Word of God that charts our course and safely steers our "boat" across the Sea-of-Life, had been replaced with "Jubilee," as the **secret** of extreme decibels of music caused a physiological reaction and the people responded and "had church" without the Word. I am praying and fasting, for I believe God would not have given me the dream had there not been hope.

Wednesday, July 4th, my unusual, first-time visitor came into my office selling burritos. We began to talk about church and the goodness of God. He said that he is a "lay minister" in his non-denominational church. By chance I asked him if he was involved in the church's music. His answer let me know that our meeting was not just coincidence. "I am over the music," he answered. "My wife and I were music majors in college."

As I explained the **Decibel Doctrine** that had contaminated Pentecost and my home church, he acknowledged the problem. Then he verified the secret that Decibel Disciples rely on to "have church." Obviously, according to him, any student of music psychology understands that extreme decibels of music have a physiological effect upon the human brain, causing an adrenaline rush that produces physical action. This learned student of music said that extreme decibels of music can "**make a person do things that they normally would not do.**"

As he left my office, I knew that he had left me with more than just warm burritos for my employees. God had sent him to edify the teachings that I had received from Pastor M.E. Burr. God continued to send more, then more,

71

messengers by "coincidence" into my life who continually edified the truth about what I was experiencing in my home church. God was revealing to me over and over that *"The Spirit of Serpent Seed Music," "The Music of the Golden Calves,"* and *"Strange Fire,"* are all from God to protect the sheep.

(These books and others authored by M.E. Burr are available in print from Amazon.com and/or **Decibel Doctrine** at P.O. Box 374 Hillister, Texas 77624.)

God used the pen of Elder M.E. Burr to warn the sheep of hidden spirits.

Spirits from the dark side? – ABSOLUTELY YES.

Spirits that circumvent biblical worship? – ABSOLUTELY YES.

Deceptive and Seductive Spirits? – ABSOLUTELY YEA and AMEN.

REAL? - Beyond all doubt VERY REAL!

Not just distasteful imaginations – BUT REAL SPIRITS that WRESTLE AGAINST GOD's SPIRIT.

My innumerable "coincidental" experiences and encounters have convinced me and compelled me to wrestle against the spiritual wickedness of the **Decibel Doctrine** in high places of religion with my pen, as did my pastor, Elder Murray E. Burr.

So, in reality the special effects of extreme decibels of music upon the human body is really no **secret** after all. Science and rock bands have known the **secret** long before New Age Pentecost. Though I guess that today's Decibel Disciples should receive some credit as pioneers of these New Paths since they are the first in history to call it "Having Church."

David Clark
7/25/02

72

A God-Destined Experience with the Decibel Doctrine

This particular page of this collection of articles, **The Decibel Doctrine**, is being written on April 8th, 2017, during a temporary pause in my writing. I was astounded again yesterday, April 7th, 2017, by signs that follow *Not-Right* Worship and the **Decibel Doctrine**.

Yesterday, without provocation, the husband of the Registered Nurse who was treating me, began to share his personal testimony with me. He had received the Holy Ghost 47 years prior and enjoyed this Pentecostal lifestyle. Then with tears, this very humble man began to astound me. With brokenness, he told of recently having to leave a church assembly he loved because he could no longer endure the new volume of music during church services. He told of visitors to his church that swore to never visit again because of the volume of music.

He told me, I repeat, with much brokenness, that he had humbly approached his Pastor three times, saying in sorrow that he felt forced to go to another assembly, where he hopefully could enjoy bringing his family to church. He spoke to me of losing his joy and desire to go to church. He shared with me the loneliness and desperation that accompanied the loss of joy for "church." He told me of telling his Pastor, who he loved and respected, that he could never bring his grandchildren to his church for fear of damaging their hearing.

This broken man did not know of my experiences with the **Decibel Doctrine**. He did not know that my God and I were both enemies of that "new path" called the **Decibel Doctrine**. He had no idea that I also went three times to my Pastor, (the one substituted for Elder Burr when he retired), begging in humbleness for mercy concerning the new volumes of music that "cranked".("cranked" is the braggadocios term used by the music director in my home church to describe the new paths of music)

This broken man that God miraculously introduced to me, did not know that I could relate to his desperation with empathy, sympathy, and understanding. I have done my best to help him. His heart is still broken, but now he understands.

Unexpected exposure to fruit of the **Decibel Doctrine** in so many unsuspected places and odd times, has forced me to acknowledge that God has chosen me to warn with my pen: the unsearchable horrors cloaked in the **Decibel Doctrine**.

David Clark
4-8-17

Eye Witness – One More Time

I have often asked the heavens: "Why Me?" Why am I always the one who witnesses the perverted demonstrations and signs of the **Decibel Doctrine**? I am seemingly always in the right place at the right time to witness the signs of wanton spiritual waste that follow the invisible force of the **Decibel Doctrine**. It always finds me. And it knows very well that I despise it.

Witnessing the deception of good men has caused me to fear the power of the **Decibel Doctrine** for my own self. Who am I to think that I cannot be devoured by that same power that has deceived men much better than I?

It was March, 2000 A.D. I had found a safe haven by going to church in Orange, Texas, with my mother, my sister, my blood kin, and childhood friends. My wife and I sat on the second row from the front on the right side. The song services were soul-washing. For months, I wept through each song service as my soul was soothed and "washed." (Washed is the only word that seems to fit.) There was melody, there was harmony, there was intelligible words that made sentences and sense, and the volume was not cranked up enough to cause pain in the ears. It was as though you would not be hesitant to invite Jesus to sit beside you. To say that the music was pleasant is an understatement. It was a wonderful "Balm of Gilead" to my soul that had been recently tortured for five long years under the leadership of a Decibel Disciple.

Exactly a year later to the month, to my dismay, the **Decibel Doctrine** kicked the sanctuary doors open and slithered into my safe haven, and without delay, in an instant, in the twinkling of an eye, the music was cranked up to extreme decibels. Sisters began to argue over whose turn it was to tend the nursery and many volunteered over and over to help keep the nursery just during the song services.

Upon the rude intrusion of the **Decibel Doctrine**, I immediately began to witness the typical tucking of the head and finger-in-the-ear responses of men and women. I was in shock that my communion with God had again been invaded by the same monster as six years ago in Faith Tabernacle of Port Arthur, Texas. Assembling in the Sanctuary was suddenly becoming an unpleasant experience for the second time in my life. Only God and I know how many times I questioned; "Why me Lord, why is this spirit following me??"

After a few weeks of enduring the new paths of the **Decibel Doctrine**, a real Christian who lived the life, came to me on the platform asking if I could do anything about the new volumes of music which now rocked the windows and walls of the Sanctuary, and assaulted the hearing of normal people. Being familiar with the spiritual tenacity of the **Decibel Doctrine** and its aggressive disrespect for sincere Christians; I looked into the desperate eyes of a friend, and sadly shook my head as I replied, "No, Sir. I cannot."

The **Decibel Doctrine** is spirit-driven and can only be subdued and eradicated by preaching against it. And a **Decibel Disciple** will NEVER-NEVER-NO NEVER preach against the **Decibel Doctrine**.

Rather, he will justify the **Decibel Doctrine** with Bible scripture, which makes him a Genius Wizard. Only a Genius Wizard can justify a brand-new spiritual revelation and a New-Age religious practice by erroneously utilizing scripture that was written centuries ago. As if God took a long-long time to decide what He liked and forgot to write it down, so He verbally told just a few New Age Pastors.

Twice now, I am an eye witness to the quick and complete invasion of the **Decibel Doctrine** into a church Sanctuary. I am an eye witness to the speed at which this spirit takes total control and total preeminence in church leadership. I am an eye witness to the massive everlasting root system that perpetually supports this new foundation, where artificial volume rules forever more.

Shortly after this rude intrusion into my heavenly nest of peace and tranquility, I was invited to go and help Pastor Shaw in Brady, Texas. Thank the good Lord. But before I left Orange, Texas for Brady, Texas, I witnessed another manifestation of the **Decibel Doctrine** worth mentioning for the reader of this article.

As the **Decibel Doctrine** began to take preeminence and control of the Sanctuary, there was naturally justified resistance. Not resistance stemming from any hint of rebellion, but just naturally motivated from ordinary common sense.

One must never forget that the spirit of the **Decibel Doctrine** is aggressive and self-seeks preservation with vengeance; identical in tenacity to the spirit of perversion that dominated Sodom. That degree of aggression was manifested during a church serve as I witnessed the Pastor "storm off" the platform and stomp his way to the sound man in the back and tell him to *get that volume up!* I was an eye witness of the fury of this Pastor as he protected and propagated the new path called the **Decibel Doctrine**.

Of course, the ever-present question in the mind of any sane reader was: "could the congregation already hear the music before being cranked up to meet the **Decibel Doctrine** standard?" The answer is profoundly, "of course." The Sanctuary sound system was plainly audible in every hallway, every bathroom, and every Sunday School room *before* it was cranked up.

BUT it just didn't have that "umph" that creates physical emotion and ecstasy and awe. So, the sound man cranked up the music some more in obedience to his Pastor. Then the music could be physically felt, enriching the agenda of the **Decibel Doctrine** as well as satiating the lust of all present Decibel Disciples.

Never forget that the leader of the **Decibel Doctrine** is the leader of the church assembly. And the concern and priority of a Decibel Disciple as he leads a church assembly is not the welfare of the saints, nor their comfort. And without exception, any appeal to common sense is pushed aside to focus on the main concern: is the music loud enough to "make it happen"? Or can the congregation "feel the power"?

And "sonny-boy" - anything or anybody that interferes with that agenda will be devoured by a toothed spirit.

This was my old home church as a young lad being raised in Orange, Texas. This church had a phenomenal Pentecostal heritage established by men like W.E. Gamblin. I remember years ago when the **Decibel Doctrine** and its agenda were foreign and unknown in this church. But that spirit found its name on a welcome mat in the Sanctuary of the most-high God, and it entered through the airways to be lifted up above the stars of God forever. And it works, they say, and it will never go away.

And I am an eye witness…. one more time.

David Clark
March, 2001

God is Robbed in His Own House

In the book of Genesis, we find many typologies that express future Types and Shadows of things that will come to pass. Typologies that reveal God's ways and also the ways of man. It all started in the beginning, and there are many examples recorded for our benefit, in the Book of Genesis.

In the beginning God created, and I contend that He created exactly what He wanted to create. Though this statement seems unnecessarily elementary, yet it is an absolute that some men cannot accept. Thus, we find "wise" men constantly changing and improving upon what God decisively created for His own pleasure; applying their own opinions of what God desires while appeasing their personal preferences.

Before creation there was a plan - a want - a desire - an idea, in the heart of God to create exactly the desires of His heart. When the Creator finished creating, He beheld it all as "very good." (Genesis 1:31)

God had completed the desires of His heart, and very possibly filled a void induced by loneliness, that could only be satisfied by creation. But presumptuous "wise" men always have a better idea of what pleases God than God Himself. And these presumptuous "wise" men consistently add the "works-of-man's-hands" as an improvement to what brought God pleasure from the beginning. They presumptuously say "the worship I offer unto God is my personal preference."

This question is FOREIGN to New Age Pentecost: Why not let God have His personal preference?

Revelation 4:11 explains that all things were made by Him for His pleasure.

> *Thou art worthy, O Lord, to receive glory and honour and power: for thou hast created all things, and **for thy pleasure** they are and were created.*
> **Revelation 4:11**

So, all creation has the God-given ability to bring pleasure unto God, from the beginning. But the fallen angel called Lucifer sought an opportunity to interfere.

It is evilly natural that Lucifer chose to manipulate the creation that had the most potential to please God. And that creation is the one that was made in God's own image, the most God-like creation, called man. And of course, that is you and I.

Lucifer's perpetual agenda is revealed in Isaiah 14:13-14: to exalt himself above the stars of God, and to be like the Most-High. Lucifer lost his first estate in heaven because iniquity was found in his heart, and ever since that fall, he has found pleasure in the allegiance of other fallen angels that were also created for God's pleasure.

Today Lucifer seeks and desires to use you and I as pawns for his pleasure and rob God of His pleasure. If he cannot take preeminence in a man's life, then surely, he thinks: "If I can pervert and distort and interfere with the original purpose of the God-like creation called man, I will have robbed God of the pleasure that He seeks from man."

When the Creator formed man with His own hands, the one true God that knows no limits, created an inherent completion of everything that He desired. Though I may forget to do so, I want to often repeat in this treatise that in the beginning, God created exactly what He wanted. (Let us agree that redundant re-iteration of such an absolute that refers to God's pleasure is justifiable.)

So, our can-do-anything God fully designed man with everything necessary to bring pleasure unto Himself, from the Beginning.

The Creation called man actively brought pleasure to God in the Garden of Eden.

Adam and Eve simply walked and talked with God in the Garden of Eden.

And they heard the voice of the Lord walking in the garden in the cool of the evening...
Genesis 3:8

Adam and Eve recognized what they had heard many times before, the voice of God.

(Please study the meaning for "walking" in Strong's Concordance. I write only the pronunciation. Pronounced **Haw-lak'**.) **Haw-lak'** is a verb. And there is a great variety of applications to the meaning of **Haw-lak'**. Most of which refer to physically-near positioning AND, as is logical, that KEY action - **"to be conversant."**

Adam and Eve did not walk together with God through the Garden of Eden in silence. It is spiritually insane to assume that God walked with man in mute silence as if for exercise. As the Hebrew definition of "walking" concludes, Adam and Eve were conversant with God. Adam and Eve talked with their Lord. Is that not what we call communion, simply talking with closeness and relationship to God?

My use of the term "simply talking" is an understatement of a sacred privilege. Rather, Adam and Eve closely communed with God. And in doing so, the creation called man, afforded to God the pleasure for which He created man. Common sense, I think, forces a learned man to understand that God desired more from man than just an exercise partner or a visual-only contact. In the

Garden of Eden, God would speak to Adam and Eve, AND God would listen to Adam and Eve.

One can envision God slipping off His throne in Heaven, turning His back on a heavenly host that worships and praises Him twenty-four hours a day; just to walk and talk with two human beings in the Garden of Eden.

One repetitive refrain continually heard in Heaven is revealed in Revelation 4:8;

> *"… they rest not day and night, saying, Holy, holy, holy, Lord God Almighty, which was, and is, and is to come."*

Words of adoration and honor spoken to God. Words from the pure lips of heavenly creations spoken of God, in His presence, for His pleasure. Angelic voices glorifying the deity of their Creator resonating in Heaven, yet God would wander away into the Garden of Eden to commune with two human beings….!

A mystery, a phenomenon beyond human comprehension! That you and I are given preeminence over the pleasure that a Heavenly Host of angels bring to God!

I contend that today, if you and I were the only two human beings in the Garden of Eden, not as Adam and Eve, but rather as John Doe and Jane Doe; The Lord of Creation would again turn His back to the praises of angelic voices in heaven, and seek pleasure in walking and talking with we two human beings. That is mind boggling! My education being limited to five years of college and only the English language renders this concept as ineffable.

It is no wonder that David, referred to by the Lord as "a man after mine own heart," wrote:

> *What is man, that thou art mindful of him? and the son of man, that thou visitest him?*
> **Psalm 8:4**

(Before I refer to the ugly words, **"Decibel Doctrine"** in this article, allow me to expound more on the untapped uniqueness of the Hebrew word *Haw-lak'*.)

Psalms 51 is the words of David as he appeals to the weakness of his Creator in his plea for mercy after his blatant sins were exposed by the Prophet Nathan. "Weakness" in God? YES!

The "Achilles Heel" of God's heart is His passion for the pleasure that He created in man: *Haw-lak'* – simply, to be in close proximity and conversant with God. To speak to, converse with, commune with – just as in the beginning.

King David had committed adultery and murder, even going as far as trying to cover his sins. David, known to God's heart, pleads with God in Psalms 51 and bargains for mercy, by appealing to a "soft spot" in the heart of his Creator.

> [14]*Deliver me from bloodguiltiness, O God, thou God of my salvation: and my tongue shall sing aloud of thy righteousness.* [15]*O Lord, open thou my lips; and my mouth shall shew forth thy praise.* [16]*For thou desirest not sacrifice; else would I give it: thou delightest not in burnt offering.*
> ### Psalm 51:14-16

David, being a man after God's own heart, knew that his best chance of finding mercy was to offer his Creator sounds out of his mouth. David, knowing the heart of God, bargained "if you will forgive me and wash me clean of my iniquity, my mouth will sing of thy righteousness and my lips and my mouth will speak your praises." *Haw-lak'*; the irresistible pleasure that God seeks from the beginning.

Haw-lak' is the same God-created pleasure that caused Noah to find Grace in the eyes of the Lord as declared in:

> [5]*And GOD saw that the wickedness of man was great in the earth, and that every imagination of the thoughts of his heart was only evil continually.* [6]*And it repented the LORD that he had made man on the earth, and it grieved him at his heart.* [7]*And the LORD said, I will destroy man whom I have created from the face of the earth, both man, and beast, and the creeping thing, and the fowls of the air; for it repenteth me that I have made them.* [8]*But Noah found grace in the eyes of the LORD.* [9]*These are the generations of Noah: Noah was a just man and perfect in his generations, and* **Noah walked (Haw-lak') with God.**
> ### Genesis 6:5-9

In the days of Noah, the creation called man had become continually evil. God was grieved and was sorry that He had created man. Why was God grieved over His creation?

Remember the very purpose of Creation, especially man, was for God's pleasure. Obviously, man no longer practiced *Haw-lak'* unto God. Talking with God, communing with God, walking with God, which all require the acknowledgement of God, are all distasteful practices for a wicked man. Since man in those days of Noah no longer brought pleasure unto God, the Lord said: *I will destroy man whom I have created from the face of the earth.*

In country boy vernacular, God was saying; "What good is man to me? Man no longer brings pleasure to me." (And the whole time the sound of angelic voices echo exaltation throughout the heavens to their Creator in perfect harmony.)

It appears that God looked over the Earth one more time before completely destroying all mankind. And He found Noah; a just man and perfect. But the distinctive attribute found in Noah was that he was conversant with God. And that signal mark saved him and his family. Being a just man and perfect in a wicked world no doubt required much prayer (talking to God). *Haw-lak'*

Noah walked with God - and that act of being conversant with God, *Haw-lak'*, moved the Lord to give Noah a Plan-of-Salvation called the Ark. The Ark saved him and his family and any and all that got on the Ark. Consequences and Rewards of **Haw-lak'**. God's pleasure.

One more short mention of another man who was Conversant with God, before I refer to the **Distasteful Decibel Doctrine.**

> And ***Enoch walked with God***: *and he was not; for God took him.*
> **Genesis 5:24**

It is as though when God found a man that would **Haw-lak'** with Him, He took him straight to heaven, before Enoch got too busy with the cares of life to walk with God.

Here I repeat a previous paragraph: It is evilly natural that Lucifer chose to manipulate the creation that has the most potential to please God. And that creation is the one that was made in God's own image, the most God-like creation, called man. And of course, that is you and I.

The most effective instrument with which Lucifer wars against this pleasure created-in-man from-the-beginning is men themselves.

God uses men to fulfill His purpose on earth. AND Lucifer uses men to fulfill his purpose on earth; to spoil God's purpose of creating man in the beginning.

There is no works-of-man's-hands more effective for spoiling God's planned pleasure, than the **Demonic Decibel Doctrine. The Decibel Doctrine** is invigorating and exciting to the flesh of the shallow and unaware, while it overrides and overwhelms the sound of human voices offered to God. As sincere men attempt to **Haw-lak'** with their God in the Sanctuary, the sounds of humans being conversant with their Creator are covered and over-powered by extreme decibels of music.

This act of "treason" in the Sanctuary can only be performed by the works-of-man's-hands referred to today as a sound system. Human voices of praise, lips that exalt Him, human mouths being conversant with their Creator, all attract God and afford Him pleasure. But when the **Decibel Doctrine** is in action, and the electronic invention called a sound system is abused, God's preference-for-pleasure, the human voice, is decimated, minimized, and then obliterated by man's preferred pleasure in the Sanctuary.

And God gets robbed of His preference in His own house.

The **Decibel Doctrine** is a nefarious substitute for the sounds of pleasure that attracted God into the Garden of Eden. The **Decibel Doctrine** is a manmade, spirit-led invention that usurps that precious act of **Haw-lak** that awarded Noah with God's Grace.

(Nefarious is a rare word to my everyday vocabulary. But I find it very fitting to grade the man-made substitute that has robbed God in His own house.)

<u>Nefarious</u> definition - Webster – adjective. *Wicked in the extreme; abominable; iniquitous; atrociously villainous; execrable; detestably vile.*

Synonyms. — *Iniquitous; detestable; horrible; heinious; atrocious*

In the beginning it was not so. No electronics, no transducers, no amplifiers. Nothing artificial. All God-created, nothing man-created, and God considered it all as "very good." This simple absolute truth is not a statement against technology, but it is a statement that absolutely declares at least a hint of God's pleasure.

It is an absolutely presumptuous act of the created to think that he can force the preference of His Creator.

A Decibel Disciple believes that he creates a Utopia of Praise and Pleasure for the Creator by practicing the **Decibel Doctrine**.

A Decibel Disciple refuses to believe that music should only accompany the human voice in song, never taking dominion or preeminence.

Maybe, just maybe, God simply prefers that the breath of life that he breathed into the nostrils of man during creation in the beginning, to be returned to Him in the form of conversation with Him, or communing with Him, or walking and talking with Him, …… **Haw-lak'.**

Poor God. He never desired complicated man-made technology in the beginning. And many falsely-taught Christians believe it will be in Heaven. This type believes that in Heaven, they will offer their **own personal preference of pleasure** to their Creator.

Yes, God is robbed of His preference every day in His own house; whether that house be the Sanctuary of a church building, or the Temple of the Holy Ghost which is Spirit-filled men.

What? know ye not that your body is the temple of the Holy Ghost
which is in you, which ye have of God, and ye are not your own?
1 Corinthians 6:19

God still longingly seeks **Haw-lak**, His preference of pleasure.

And every sane man groans: "Poor God."

David Clark
September 2001

Metamorphosis of Pentecost

Most Bible scholars agree that the New Testament Church was birthed in the Second Chapter of the Book of Acts. The "pouring out" of God's Spirit profoundly changed Religion.

*¹And when **the day of Pentecost** was fully come, they were all with one accord in one place. ²And suddenly there came a sound from heaven as of a rushing mighty wind, and it filled all the house where they were sitting. ³And there appeared unto them cloven tongues like as of fire, and it sat upon each of them. ⁴And they were all filled with the Holy Ghost, and began to speak with other tongues, as the Spirit gave them utterance.*
Acts 2:1-4

And they continued stedfastly in the apostles' doctrine and fellowship, and in breaking of bread, and in prayers.
Acts 2:42

*Praising God, and having favour with all the people. And the Lord added to **the church** daily such as should be saved.*
Acts 2:47

Since God chose the Day of Pentecost for the day of birthing the New Testament Church, the term "Pentecost" is commonly applied to similar churches of today that have been *filled with the Holy Ghost, and began to speak with other tongues, as the Spirit gave them utterance*. This Pentecostal Experience has been cuddled in the hands of man with reverence for nearly two thousand years as a precious ruby without price. But in the hands of the New Age Priesthood of the Twentieth Century, Pentecost has suffered METAMORPHOSIS.

We Pentecostals have earned the reputation conveyed in the following true story:

My close church friend, Kevin, was asked by a young man in a store if he was Pentecostal. When Kevin replied yes, the man became excited and began to explain to Kevin that the Baptist church he attended was now just like a Pentecostal church. With exuberance, he continued to explain that his church had just purchased and installed a very expensive and powerful sound system with large speakers and that they now "really cranked it up." "It is awesome," he said, **"we are just like you."**

At this time, Kevin and I were attending the same church together in Port Arthur, Texas. (As referred to in this Collection of Articles, this is the church where the authority of the Word of God was usurped with the authority of the **Decibel**

Doctrine in 1995.) As Kevin relayed this story to me, we both realized that it was another God-Sign that something was now very much awry in our beloved home church. We did not realize that the change we were witnessing in our home church was only the beginning of complete METAMORPHOSIS.

Searching for a wise response to this real-life testimony, I am speechless. The damage and deformation to the kingdom of God is forever settled. I wished that I could say that the METAMORPHOSIS has stalled or ceased. But the insatiable lust for the fruit of the **Decibel Doctrine** supersedes man's desire for God and His established paths.

METAMORPHOSIS continues today throughout an unaware religious movement, at W-A-R-P SPEED.

I am more convinced today than ever before, that the **Decibel Doctrine** is an abomination unto God. And that men, even good men, become deceived as they embrace it and share this consuming deception with many-times-many innocent souls unto pandemic proportions.

Metamorphosis of Pentecost has provided the world with Epic Deception.

My heart mumbles: "Poor God."

David Clark
5/5/10

Humorous/But Not Funny

The Preacher's message was invigorating. Just the message title, *"I Want My Old Church Back,"* stirred my already ravenous appetite for the Old Paths of Inspired Scripture. But in the midst of such a hopeful possibility, this Pastor of a large church, revealed a sign with just a "few words" that painted a picture geometrically positioning his church as traveling a path diverging from the Old Paths. Diverging from the path less traveled today, the unpopular narrow path that makes all the difference. Those "few words" ridiculed and mocked a Sunday morning visitor to his church.

Sardonically, with a touch of crowd-pleasing humor, he told the story to a very large crowd, from an Apostolic pulpit; How he had shredded and put-in-place, a first-time female visitor to his church.

The story was told: *I greeted a lady on her way out after the morning service and she asked me, "Are you open to criticism?" I said yes, and she told me, "Your P.A. (public address system) is too loud." I told her the truth: "If you think it was loud this morning, you should be here tonight."* And the large Apostolic crowd attending the ARK 2002 Conference all laughed and shouted "Amen."

Seemingly all the crowd considered this story told in that church service to be funny except me. I thought to myself: *How disappointing it is to drive so far and find this in the pulpit!* I had been preaching for a Pastor near Denver, Colorado, and we had decided to attend ARK 2002, in Tulsa, Oklahoma; realizing too late that we had wasted good gasoline and precious time.

Had this visiting lady been of an arrogant nature, she would have blurted out "Hey, your "####" sound system is so loud it hurts my ears. Are you deaf? I have read about Pentecost in the Bible, but this is not THAT." But she probably was a learned lady. A polite and mannerly and proper lady. A lady who would have politely smiled and not spoken had she even remotely thought that the Pastor would not be concerned. And had she complained about the Acts 2:38 salvation, the Pastor would have shown concern and scripturally explained. Had she been hurt by the One God Truth, or Jesus Name Baptism, or even Holiness Standards, this "kind Shepherd" would have shown compassion, diplomacy, and great concern for her soul and scripturally explained. But there is no scriptural defense or explanation for the **Decibel Doctrine**; only defiant defense.

Her honest and sincere complaint was a "No-No" among modern Neo-Pentecostals. She committed the unpardonable. She had failed to worship the music of the Golden Calves. She had blasphemed against the Spirit of Serpent

Seed Music. She had failed to embrace Strange Fire. She had questioned New Age Pentecostal Sacred Worship. Her complaint was regarding the most prominent and dominating experience a visitor encounters in more and more churches today; excessive volumes of the sound system, especially involving music.

Unknowingly, she had touched the raw nerve of Hell itself. Unknowingly, she had challenged the sacred cow of the **Decibel Doctrine**. Unsuspectingly, her open-hearted honesty was crushed by a spirit she did not even know existed in religion; the Spirit of Serpent Seed Music. But she left the First Pentecostal Church of Durham, North Carolina, and went home with new knowledge; IT IS TABOO TO QUESTION THE POWER OF THE DECIBEL DOCTRINE IN A PENTECOSTAL CHURCH.

With braggadocios fervor, this Pastor by the last name of Godair, repeated (yes repeated) his response to this God-searching soul for the crowd's pleasure; "Lady, if you think it was loud this morning, you should be here tonight." With intentional ridicule, the Good Shepherd was in essence telling the now embarrassed lady: "Tonight is Sunday night, that is "worship" night around here. And "worship" requires extreme decibels of music. The more powerful the sound system, the more powerful the "worship." Lady, you don't understand the great power that the sound system can usher into a church. Go find yourself a dead church that doesn't have a powerful P.A. system. We don't need your kind around here."

The crowd of hundreds attending the ARK 2002 Conference that night applauded and gee-hawed at such a humorous story.

All cheered the occasion, except me and the few with which I share a kindred spirit.

And all the sane saints please whisper to yourself: "S-H-A-L-L-O-W."

All the sincere say: **That is Humorous / But Not Funny**

And then all the real men say: "Poor God."

Signs, Signs, Signs. Signs that follow *"Not-Right"* worship. Inescapable signs, irrevocable signs, established in Genesis for eternity. Signs that are the fruit of a deeply rooted power.

Like unto Cain, Decibel Disciples are very touchy about what they prefer to offer God. The decibels produced by their P.A. system is their offering of oblation to the One who died for them. Criticize their favorite dog, their car, their boat; criticize the way they walk, talk, or part their hair. Even criticize their mother.

Just don't criticize the volume of their music. Do not discredit the power that they call worship.

Don't try to rob them of their "worship." To do so is to reap the deepest of spiritual animosity. An irrational anger like unto Cain's anger when his *"Not-Right"* worship was challenged by God.

I wish that I could find this lady and repair her perception of Pentecost. I think that I would tell her the spirit of our culture has changed the environment of Pentecost, but the true Pentecostal experience remains the same. I would explain that all Decibel Disciples are not bad men, but that perverted dependence upon extreme decibels to ignite "worship" has perverted the sanity and reasoning skills of many good men of God. I would try to convince her that the God-of-Old is still the same, His promises are still the same, and the worship that He desires was written long-long ago, and is still the same.

Maybe I would explain that God had mercy on the dead Sardis Church which claimed to be lively. All the Sardis Church had to do was remember the teachings received of old, hold fast to them, and repent of their new paths. (What a novel idea!)

But most likely I will never meet this lady, although I have met many others in her shoes. Nor am I likely to meet the many friends that she will indelibly impress with her experience of New Age Pentecost.

But Decibel Disciples think: *What is the cost of a few souls when compared to the value of the "worship" that extreme decibels of music can bring to the Sanctuary? And if it is true that extreme decibels of music will "keep" the youth, isn't a few lost souls worth trading for a new path that will save this young generation?*

A small price to pay, in the dim eyes of a Decibel Disciple. A gentle turn of the knob, a deft slide of the lever, and the power that will "keep" the youth begins to control the airways as the sound system brings life to the creations of God assembled in the Sanctuary.

Perversion personified. I puke.

The mean streak in me wants to explain the difference between a Disciple of Christ and a Disciple of the **Decibel Doctrine**.

To oppose the **Decibel Doctrine** (to be a Disciple of Christ), one's reasoning skills, common sense skills, and spiritual discernment must exceed that of a cheap laptop computer.

But rather I shall be nice and pray, lest an even more evilly-asinine doctrine pervert my own understanding.

And all the Decibel Disciples Chant:

I LIKE MY MUSIC SO LOUD

I CAN'T HEAR MY THOUGHTS.

Again, the Thinkers think: "Unfinished Men."

David Clark
2002

Pulpit Abuse

As the **Decibel Doctrine** is embraced and promoted by more and more New Age Pentecostal church platforms, Christians will begin to witness the pulpit used more frequently to rebuke those who complain about the intensity of the new volumes of music. That same pulpit will mock the sheep who use ear plugs in their ears. The sharp rebukes will silence the sheep, for sheep are meek and humble and seek to please God. The goats will jump and buck and bump heads as only goats do. And with a smirk, the goats will shout "Amen" when the sheep are rebuked from the pulpit for their honesty concerning the **Decibel Doctrine**.

But that same pulpit shall <u>NEVER</u> be used to rebuke those who suddenly begin to complain that our music is not rock-concert-loud like other churches. These New-Path Pulpits will <u>NEVER</u> rebuke saints who complain because the sound system music "ain't cranking." <u>NEVER </u>shall a **Decibel Doctrine** propagating pulpit be used to rebuke those who complain that the music volume for the past 30 years was boring and void of life.

The adverb "never" used here might be too absolute, for hopefully there will be Pastors in time who have enough discernment to perceive the root of the **Decibel Doctrine**. Therefore, rather than say NEVER, I should rather say that pulpits that rebuke those who seek and thirst for the ecstasy produced by intense volumes of music and beat will become more and more rare. More rare than seeing a spotted ape roller skating on a graffiti-covered sidewalk in downtown New York City, wearing red high-top tennis shoes and a pink bow tie and whose smile reveals a gold tooth with the inscription, "I love Jesus." Oh, and of course, a T-shirt that says "Crank Up the Music and Let's Have Church." So, rather than say "NEVER," I should rather say: PROBABLY NEVER.

On March 23, 1775, Patrick Henry addressed the Second Virginia Convention in Richmond, Virginia. A quote from his speech that day became famous for generations afterward: "Give me Liberty or give me death." Patrick Henry spoke those words with bold resolve from the depths of his heart.

When lust for extreme decibels of music finds freedom on the platform, it will satisfy its thirst or die. The same bold resolve evident in the words of Patrick Henry when he said, "Give me Liberty or give me death," can be witnessed when proponents of the **Decibel Doctrine** speak from the depths of their heart: "Give me intense volumes of music and beat or give me death."

All Decibel Disciples consider that withholding rock-concert volumes of music from the Sanctuary assassinates the spiritual life of a church service, in first degree murder. Therefore, Decibel Disciples plead from the depths of their hearts with resolution equal to Patrick Henry; "Give me extreme decibels from my sound system or give me death."

How does such innate lust evolve? How can musicians and singers who have been praising God for ten or twenty years or longer, in the same church, with the same acoustics, on the same platform, suddenly one day say "our music is not loud enough," "we want it louder," or "give us loud music lest we die"? Or worse; they LIE and say, "we have never had a move of God without loud music" and THEY BELIEVE IT.

Surely, they have tasted the addictingly deceptive ecstasy of the **Decibel Doctrine** somewhere along the way. (I can now better understand why Pastor Murray E. Burr guarded our home church from many religious meetings and conferences.)

I am told that "special effects" from the drug referred to as "crack" is so addicting that the user is addicted immediately upon the first use. Could it be that the physiological effects of loud music and beat upon the human body can cause first-time spontaneous addiction? Taste it once, and forever thirst for those special effects?

Maybe that is why peer pressure from the addicted can influence, in time, even the least suspected pulpit.

Pulpit Abuse – when the pulpit is used to mock and intimidate and rebuke the resisters of the **Decibel Doctrine.**

God give us men who are above **Pulpit Abuse**.

Signing off with a Krazy Equation:

A Red-Hot Sound System + A Lukewarm Soundman = Special Effects that make Hollywood salivate.

David Clark

A Most Sobering Discovery That Found Me

On April 12th and 13th, 2010, I attended the UPCI men's conference in Lufkin, Texas. I was blessed to have my friend, Caleb with me from Colorado. The theme of the meeting was STEADFASTNESS. The preaching seemed to be heaven-sent just for my soul. I believe that there was much accomplished that day through the Word of God.

As I entered the sanctuary that night, I did what I have done for at least 20 years. Prior to choosing a seat I scanned the positioning of the powerful speakers mounted in the ceiling; seeking a seat that hopefully might be the least targeted by the power sent down by the hands of the sound man. I chose the seat that appeared safest from sound-system-assault and knelt to pray.

But during the meeting, I was pleasantly surprised. Not one song was obnoxiously loud or physically painful. In years past, I have often sought safety during the music service by exiting the auditorium and perusing the books for sale or counting the blades of grass on the landscape.

After the last day-service that Friday, Caleb and I went into a local music store called Sound Tech. I was questioning Tim, the in-house sound technician, about recommended speakers for our church in Hillister, Texas. In the middle of our discussion, Tim asked me what kind of church I pastored. When I answered Pentecostal, he said that those particular speakers that I was inquiring about were not large enough. I asked, "Why do you say that?" He told me that their store ran the sound system for the Pentecostal campground, and he knew what we liked.

With calm, almost-controlled anger, I began to explain to him the deception in the **Decibel Doctrine** and that it didn't matter what he liked, or I liked, or they liked; but what God liked did matter. I finished by saying that God is not impressed by man's technology; He is not touched by the artificial electronic volume; "loud" in the Bible was not prophetic of what man's technology would produce 4000 years later; and much more. When I finished, he could tell that he had touched a conviction in my life and just stared at me confessing, "I agree, I agree."

Now knowing that it was his store that ran the sound system for the campground, I told him that the volume was abnormally pleasant at camp meeting this year and asked him to be sure to compliment the sound man. Tim replied that Mark was the sound man for the campground conference and that he just happened to be in the store at that time and would be glad to receive a compliment. I was introduced to Mark and gave him my compliment, and then he disturbed me with some Most Sobering information.

This professional sound man that was hired to run the sound at our UPCI Conferences disturbed me by confessing, "It is not I". I just do as "**They**" say. "**They**" want it hot; "**They**" want it loud. Sometimes "**They**" tell me to step back, and "**They**" crank it up. (**They**, of course being the UPCI authorities over the conferences).

As I have written in times past, this war of good against evil, right against wrong, light against darkness, is very vicious, and only the alert and the aware survive. Of all the battlefronts in this war, the most vicious is the war over worship, because of the loot at stake. Spiritual warfare over what is Biblical Worship and to whom it will be offered. A contest of *Right* Worship versus *Not-Right* Worship.

"What Does the One True God Seek and Deserve" could be the historical title of this perpetual war. "Worship" is mentioned 14 times in Revelation; the book that vividly exposes the war over worship and awards God as the conclusive victor.

If there was a "War 101" class, the first lesson taught would cover three elementary truths.

1. Is there an enemy? - If no enemy, no war.

2. Who is the enemy? - Without this information there is no defense, no offense, and no victory. Identifying the enemy is most crucial.

3. IDENTIFY, then REMOVE FIRST, the most dangerous enemy. - In "War 101," they would teach that **the most dangerous enemy is an enemy found within your own ranks.**

Below, I surmise my discovery, repeating the identical word "they" used by the soundman in Lufkin, Texas, referring to us Campground-Pentecostals.

"**They**"- are the enemy of Biblical worship.

"**They**"- are the enemy of ancient landmarks and old paths embraced and preached by Patriarchs such as V.A. Guidroz who is memorialized at the entrance of this beautiful edifice in Lufkin, Texas, called The Tabernacle.

"**They**"- are the enemy of *"shachah"* - Old Testament worship AND *"proskuneo"* – New Testament worship. (Pronunciation used in place of Hebrew and Greek lettering for worship.)

"**They**"- are the most dangerous enemy in this war over Biblical worship because "they" are among us.

"**They**"- are an enemy to us who seek Biblical worship and hunger for the old paths and old principles found in the written inspiration of our God and preached by old warriors as they defended God Himself

"**They**" are us. We are the enemy of Biblical Worship.

For years I have wanted to choke the sound man at conference meetings. I have wanted to pray for him, cast the devil out of him, enlighten him, rebuke him, or pray for a power outage. But most of all, I have prayed that his master who manipulates him would be bound and sent far, far, away. Far enough away to not rob me of the joy of assembling with brethren of like precious faith. Far enough away to not rob God of the pleasure of the true sacrifice of praise, the fruit of the lips of His people.

And now I know that it is not he, but **THEY**.

So, **To THEY, I SAY:**

The volume of our music is not worship unto the One who is worthy of worth.

And except we de-program ourselves and begin to defend our God and the Biblical Worship that He is worthy of…., Selah.

The horror of eliminating an enemy in our own ranks goes unspoken.

Long distance weaponry often minimizes the reality and horror of the elimination that is a necessity in worldly war.

But when the enemy that challenges Biblical Worship - is in our trenches… among us…??

It is a horror to think of hand-to-hand combat with a friend or brother.

And, of course, spirit to spirit combat with a fellow brother is even more horrific.

David Clark
2010

I did not write the Bible. I just try to live by it. And I am sometimes successful.

If Non-Biblical Worship makes a Christian *Not-Right*, as established in Genesis, we all need to re-evaluate our stance in this war. Including "**THEY**."

Cop-Outs

cop–out, noun\\\ˈkäp-au̇t\\

Definition

- **an excuse for not doing something**
- **something that avoids dealing with a problem in an appropriate way**

Synonyms

Cop-out, dodging, ducking, eluding, elusion, eschewal, eschewing, evasion, out, shaking, avoidance.

Related Words

bypassing, circumvention, runaround, sidestepping, skirting, averting, deflection, obviation, precluding, prevention

Slang – "beat around the bush"

Decibel Doctrine Pastors will naturally be quizzed by sincere saints who have a reasonable aptitude of common sense. The necessity of extreme volumes, especially volumes of music, will be questioned by the genuinely sincere church member, or even a visitor who has not been exposed to the power of special effects in New Age Pentecost. The questioning, the confession of pain in the ears, and the polite respectful complaint reflecting genuine concern, are always responded to by the Decibel Disciple. But the response to even the most humble, sincere saint begging for "common sense" mercy from a Pastor who highly regards his sound system is often a **cop-out.**

No matter the level of gross abuse concerning the music and drum volume; the answer from a Decibel Disciple is habitually a **cop-out.**

Real-Life Cop-Outs

First Place Winner

Cop-Out. The most exaggerated cop-out I've heard so far in my lifetime, came from a Pentecostal pulpit: "**It is going to be loud in heaven!**"

Of course, these words were forced upon the submissive crowd with an intimidating force of extreme decibels using a "hot" microphone invented by man's hands. Similar, and much like unto the intimidation that the wily wizard used upon Dorothy and her friends in the Wizard of Oz fairytale.

No **cop-out**, that I know of so far, exceeds the mystic absurdity lurking within the **cop-out** phrase: **"It is going to be loud in heaven."** (And they refer to the technology of transducers and amplifiers created by man, not the precious human voice created by God and purchased by God and preferred by God.)

Most **cop-outs** used by Pastors are initially not even believed by themselves. Surely they initially don't even believe it themselves. Yes, I'm saying they are putting you off with a statement that they know is inaccurate.

For example, Pastors sometimes say, **"the Bible says to make a loud noise,"** claiming that their sound system fulfills this commandment. They know that their 20th century technology, which has the ability to "rock the house," is not inferred by ancient scripture.

I think when they first use this **cop-out** to sidetrack a saint, and I say again, I think; they really don't believe that the power of their sound system is referred to in ancient scripture inspired of God. But in time, they become so very defensive and deceived because excessive volumes do accomplish a "work" in the Sanctuary. And their only defense is to teach that their doctrine is in the Bible. And, in time, God turns them over to believe that their **Decibel Doctrine** is found in the Holy Scripture.

(Just out of curiosity, will the massive sound systems that Decibel Disciples hope to find in heaven be powered by 110 volts or 220 volts? If any leaders of the **Decibel Doctrine** are allowed into heaven, maybe even 440 volts sound systems will be available for those who really want to impress their God.)

Can one imagine a Decibel Disciple being a worship and praise leader in heaven??!! Poor God. Poor Angels. Poor Elders. Poor Apostles. Poor Martyrs. Poor Saints. Poor Bride of Christ.

Second Place Winner

Cop-Out. The most perverted cop-out I've heard in my lifetime, came from a Pentecostal pulpit in North Little Rock, Arkansas: **"Of course the music is loud, church is a party."** And the unaware and gullible sheep received it as Truth... And PARTIED IN THE SANCTUARY.

I hesitate to mock this Cop-Out. The words necessary to expose the injustice that this Cop-Out does to our precious Blood-Bought Gospel might appear on the verge of that gross darkness called Blasphemy. I have faith in God to have a people in this day and time, even in Caesar's house.

Third Place Winner

Cop-Out. The most wily and sneaky and subtle cop-out fabricated to facilitate a lie and deceive the sincere: **"You can't please everybody."**

This statement is critical in the secular world, as in a club where people want their money's worth. But it is completely irrelevant in a Sanctuary where God dwells. God Himself is the one who should be pleased with the offering and sacrifice of praise in His presence. **(Of course, if God is not present, then it only makes sense that the Decibel Disciple should seek to please the flesh in the house.)**

It remains easy for me to believe that the Lord should take preeminence in all that Christians do, especially in the Sanctuary. When one is able to receive this simple spiritual perception, then he can see the wily, sneaky, non-spiritual intent of such a cop-out.

Interestingly, Decibel Disciples force obnoxiously loud music upon people only in the Sanctuary.

Amazingly, only-in-the-Sanctuary.

Intentionally, only in-the-Sanctuary.

Surely the defining spirit of a Decibel Disciple is plainly identified in this cop-out from low places.

Fourth Place Winner

Cop-Out. "Church should be like a football game, very loud."

KRAZY! - FUNNY! - Until one realizes that they mean it.

First of all, the attending band at a football game is not amplified above their natural level. (Like in Church). Secondly, the excitement of the crowd often drowns out the music as they cheer for their team. (Not like in Church.)

The sound that stirs contagious excitement at a football game comes from the people, not from artificial, synthetic, electronic volumes and beat from a church band.

****

Excerpts from real-life (Cop-Out) scenarios that I have witnessed in Church.

1. "Pastor, my family will not come back to church with me because the music hurts their ears." (Usually spoken in submissive desperation).

Answer (**cop-out**): "We are not having dead church around here." (never spoken with compassion.)

2. "Pastor, why is the sound system so much louder now than ever before? This has been my church (safe haven of peace) for 30 years. The music gets louder every year!" (Usually spoken in submissive desperation).

    Answer (**cop-out**): "Be patient, we're working on it."

    This **cop-out** often appeases the cringing humble Christian begging for mercy. Truly, they are working on it, but not in favor of the sincere who love God. The "working" is the works of carnal hands to force greater power from the music, as much power as the hands of man can create with physics and money.

3. "Pastor, I want to ask your permission to stay home on Sunday nights. That is when the sound man really cranks up the music even louder." (Usually spoken in submissive desperation).

    Answer (**cop-out**): "Sunday nights are Jubilee nights!" (Often spoken with red-faced anger.)

4. "Pastor, do you really believe these new volumes of music brought spiritual life to our Sanctuary??? And will help save our children???" (Usually spoken in unbelief).

    Answer (**cop-out**): "It works." (Spoken with a face red from anger to the point of fiery tears.)

5. Saint yelling loudly to be heard (holding both hands over ears) "The music is too loud!"

    Answer (**cop-out**): "You are sitting in a HOT spot; try sitting somewhere else!"

    My thinking mind questions: If the **Decibel Doctrine** is correct, then that saint should feel super-spiritual sitting in the HOT SPOT!

****

I have witnessed far too many **Cop-outs** by **Decibel Doctrine Pastors**; in response to those saints who cannot accept the **Decibel Doctrine** and dare to think that Old Biblical paths really do please God.

Decibel Disciples are getting more and more creative with their **Cop-Outs**. Their **Cop-Outs** have birthmarks from the Dark Side and can all be classified as "Fake News."

I list a few more for humor's sake.

1. **"This sanctuary is a soundman's nightmare."** Again, the thinkers think: "Hmmm, same building for 30 years."

2. **"These bigger speakers will help keep our youth."** Decibel Disciples believe that God forgot to include this salvation principle in the Holy Scriptures.

3. **"If you want dead church, go to the church down the road."** (I cannot refrain my pen here. Third-grade common sense retorts; "Then bring your sound system to the "dead" church down the road and give them life…if you have a burden for the lost.")

4. **"The volume of our sound system is like the thermostat that controls the temperature. You just can't please everybody."**

Again, my pen mocks the Decibel Disciple. If the thermostat could be adjusted cold enough to cause pain to unprotected body parts, then and only then, could a parallel of perversion be drawn between the **Decibel Doctrine** and the thermostat. Of course, the trusting sheep would have to be told that the pain of frostbite that they are experiencing is the power of God, or better yet, tell them it will help save their children.

It is ludicrous for a **Decibel Doctrine Pastor** to compare the intentional abuse that saints endure, while under his leadership, to the thermostat that controls the temperature of the Sanctuary.

Decibel Doctrine Pastors think that sheep are dumb enough to believe their **cop-outs**. Real sheep are not dumb, nor ignorant as supposed by Decibel Disciples. However, they are humble, and they are easily taken advantage of.

Attendees of **Decibel Doctrine** churches will hear various inspirations from the pulpit that leave a queer feeling in the spirit of the hearer.

Though not a Cop-Out per say, the queer phrase: **"You haven't worshiped God until you are wet with sweat,"** is often used by misled **Decibel Doctrine**-worship-leaders. It confesses in shorthand, that extreme decibels and aggressive rhythm are essential stimulants for the ecstatic physical exertion necessary to fulfill the Decibel-Doctrine-Pastor's definition of worship. This phrase paints the most vivid panoramic view of just how mindless and void of godliness man-made doctrines really are.

I have witnessed times that **cop-outs** do not appease the sincerity of a precious, humble, blood-bought part-of-the-bride. And they dare to question the presence of such power as being even a small part of heaven. Their cry of desperation to the **Decibel Doctrine** Pastor is answered with a fierce anger that arises from the deep, in defense of this new doctrine called the **Decibel Doctrine**.

The ferocity of a cornered Decibel Disciple is greater than a she-bear robbed of her whelps; as the promoter of *Not-Right* Worship feels pressure to defend his source of "power." Therefore, the spirit that drives the **Decibel Doctrine** attacks and subdues the questioning bride with a force of anger unmatched in the physical realm. And the Decibel Disciple finds this an easy feat, because saints that do not embrace the **Decibel Doctrine** as Biblical, are usually meek and humble and submissive (even to perverted leadership).

I want to help the reader by encouraging you to study the word "worship" in the Bible for yourself. Study the meaning of the word. Study the examples of worship being performed in the scripture. It will enlighten you as only the Word of God can.

There is no reason to study the word "loud" in the Bible. It is a no-brainer that power of our 21st century sound systems are not referred to in Holy Scripture that was written long before electricity was even discovered.

If you as a reader of this collection of articles have questioned the Biblical validity of the **Decibel Doctrine**, then a Biblical study of "worship" will help you. But if you have already embraced the **Decibel Doctrine** as Biblical, the Word of God cannot help you. Remedy from this deception will continue to escape you.

The rarity of men capable of a self-diagnosis of deception is frightening. So far in my life time, I have yet to witness even one Decibel Disciple recover from the snare of total deception hidden within the **Decibel Doctrine**.

I cannot help but believe that my Lord is very serious about what is offered unto Him in His Sanctuary, especially under the guise of worship.

I have lived long enough to witness the distasteful self-generated power in the airways when a Decibel Disciple is in control of a church service. And I am old enough to have also witnessed the ordained power that comes from only God above.

David Clark
3-7-2017

Long Forgotten Insightful Warnings From Old Pentecostal Patriarchs

The Pentecostal Experience began over two thousand years ago. Documentation of its birth is found in the second chapter of the Book of Acts in the Word of God that we call the Bible. This Pentecostal Movement continues today as hungry souls still experience the baptism of the Holy Ghost.

God, as the giver of the Holy Ghost, also gave us strong, spiritually sensitive men for guidance, encouragement, and admonition. We have depended upon these men of prayerful insight and wisdom to defend us against the never-ending innovative wiles of the enemy-of-all-righteousness. One of these Pentecostal Patriarchs upon whom we have leaned heavily for wisdom is Reverend David F. Gray.

Reverend Gray was ordained by the United Pentecostal Church International in 1939. He earned two degrees: Bachelor of Arts in Theology, and Doctor of Christian Literature. He went to be with his Lord on April 23, 1996. The United Pentecostal Church International rightly esteemed Reverend Gray as "a giant soldier of God." The fruit of his ministry edifies this honorable title and much more; Reverend Gray became the "Go to man" for spiritual advice and Biblical questions.

Thus, his God-given wisdom found within the publication *Questions Pentecostals Ask* became a Landmark Guide and Directive in the 1980's for the Pentecostal Movement.

****

Below; This Article contains **Brief Quotations in Literary Review** of the spiritual wisdom and insight that Reverend David F. Gray shared with God's Church that he loved.

SUBJECT – CHURCH MUSIC

As indicated by his words, this Landmark Patriarch believed with most of his contemporaries; that rock-and-roll was the pornography of music. Rock-and-Roll Music: Music built upon excessive volume and exaggerated beat.

Insightful Warnings From a Spiritually Wise Pentecostal Patriarch

QUOTES (from page 173 of *Questions Pentecostals Ask*)

Rock n Roll Music – "It works upon the nervous system of individuals, producing disorientation and the breaking down of restraints." "It is hand-in-glove with the drug culture, with occult and devil worship." "...the heavy beat, repetition, and broken rhythm is so hypnotic that the words are not even heard or considered..."

QUOTE (from page 170 of *Questions Pentecostals Ask*)

"It is 'strange fire' indeed to try to worship God by means of music which brings demon spirits into operation and which unleashes the lower bodily passions."

QUOTE (from page 166 of *Questions Pentecostals Ask*)

Here, Reverend Gray, our Honorable Landmark Patriarch, quotes from the Pentecostal Paper titled the *Sentinel* as follows: "Our own churches are being invaded by the beat of the Beast and the twist of the Tempter!"

In the closing of page 171 of *Questions Pentecostals Ask;* Reverend Gray addresses Christians who feel that adding Christian words to corrupt music makes it an acceptable offering to the Lord. To this subject group which is prevalent today in our Pentecostal ranks, our Honorable Landmark Patriarch leaves another Landmark of wisdom and warning.

QUOTE – "Remember the first sin - the one that plunged the whole human race into depravity and despair? Today, as then, Satan is a past master of getting people to eat of the tree of (a **mixture** of) **good and evil.**"

End of Quotes

****

The effect of aggressive rock-n-roll beat upon people is documented repetitively in professional research sources. This voluminous information is available to anyone willing to search it out.

We Pentecostals have discovered a new-way of technology that enhances the effect of the beat; EXCESSIVE VOLUME will exponentially increase the works of the beat upon the human mind and body.

And thus, the **Decibel Doctrine** has come to fruition as our worship, because of the fruit-of-its-works that we now accept as Biblical Worship.

I borrow a truth from my Pastor Elder Murray E. Burr: "Rock-n-Roll music, if one can call it music, is simply *Beat and Volume*. Words or lyrics do not designate the identity of Rock-n-Roll; simply *Beat and Volume*, with or without words."

Perpetual evidence has convinced me that the spirit of Rock-n-Roll rules our worship today. And I am not convinced that we are even aware, because it crept in, stealthily. A little here and a little there.

Warnings from our Forefathers and Honorable Landmark Patriarchs were heard with a smile, but their words of warning have passed into the night, unheeded.

Oh God save us. Even in our resistance to our Forefathers. Save us from the Spirit of Serpent Seed Music, save us from Strange Fire, save us from The Music of the Golden Calves, save us from Rock-n-Roll Music, save us from The Beat, save us from The African Siguco, and save us from the **DECIBEL DOCTRINE**.

The publication *Questions Pentecostals Ask* is available on Amazon. It is a source of expository of Biblical Principles for the Christian life.

Secular Definitions of Worship

Worship: Whether used as a verb or a noun, the language is of the same essence.

<u>Webster – 1913</u>

worth; worthiness, Honor; respect, the act of paying divine honors to the Supreme Being; religious reverence and homage; adoration, or acts of reverence, paid to God, obsequious or submissive respect; extravagant admiration; adoration, to pay divine honors to; to reverence with supreme respect and veneration, to honor with extravagant love and extreme submission, as a lover; to adore; to idolize.

<u>Oxford English Dictionary</u>

The feeling or expression of reverence and adoration for a deity.

Religious rites and ceremonies

Great admiration or devotion

His/Your Worship – chiefly a British title of respect for a magistrate.

<u>Merriam-Webster</u>

To honor or show reverence for as a divine being or supernatural power

To regard with great or extravagant respect, honor, or devotion

Reverence offered a divine being or supernatural power, *also* an act of expressing such reverence

Extravagant respect or admiration for or devotion to an object of esteem

****

Words of Wisdom for Reflection

Music is a language that homogenizes religions.

Music mixes and mingles opposing beliefs together, causing each to lose its identity and become one with all.

The Word of God is the language that separates religions and opposing beliefs.

The Word of God identifies and exposes core beliefs, thusly separating the False from the True.

****

Within the operations of the **Decibel Doctrine**, **M-U-S-I-C artificially declares authority over the Word of God.**

Even proclaiming itself to be "worship"- justified by the deception of the Decibel Doctrine.

Below is a published quote on the *Ministry of Music* from the *IBC Perspectives* magazine, volume 18, NO.3, page 77;

"First and foremost, music is worship."

This Public wresting of Scriptural Principles burdens me for this current New-Age generation.

****

I appeal to sane commonsense. Can worth, worthiness, honor, respect, homage, adoration, acts of reverence, admiration, adoration, submission, esteem, be found in the ecstatic motion demanded by New-Age Pentecostal music volume and ordered by the beat?

Again, I ask: Where is Biblical Worship of God in our Christian Sanctuaries?

Surely God still seeks Biblical Worship.

Surely God still seeks what He asked for.

At best, the **Decibel Doctrine** is a mocking substitute and a thief.

David Clark

SECTION TWO

Experiences In My Home Church

Signs That I Witnessed in My Own Home Church

This article lists only a few of the initial signs I experienced in my own home Church as the **Decibel Doctrine** was being transplanted and rooted. Remember, I was introduced to the **Decibel Doctrine** in my beloved home church, as were many of you. This section also includes both *The Yellow Envelope* and *The Night My Pastor Was Crucified in The Sanctuary*; which are detailed articles that describe at length other distastefully bizarre signs that followed the **Decibel Doctrine** into in my home church.

1. The sign that manifested as a prelude or warning that the **Decibel Doctrine** was on its way to my own church were the words of Mark, our music director: "When Brother Hammer gets here, this music is going to CRANK!" (Pastor Burr had recently announced his retirement.)

    Of course, the word "CRANK" is not in the Bible, nor is the intended meaning of that word in the Bible, nor is the principle implied by that word even remotely biblical. It seemed weird to apply the word "CRANK" to Sanctuary music offered to God, but the new-coming pastor's thoughts were above my thoughts. I soon discovered that the premeditated plan was to establish the **Decibel Doctrine** in my own precious Church. And that plan needed the music to "CRANK!"

2. Abnormal sums of much money were spent installing a more powerful sound system and larger speakers. But they reasoned; if it saves one soul, that one soul is worth more than the thousands of dollars spent on equipment. Still to this day, I'm not sure to whom they credit the salvation of souls; equipment and technology OR a lukewarm soundman OR a Pastor who embraces the **Decibel Doctrine**??

3. One of the beginning signs was of course shocking volumes of music that caused many to tuck their heads and try to stop the pain with their fingers. The New Crank Music dramatically changed our church services.

    When the **Decibel Doctrine** entered my home church in 1995, the congregation was at first stunned into silence during the new music. As the force of the rock-concert volume music would subside and people momentarily recovered from shock; hands would be lifted as usual, and the true sacrifice of praise would become a joyful noise as they offered the fruit of their lips, as was a custom for forty years.

    But then, in the midst of such a heavenly contagious sound of praise, the Decibel Demagogue that walked into my home church with the **Decibel**

Doctrine would signal a call for all musicians to get back in their place. And the sounds of praise would again be replaced with music that rocked the house.

The congregation would again be stunned into silence by the foreign force of rock-concert volume music; at a loss of how to respond to such forceful music. After suffering much anger and rebuke from the pulpit, the congregation of my home church became convinced that their way of praise had been wrong for forty years and submitted to the New Way.

4. The Sanctuary walls were covered with sound board to prevent the distortion of fractured sound waves as the new "cranked-up" volumes were forced upon the saints.

5. When we thought the volume could not get worse in our church, the leadership bought more large speakers. I heard these words from the pulpit; "I know the music is already hurting some of your ears, but these additional speakers will help keep our children." Spoken in anger of course.

6. Pulpit words and phrases: (Rehearsed to appease only the spiritually unconscious.)

    "If the music hurts your ears, buy some earplugs or leave."

    "Some of you have ear pain and headaches because you are sitting in a hot spot"

    "This building is a soundman's nightmare"

    "We are working on it"

7. Words from the pulpit with anger: "You cannot worship God standing in the pews. You have to get into the aisle and move!" The thinkers thought; poor Adam, poor Enoch, poor Noah, poor Moses, poor Abraham, poor Elijah, poor Daniel, poor New Testament converts… they never knew this secret to pleasing their God.

8. One early-on sign was experienced while helping change the chandelier light bulbs in the tall cathedral ceiling of the Sanctuary. As I was helping my friend, Skip with the tall ladder, he said "The sound system keeps shattering the light bulb filaments. But as far as I am concerned, they can crank it up some more." I thought, how oddly weird.

9. The continual increases of amplified music volumes quickly out-ran the ability of the drums to dominate, even with vigorous beating. So, three microphones were added to amplify the drum beat. The microphone-

enhanced drums could then produce volumes that were able to make even a strong man flinch. Much too soon after this addition of three mics to the drum-set, the continual increase of music volume again out-ran the microphone-enhanced drum volumes.

So, the real drums were replaced with fake electronic drums that had an unlimited source of volume. Interestingly, the excuse given from the pulpit for installing fake electronic drums was that the real drums were too loud. Even we lower-IQ saints thought; "why not remove some or all of the microphones that you recently added to make the real drums louder??"

My experiences such as this have convinced me that one of the signs that follows the **Decibel Doctrine** is the Decibel Disciple treats the sheep as though they are dummies.

10. I witnessed the tempo of commonly sung hymns increasing to an unusually fast tempo and then trending to even faster tempos. For effect.

I found it funny that my drummer friend became angry one night when the song leader kept beating out an accelerated rhythm with her hand against her hip. Then she turned to him with a "Get with it!" look. For years my drummer friend had accompanied the same song many times with his drums, but that night, the beat was rabidly increased. He had the skill to keep up with the new beat, but not the heart.

11. This same drummer friend told me that the music director told him to start making song practice because "we now have a new beat." Of course, the new beat was chronically faster than normal. Fruit of the premeditated "CRANK!" that came with the new Pastor.

12. During church services, supporters of the **Decibel Doctrine** would signal thumbs up and smile at the soundman as they watched saints grimace and tuck their heads or put cotton in their ears or even walk out of the Sanctuary.

13. A young man stood in my house one day in Bridge City, Texas, saying, "I don't know why the old people complain about the drums (referring to the recent excessive increase in volume), "**it is the drums that set the mood for worship.**" Stupid young man? No, intelligent. Aloof? No more so than the average American youth. Uneducated? No; educated by a Decibel Disciple.

14. Music Director's wife speaking of her husband: "He keeps playing the music in our van louder and louder. I keep telling him to turn it down." Insatiable thirst seeded in his heart by the **Decibel Doctrine Pastor** he trusts with his soul.

15. I witnessed the removal of all Sanctuary altars which leaders of the New Way said "got in the way of worship". A world-wide church evolution; the **Decibel Doctrine** comes in, and the altars go out.

16. I witnessed the removal of the front two rows of pews in the Sanctuary to make room for the New Way of "worship."

17. Too often, while I would be praying before church, the lead guitar player, Daryl, would come whisper in my ear: "we are going to play you some rock-n-roll tonight." I never knew his motive for I never asked, but I knew he was referring to the new music and new beat recently introduced to our church by the new Pastor, a strong advocate for the **Decibel Doctrine**.

18. Over and over, I witnessed the motion they called "worship" cease to a dead stop when the music and beat stopped.

19. Words heard from the pulpit – "All worship should end in total exhaustion."

20. I insert here a sign that never follows the **Decibel Doctrine** in the pulpit – Revelation 4:11 is never taught or expounded to discover the nuggets of gold therein. To expose the foundational principle in this biblical scripture, the teacher would have to confess that – **in the beginning God created exactly what He wanted for His pleasure.**

Thou art worthy, O Lord, to receive glory and honour and power: for thou hast created all things, and for thy pleasure they are and were created.
Revelation 4:11

21. Another sign that never follows the **Decibel Doctrine** - Bible Study on the word "WORSHIP." It seemed taboo to study biblical-worship scriptures in my home church.

22. The initial evidence of the baptism of the Holy Ghost changed from "hearing them speak in tongues" as found in the Bible, to "seeing them speak in tongues." I am embarrassed to admit that people seeking the baptism of Holy Ghost were sometimes told to run around the Sanctuary. This action seemed to align itself with the thunderous volume of music and aggressive beat. Totally void of any Biblical Certification.

23. The sound of congregational singing disappeared. Any individual singing unto the Lord was like singing at a railroad crossing as the engine roars past. You feel your mouth moving, but no sound is heard. Yet in obedience to the Decibel Doctrine Pastor angrily screaming "EVERYBODY SING," everybody opens their mouth and pantomimes. (It is the thought that counts, the fruit of your lips is not important.) "Yeah Wight," said the little boy.

24. On at least three occasions, men borrowed decimeters from their job's safety department and brought them to church to prove that the new volumes of music were damaging the ears of their families. The response from the Decibel Disciple pastor was much anger in the pulpit against those who dared to say anything negative about his new volumes of music.

25. One night after church, I sat with the soundman, a drummer, and a song leader while eating at Burger King on Highway 365 in Nederland, Texas. (That Burger King building is currently a Starbucks Coffee Shop.) The focus of our new Pastor had continually been upon ways to increase the volume of our church music. Visitors were complaining, saints were complaining, saints were walking out and a plague of confusion was evident. So naturally, the discussion at our table that night after church was the increased volumes of music.

    I made the fatal mistake of stating that I did not believe that excessive volumes of electronically induced music brought a true move of God. The response of the young song leader sitting across the table from me, literally nauseated me to a point that I could not finish my meal. I will always remember his words verbatim; "we have never had a move of God in Faith Tabernacle without loud music." Words that defied not only a God of common sense, but also defied the forty years of teachings of his previous Pastor, Elder Burr.

    Those words of my song-leader-friend that night portrayed with concise accuracy the subtle teachings of the **Decibel Doctrine.** That young man had been beguiled by the present pastoring Decibel Disciple.

26. There was much anger used in the pulpit to intimidate those who did not support the **Decibel Doctrine.** Anger-anointed words such as; "*It is of the devil to say the music hurts your ears. Saying the music hurts your ears is the first sign of backsliding. Complaints about the volume of music is stopping revival.*

27. Brother Dave, a wise elder and a real Christian friend of mine, warned the father of his grandchildren: "Son, teach your children at home, they will no longer receive it at church."

28. A dedicated prayer warrior said to me one day, "You know, we have moves of God, but they don't have the depth they used to have." (Referring to **Pre-Decibel Doctrine** Faith Tabernacle.)

29. I witnessed an evangelist walking the back of the pews, screaming, "You have not worshipped God until you are wet with sweat." With the approval and admiration of the new pastor, a Decibel Disciple.

30. One night I was blessed to hear a godly Evangelist by the name of Battrell preach at my home church. During his sermon, he made light of the song; *Crank up the Music and Let's Have Church.* And as we all suspected, he was never invited back.

31. One night, I witnessed an Evangelist preach that "complaining about the music volume" was one of the Three Things Preventing Revival. He had very recently shared vacation travel with our music director where I presume he had received erroneous spiritual inspiration.

32. Many visitors to my church made a wise choice to never come back. I remember a visitor named Lee came to get baptized. We were trying to discuss water baptism in Jesus Name as in the Bible, and this first-time visitor got into an argument with Craig-the-sound-man, when Lee told him the music was hurting his ears. It was difficult to share a Bible Study conversation even in the vestibule. Lee left to find a church to baptize him in the Name of Jesus, but "where the music was not so loud." (His departing words)

33. I brought three young boys from a homeless shelter to church on a Sunday morning. They wanted to sit on the front row with the other kids and did so. The music got so loud so quick that they began to cry in fear and ran to me to carry them outside.

    The dark spirit behind the **Decibel Doctrine** would say to them: "Fear not little one, it is I, thou shalt not surely die." But the angel Gabriel would say, "Run little boy, as fast as you can. Don't let them catch you, run like the gingerbread man."

34. My first cousin Steve, was diagnosed with a cancerous tumor in his jaw. He began to show interest in salvation and would cry during Bible studies. I wanted to bring him to my own church, but he had attended a Pentecostal Church two years prior and told me that he had felt like he was at a rock concert. Then he asked me if this is what Pentecost is today? So, the **Decibel Doctrine** prevented me from bringing my blood kin to my own home Church.

35. A highly respected couple who were long-time members of my home church loaned me a book titled *The Roaring Lion of the East: An Inside View of the Hare Krishna Movement.* This Elder and his wife somehow knew that my spirit had been suffering from the **Decibel Doctrine** that had become a precedent in our church Sanctuary, and they wanted to help me.

When the **Decibel Doctrine** began to replace the teachings of the previous pastor, this couple began to spend a lot of time in their get-away-home out of state; finding more God on a country porch. The wife was known as a praying woman, and my spiritual distress became revealed to her. Prior to sharing this subject book with me, they mailed me a very kind card to which was added hand-written words of encouragement. Kind and gentle spirits, they never publicly spoke evil of the new paths forced upon the sheep by Elder Burr's substitute, but chose rather to silently run far away.

The book titled *The Roaring Lion Of The East: An Inside View of The Hare Krishna Movement* is a publication by the Word Aflame Publishing House and authored by Marvin Yakos. The book is also available on Amazon.com.

Listed below are a few select phrases from *The Roaring Lion of The East*, a book detailing a sect of pagan worship. Shared with me by a friend in my home church, obviously to warn me against our new paths of Sanctuary Worship forced by the **Decibel Doctrine**.

Quoted Phrases of Paganism That My Friends Wanted to Share with Me

Page 116 "devotees dance ecstatically before the deities, and the chanting is tumultuous"

Page 134 "A person may even worship Satan without realizing it, …astrology, clairvoyance, astral projection, and related spiritual sciences. (A spiritual science would be the power in rhythm and decibels of music)

Page 153 Congregational assemblies "consist of group chanting accompanied by drums, cymbals, or harmoniums. These (assemblies) usually build in spiritual intensity and in a frenzied crescendo. Their effects are subconscious and quite euphoric. They often lead the devotees to dance in ecstasy. The devotees cherish this activity, as it pumps them up spiritually."

Page 154 "Chanting is not just harmless repetition, but it opens the mind to evil spirits."

These select phrases from *The Roaring Lion of the East* describe pagan-style worship inside the Hare Krishna Movement as well as the worship newly begotten on the inside of my home church.

I really don't know who copied who, nor when, but one has to acknowledge that New Age Pentecostals are probably not the pioneers of these worship types inside the Hare Krishna Movement.

History gives much age to the worship of pagan deities; EONS before Pentecost. However, we could be the first to add extreme decibels of music to their pagan-style worship as a catalyst to enhance and effectively multiply the power of rhythm and volume in the Sanctuary.

36. The most devastating sign of the **Decibel Doctrine** that I witnessed in my home Church affected a dear friend of mine who was struggling to regain his walk with God. He came to Church with his heart hungry for repentance and mercy and the renewing of his soul. He sat on the back row, his heart in need of preaching and an altar. Neither were available that night.

Rather than receiving the Word of God or a place of repentance, my struggling friend was offered the special effects of the **Decibel Doctrine**. The pastor ordered a few of the men "worshipping" up front to go to my friend and "run him." To "run him," in a **Decibel Doctrine** Church, means to lock your arms with another man and run around the sanctuary. I was quickly learning that Decibel Disciples believe that "running" a man accomplishes more than bringing him to an altar to pray. My friend broke free of their grip that night and walked out of the sanctuary, never to return. A sad, but common sign that follows the **Decibel Doctrine**, and I witnessed it in my home church.

That particular sign makes me feel like singing:

When your heart is full of sin
And you just can't get it out,
Step into the aisle with me,
And shout, shout, shout.

[Not Biblical shout as a sound out of the mouth,
but rather meaning physical movement.]

37. When I could bear the **Decibel Doctrine** no more and left my beloved home church for good, the Pastor tried to separate my wife from me, but was unsuccessful, thank God. With the help of his Decibel Disciples, the Pastor was temporarily successful in separating my daughter from me, until through prayer, her eyes were opened. The spirit of this unnatural separation was so vicious and self-preserving that my own daughter was afraid to hear any of my words. That is until God intervened. Oh, the ugly horror of the Decibel-Disciple-Producing **Decibel Doctrine**. The spiritual carnage is unmatched.

38. Soon following my decision to escape the **Decibel Doctrine** that had invaded my home church; my Faith Tabernacle friends, which I still esteem as dear, were instructed by the Pastor to not greet David Clark anywhere with a handshake. They were instructed to "say hello and keep walking." A year later, I attended the funeral of a precious saint and was embarrassed when a

man from my home church refused to shake my extended hand. (I'm not asking for a pity party. I am revealing real working signs that follow the **Decibel Doctrine**.)

One of my close friends from Faith Tabernacle told me that this man named Terry who embarrassed me at the Funeral Home, told his story to the new pastor. Terry received applause from the church assembly as a reward from the pulpit during a church service "for not shaking David Clark's hand." This sign further defines the spirit that rules where a Decibel Disciple pastors and the **Decibel Doctrine** dominates.

39. I silently witnessed many hidden agendas that protected the Spirit of Serpent Seed Music which propagates the **Decibel Doctrine**. I witnessed that spirit go beyond reasonable limits of self-preservation.

    Being a spirit, it knew that I knew. (I am saying it the best way I can.) And because that spirit knew that I knew, it also knew that when I ran for my life, I could not be left to live.

    And, as soon as I ran for my life, it came to pass. As a resister, my character had to be assassinated.

    My brothers and sisters in my beloved home church were told that I was possessed with an evil spirit.

    The same brothers and sisters were told that my precious God-fearing wife, a Faith Tabernacle Sunday School teacher, had the spirit of a "witch."

    The brothers and sisters of my beloved home church, Faith Tabernacle of Port Arthur, Texas, are very good people. The best of the best. They loved me, and I loved them. But the Spirit of Serpent Seed Music thriving within the **Decibel Doctrine** knew that I knew. And to self-preserve, it had to destroy my life. And what better way to assassinate my person than false accusations of evil in the spiritual realm.

    Time has proven that this SIGN of **Desperate Self-Preservation** will always follow the **Decibel Doctrine**.

40. Church gatherings such as the new Pastor's birthday and holiday parties were used to mock church members who did not embrace the **Decibel Doctrine**. Humorous skits were written and acted out to mock and intimidate me and others who could not comprehend the spiritual value of loud music. The actors (brothers and sisters in my home church) were of course awarded "brownie-points" by the present Pastor as he nodded his approval. Some of

these skits were based upon a very entertaining audio comedy series called *Hank the Cow Dog*.

Amazingly to me, I never angered over the public mockings. I think I was just beginning to accept the price that any man will pay for standing firm in the "Old Paths" and being known as a declared "RESISTER" of the **Decibel Doctrine**.

Even in my "Golden Years," I still enjoy listening to *Hank the Cow Dog* for clean casual amusement. AND, even in my "Golden Years," I still despise the **Decibel Doctrine**. So, as a "RESISTER" of the **Decibel Doctrine**, I have learned to live for God without any "brownie-points" from a Decibel Disciple and have suffered no regrets.

These are common-to-all signs that I initially witnessed in my own beloved home church as the **Decibel Doctrine** took preeminence.

David Clark

Seeking A Relevant Comparison to the Decibel Doctrine in Action

When all restraints were gone, and the **Decibel Doctrine** began to freely have its way in the Sanctuary of my beloved home church; My mind searched for words that could describe the **Decibel Doctrine in Action** to an outsider.

To what exactly would one compare the **Decibel Doctrine in Action**? Using relevant terms?

What picture would a teacher paint with graphic words to help the student relate to the **Decibel Doctrine** in unrestrained performance? Definitions alone fail to adequately convey this New Age concept to common people because the **Decibel Doctrine** is so foreign and bizarre to all that is natural.

Many Christians have never been to a rock-n-roll concert where loudness rules and afflicts the hearer with addictive beat and volume. So, just how would one verbalize a relevant comparison of the **Decibel Doctrine in Action** for clarity to the innocent and unaware?

Jesus, in teaching His Disciples, would often use an example to which the Disciples could relate and compare in order to clarify a subject principal.

For example, Jesus often started a Lesson of Principal with these words: "The kingdom of heaven is like unto….," and then He would speak a parable that the Disciples could relate to.

Seeking A Relevant Comparison to the Decibel Doctrine in Action, I revert back to my original experience with the **Decibel Doctrine** in the Sanctuary of my beloved home church.

When I first found myself face to face with that repugnant irritant called the **Decibel Doctrine**, my first thoughts were: This is like standing at a Railroad Crossing, and the train is roaring past, only a few feet from you. You can literally feel the vibration of its Power. The train horn/whistle that eventually deafens all train Engineers is causing you to flinch and put your fingers in your ears. And because you love God, you still try to sing the songs of Zion unto Him.

A simple country boy would say, **"Get the Picture?"**

David Clark

But It Works

This particular article was inspired by a response from the music director of my home church. The subject of our conversation was the recent increase to new levels of music volume in our church. Something he said made me inquire with suspicion: "Do you really believe that the new volumes of music in our church have brought revival?" His response was two words; **"It works."** I digested those words in muteness.

It was August of 2001. The conversation was via CB Radios as we caravanned to San Angelo Texas to help a church. Ten years later, I found notes in my office that I had scribbled in pencil while contemplating our music director's words: "It works." Those scribbled notes are here shared for the reader.

Long before medical advancement discovered the scientific process of physiology that occurs in the human body when exposed to extreme volumes of music, uneducated men had witnessed these visible effects many times and in many places. The worldly proponents of loud music that use extreme volumes for desired effects, really don't care what or why; they just know that **it works. It works** in the dance halls, **it works** on the disco floor, **it works** in rock concerts, and **it works** in any assembly of people. **It works** anywhere humans are gathered and subjected to the "power" of loud music. When this predictable effect is desired and promoted as the power of God in a religious assembly, it is the practice of the **Decibel Doctrine**.

The **Decibel Doctrine** is gaining popularity today in many church Sanctuaries because **it works**. Meaning that extreme decibels of music produce the results that the promoter of the **Decibel Doctrine** desires to see in the assembly.

Managers of beer joints, drug parties, dance halls, rock concerts, and suchlike, should get the credit for being first to discover the effect of extreme decibels of music upon humans. They knew before medical science made the discovery. But judging from my limited experience of the last twenty-five years, the Pentecostal Churches of my latter days were the first among the religious world to discover and employ the **Decibel Doctrine** in Church Sanctuaries.

Multiple denominations have now discovered that **it works** and have wholly embraced the **Decibel Doctrine** and its fruit as "the works of God." Their church signs advertise two worship services, one being Traditional Worship, the other being Contemporary Worship. The contemporary being a "worship" service in which the **Decibel Doctrine** is practiced.

We Pentecostals got it from rock-n-roll stages because **it works**, the denominal church world got it from us because **it works**, and this delusive virus is spreading among us all because **it works**.

And All Will Keep IT, because **IT WORKS**.

Of course, the term **"it works"** indicates the carnal agenda of Decibel Disciples who are shallow, unfinished men at best, and do injustice to the biblical definition of worship.

David Clark

Wisteria Vine Vision

I experienced this vision on the Sunday of Thanksgiving week, 1997, in my own beloved home church.

Many Sunday nights during "worship," I would stand in a corner near the back of the Sanctuary of my home Church. My corner was safe from collisions with "worshippers," but no place was safe from the rock-concert decibels of music that dominated the atmosphere of Sunday night "worship."

Often during Sunday night Jubilee, I would tell God in frustration: "If the enemy that I can feel trying to squash my peace and love for the House of God would just stand in front of me and identify himself, I will fight it." It was during one of these times as I was trying to reject the carnal adrenalin administered by the sound man as prescribed by the Pastor, that I experienced a vision. I have preached this vision and its moral many times.

The vision that God gave me in the Sanctuary of my home church in Port Arthur, Texas, was as follows:

I saw a very tall and stately oak tree standing alone. For some reason, there were no limbs until very high up the trunk. The bark was almost white, similar to a White Oak tree. The tree trunk was very straight.

A small vine began to grow at the root of the tree. It was a wisteria vine. The vine grew rapidly upward, spiraling around and around, until the oak tree was completely covered by the beauty of the wisteria. The trunk first, then the limbs, and then the leaves.

Then these words came so forcibly to me: "The beauty of the latter is greater than the beauty of the former."

The interpretation of the vision seemingly came also in a moment. The interpretation was as follows: *The tall and straight tree is the true old paths of Apostolic worship. The beautiful vine that enveloped the stately tree is the spirit of serpent seed music. To the casual observer,* **the beauty of the latter is greater than the beauty of the former.**

What I saw ended with the understanding that a wisteria vine eventually squeezes and chokes its host to death. The vine that wraps around the trunk so methodically, squeezes the cambium layer, impeding the flow of nutrients from the original soil, or foundation, from which the tree was birthed. The beautiful flowering foliage of the wisteria shades out sunlight which is the tree's source of life from above, and hinders that God-created process called Photosynthesis.

I did not see the majestic oak tree fall; the vision only revealed the immanent cause of death. The explanation or interpretation is that a tree killed by the unchecked growth of a wisteria vine continues to stand until its strength to stand upright decays away. An oak tree killed by an aggressive, uncontrolled Wisteria Vine, dies "standing on its feet." And until the day the oak tree crashes to the ground, long time dead, the casual observer considers the present beauty to be greater than the former beauty.

It is commonly natural for most of the vine family to exhibit vigorous acceleration of growth when trimmed or cut back. The only way to destroy an unwanted vine is to destroy the roots. The only way to destroy the roots of an unwanted spiritual vine is to preach against it. Most unfortunately, Decibel Disciples will never preach against the **Decibel Doctrine**, because it is their source of power, and its beauty exceeds that of any former power.

A casual observer fooled by a Decibel Disciple, can be convinced that the physical ecstatic commotion facilitated by rock concert volumes of fast music and aggressive drum beating is BEAUTIFUL. A saint duped by a Decibel Disciple will compare his church of former days when the Word of God took preeminence and dictated WORSHIP in the Sanctuary, to the present practice of the **Decibel Doctrine** in action and say: "THE BEAUTY OF THE LATTER IS GREATER THAN THE BEAUTY OF THE FORMER." In other words, "rock-concert-volumes of music and a dominating beat has brought life and excitement to our sanctuary. The beauty of the New Way is greater than the beauty of the Old Way."

When a church assembly embraces the **Decibel Doctrine** and the non-biblical worship that accompanies, the casual observer considers the present Beauty of the Bride as greater than the Beauty of the former Bride. Outward holiness may be maintained, causing the casual observer to utter "Shalom," while the slow death-by-starvation continues incognito, as feeding-the-sheep transgresses to exercising-the-sheep to the beat.

123

The casual Christian observer boasts: "We rock the walls with our music, offer our cranked-up-crazy worship to God, and sometimes receive preaching. We see Beauty in our New Paths."

And I say: "In Genesis, God proved to Cain and to the whole world… When Your Worship Isn't Right–You Aren't Right. *Not-Right* worship leads a man out of the presence of God."

Again please, in closing: <u>The chilling reality of this vision is that the Old-Path-Strongly-Upright Oak tree that hosted the beauty of the Wisteria Vine, is always</u> **long-time dead before it falls**.

Deception is to be feared.

David Clark

The Night My Pastor Was Crucified in the Sanctuary

Introduction

Though it be very bizarre to all sane reasoning, I seriously doubt that the following scenario is an isolated case amidst the signs that follow the **Decibel Doctrine**.

My beloved Pastor, Murray E. Burr, was crucified on a Sunday night from his own pulpit before the assembly of saints that he had fed with Truth for 42 years. He had been retired less than five years and was living in Junction, a small town in West Texas. I was present in my home church that same Sunday, praying that the Word of God would receive preeminence. So the nefarious violence that came from the pulpit that night was completely unsuspected.

Witnessing live, the crucifixion of my "Old" pastor, a true man of God, was an unmatched horror in my life. I will carry this indelible branding of my mind to the grave. The words of a few saints after that church service spoke of a very odd feeling in the sanctuary. When I got home, I began to vent my frustrations on paper. For it seemed inappropriate to vent to others, not even to my wife. My wife and I drove our twenty-minute trip home in complete silence.

I do not know if there are Christians anywhere in the church world who have witnessed a similar nightmare, but I do not wish such an experience upon even my worst of enemies.

The following article includes a few of the words and thoughts I scribbled late that same night in my office. These random thoughts give only a glimpse of the anguish a saint suffers when the teachings and character of his "Old" Pastor are openly attacked from the same pulpit that fed him and his church family words of eternal life.

Oh, the horror of a false teacher. Oh, the spiritual carnage wrought by a deceptive ministry. Surely Angels flinch.

My, oh my, the cruel signs that follow *Not-Right* worship and the **Decibel Doctrine**. Selah.

The igniting catalyst that forced the crucifixion of Elder Burr was like unto that of Jesus' Crucifixion; TOO MUCH TRUTH WAS SPOKEN. Jesus spoke words of life to the religious and to the pagans. But it was the religious who crucified Him for the Truth that abided in His words.

The spirit of Elder Burr had consistently taught the saints of Faith Tabernacle of Port Arthur, Texas with both spoken words and written words. Words of Truth that were too plain for some men to receive. When Elder Burr's book *"The Music of the Golden Calves: The Bride and the Beat"* found its way into the hands of the people he had taught for 42 years, the dark side had to crucify him, for his pen had spoken too much Truth.

And they (the dark side), Pastor Burr's replacement and the ministry of Decibel Disciples, did an outstanding job. Elder Burr's character was crucified, his core beliefs were crucified, the fundamental principles of his life's teachings were crucified, all from a pulpit that was sacred due to the 42 years of TRUTH proclaimed across it. And like unto Calvary, he was crucified before those he loved and desired only to help.

The crucifixion that night in the sanctuary was complete. He was mocked, ridiculed, falsely accused, and referred to as used-of-the-devil. Virtually, Elder Burr was beaten, spit upon, buffeted, and assassinated. The only thing that remained the next day of my former Pastor, Murray E. Burr, was distant echoes of TRUTH spoken and written through a life-time without compromise. Echoes of God-inspired TRUTH, eternally established in sacred granite.

Elder Burr's absence that night made the sinful act even more abhorrent. The night that Elder Burr was crucified in a Sanctuary in Port Arthur, Texas, he was peaceably sitting in his residence with his wife in Junction, Texas. Probably praying, as always, for the Faith Tabernacle congregation in Port Arthur, Texas.

Cause of Death. Speaking-Truth-Concerning-the-**Decibel Doctrine**-with-his-pen.

His numerous assassins, even today, keep trying to bury the Truth in prepared tombs scattered throughout the ranks of Pentecost, but the Truth keeps resurrecting. The God-inspired words of the Servant of God named Murray E. Burr continue to speak.....even from the grave.

End of Introduction

****

Some of My Thoughts the Night My Pastor Was Crucified

These are vented words of frustration, scribbled in the wee hours of the morning following that Sunday night church service when I witnessed my honorable Pastor crucified from the pulpit.

I still have the notes of that night. Handwritten with pencil in a spiral note pad, while on my knees in my office. Every time I scan these eight pages of "field notes," I am reminded of the multitude of ugly truths that I chose to not share with the readers of this collection of articles. The Spiritual Carnage left behind on the trail of an unchecked progression of the **Decibel Doctrine** is nauseating.

Let the reader evaluate the desperate cruelty of the Decibel Doctrine

As it seeks self-preservation.

I have previously explained my intended audience and also my agenda to help the unaware by exposing the exercising spirit of the **Decibel Doctrine**. However, this particular article may or may not help you. It is a sharing of an experience that wounded me almost beyond repair. It is a scar that I will carry to the grave. If my sharing helps the reader glean a smidgeon of understanding of the gross darkness within the **Decibel Doctrine**, then God Speed.

Kneeling late that night in my office, I began to write with trembling fingers…

Old Pastor,

I fear, I quake, I ache. Simultaneously I am numb. Maybe numb with fear of unchecked injustice, maybe numb with fear of confusion. Might I add, nauseated as well as angry. All of these feelings and more, that I have carried inside for 4 ½ years were compounded tonight, as I watched the pulpit that you once stood behind, used to slander and belittle you. My Old Beloved Honorable Pastor.

I observed in horror as the religious leaders on the platform called your GOOD efforts to warn the sheep that you loved, EVIL. Never had I been face-to-face with a manifestation of the God-inspired words of Isaiah *5:20: Woe unto them that call evil good, and good evil; that put darkness for light, and light for darkness; that put bitter for sweet, and sweet for bitter!*

Here I must add to my internal feelings the word, dirty. I felt dirty and odd; like it had to be a bad dream. Like – "This is too distasteful to really be happening!" I feel dirty from just having been in the congregation as a witness.

The pulpit from which you fought Hell itself for 42 years, being used to rally the ones that you love, to chant against you; "Crucify him, Crucify him." The "chant" that I refer to is the raucous cheering from the crowd as they responded to the false accusations spoken against you, and their fervor in defending the new "worship" that the **Decibel Doctrine** had newly begat in Faith Tabernacle.

Searching for the positive, maybe the chant did not come from the heart. Maybe their thinking was temporarily irrational; only momentum of uncontrollable ecstasy induced by the crescendo of rock concert decibel music that had just ceased. Maybe the Saints that my Old Pastor loved were just mindlessly taking orders from the beat as they have become accustomed to do on Sunday Nights.

I wish that I had words Old Pastor, to undo the hurt. Maybe, just maybe, this is what you meant when you wrote about Old Prophets "passing in the night."

Where do I stand? Not for a man nor against a man, for man is fallible. But I stand for Truth because "WHEN TRUTH NO LONGER MEANS EVERYTHING, TRUTH NO LONGER MEANS ANYTHING." And it is a truth that we do not battle against flesh and blood, but spiritual wickedness. Unfortunately, willing men will forever be a part of the battle because Satan chooses to use fallible man as also does God.

Old Pastor, I honor and highly value every word that you have ever written or taught. I have not yet read your latest writing, *"The Music of the Golden Calves: The Bride and the Beat,"* which ignited your crucifixion. The reason being is that I feel a foreboding that soon I will be pressed to state my position. It is spiritually impossible to stand with both you and the pastor substituted in your place. His beliefs are too diverse from yours; there is not enough common ground between the two beliefs for me to stand upon.

But decide soon I must, I can feel it in my bones. I want my words to come from your teachings settled within my heart and not be influenced by only the written words of a single book. I need to have my own conscience before God, molded by teaching and preaching and the Word of God. I can feel the urgency.

If your effort with your latest book *"The Music of the Golden Calves: The Bride and The Beat"* is to keep that spirit out of Faith Tabernacle – too late. Your preaching of 42 years warned us, but it was forced upon us. Your latest and final warning to the Bride, *"The Music of the Golden Calves: The Bride and The Beat,"* is at least four years too late. For it was approximately that long ago that I asked our director of music this question, in response to a declaration he had made; "Surely you don't believe the new volume of our music brought revival." He responded "It works."

I wonder why the volume of music does not excite me in church. Do I really have the Holy Ghost? Why don't I believe that the presence of God is proportional to the volume of the sound system? Hopefully it is because I have too many years of teaching from you in "Biblical Paths." Or maybe I have the logic of at least a fourth grader, and hopefully the spiritual IQ to match.

Back to the intention of the book *"The Music of the Golden Calves: The Bride and The Beat."* It is too late to prevent the intrusion of the *"Spirit of Serpent Seed Music"* into the bride's room that you spent forty-two years protecting. And it is too late to protect that beautiful bride called Faith Tabernacle from being soiled by that spirit.

And if your hopeful intent is to eradicate that Spirit, I say also, too late. But at one time, I had faith that words from my "Old" Pastor would bring a reality check to the new leadership in Faith Tabernacle.

That spirit is too rooted now and well grounded. Too much money and time has been pumped into it like a series of steroid injections into a prize fighter. The sound system has now been the focal point too long to minimize its necessity to "have church." To reduce the rock concert volumes of music would be like pulling up a favorite plant that someone has nourished from a seed and diligently protected as it grew. The void would be just too uncomfortable to the new gardener.

I cannot vent farther.

My tomorrows are insecure.

The teaching priest is no longer near for strength.

Fear and confusion assail my mind.

Somehow, I have successfully avoided vomiting, though the feeling is compulsive.

I must lay me down and seek rest, if God will allow me to find this elusive need for this time in my life.

God help me save my family.

David Clark

From my office, in the wee hours of the morning, still on my knees, pen in hand.

6/20/99

The Yellow Envelope

The Introduction of this collection of articles called **The Decibel Doctrine** states that in 1995 the man of God in my life was replaced with a Decibel Disciple. About four years after Pastor Burr's retirement from Faith Tabernacle of Port Arthur, Texas, one of his current writings was mailed to members of that assembly by an Elder in that church. The writing that was mailed was a booklet titled *The Music of the Golden Calves.* It was dreaded by the new residing Pastor. The book was mailed in a yellow envelope, and it dispelled the principles of the **Decibel Doctrine**.

This article describes a moment in History. It reveals the hidden force behind this specific moment in History. And of course, it describes signs that follow *Not-Right* worship. This particular moment in History is now history, yet the stench lingers. Repentance being the only per-chance remedy; the lack of which, is inherent to the signs that follow the embracing of the **Decibel Doctrine**.

The real focus of this article is not the violent resistance of the new pastor against the teachings of his old pastor, Murray E. Burr, **But rather WHY?**

The New Pastor was a strong advocate of the **Decibel Doctrine**, and the Old Pastor Burr was a long-time-strong adversary of the **Decibel Doctrine**. I was a witness of the spiritual insanity in the pulpit this particular day in my own beloved home church. The words "Yellow Envelope" are just a part of the script used in the pulpit that Sunday morning referring to the envelope that was used to mail the booklet titled *The Music of the Golden Calves.*

The first Sunday following the arrival of **The Yellow Envelope** in the mailboxes of Faith Tabernacle members, our new Pastor reacted with rabid rage from the pulpit in resistance against the book titled *The Music of the Golden Calves* with these words: **"If you got a yellow envelope in the mail, THROW-IT-AWAY!"**

Words spoken from the pulpit with so much force and animosity that fear immediately gripped the heart of the congregation, imminent fear of **The Yellow Envelope**. Sensing the urgency of their new Pastor's rabid warning against **The Yellow Envelope**, no doubt some Saints had thoughts of panic similar to "Oh My God, I hope I did not receive **The Yellow Envelope** in my mail" or "Lord please protect my children if they have touched **The Yellow Envelope**."

Surely the mind of the reader of this article begins to race as he tries to perceive the necessity and underlying intent of these pastoral words of instruction recorded in History, **"If you got a Yellow Envelope in the mail THROW IT AWAY!"** What-in-the-world could make **The Yellow Envelope** so threatening and dangerous? Explosives? Anthrax? Nuclear Waste? Biological Warfare? Or worse?

The warning "**If you got a Yellow Envelope in the mail, THROW IT AWAY,**" indicates that **The Yellow Envelope** did not have adequate warning of its own. To necessitate such an adamant and violent command from the pulpit with no explanation, **The Yellow Envelope** must have been deceptive in appearance to the sheep; harmless as a dove outwardly, yet deadly as a viper inwardly. Maybe a classic example of a wolf–in–sheep's–clothing.

Obviously, our new Pastor believed **The Yellow Envelope** received in the mail by many of the saints was of such evil that it should not remain in one's presence for even moments. The more-than-fierce order from the pulpit was to treat **The Yellow Envelope** as dangerous refuse, "THROW – IT – AWAY!!"

I was in the congregation of Faith Tabernacle of Port Arthur, Texas that day when the trumpet proclaiming this insinuated danger sounded violently across the pulpit. I was a part of the congregation that still remained after the replacement of Elder Burr, our pastor for 42 years. I heard and felt and witnessed the rabid anger from the new Pastor toward the **The Yellow Envelope**.

I saw **The Yellow Envelope**. I even touched the forbidden **Yellow Envelope.** In appearance, it was a normal store-bought yellow envelope; actually manila, not yellow. The feared **Yellow Envelope** was not laced with anthrax, nor was it impregnated with biological cultures of incurable diseases. **The Yellow Envelope** was a harmless consumer shelf item.

The enemy of the new Pastor, against which he warned the congregation that day, was of course, the content of **The Yellow Envelope**. The content was a booklet written by Elder Murry E. Burr, our new Pastor's Pastor.

So, I witnessed in horror that morning, in my beloved home church, the betrayal of the teacher by the student. The betrayal of an honorable man of God by an ingrate. I witnessed invaluable relevant truth, biblical truth, subtly withheld from the sheep to protect new paths of "worship."

(I am attempting to reveal insane signs that follow the **Decibel Doctrine**).

Unfortunately, as according to the ways of man, Elder Burr is no longer with us; yet his voice is still heard, for truth is relentless and never ceases to exist. (I write in future tense concerning the passing of Elder Burr, for this article and many others that reveal the evils faced by Elder Burr as he stood for true worship, will be printed and reprinted and reprinted again. Elder Burr's teachings will be read and read again. By many before his passing and by many more after his passing.)

Obviously, somewhere along the way, the New Way; the student, the new Pastor, had defected from Biblical old paths. He had turned from the old paths taught by his Old Pastor/Teacher and this day he was violently angry against his old wise Pastor, Murray E. Burr. The content sealed within **The Yellow Envelope** was an antidote to cure the infection of deception among the sheep that was being spread by the **Decibel Doctrine.**

Oddly enough, the content of **The Yellow Envelope** was as harmless as the manila envelope which contained it. Harmless that is, until one opened it and began to read. Then it became dangerous to its antagonist, for Truth always cuts like a two-edged sword.

Dangerous to those who taught non-biblical doctrines of worship. Dangerous to those who feared having the roots of their artificial worship exposed. Dangerous to those who secretly fear having their spiritual picture taken. This book enclosed within **The Yellow Envelope** that was to be treated as hazardous refuse, exposed the new paths of worship that been recently forced upon the congregation by the new Pastor who was now screaming, "THROW IT AWAY!" The fury in the pulpit that day was fueled by the Spirit of Serpent Seed Music that thrives within the **Decibel Doctrine**.

The complete title of this feared book is *"The Music of the Golden Calves: The Bride and the Beat."* In reality, the book was nothing new, just the same God-inspired revelations that the author had taught and preached for 42 years while pastoring Faith Tabernacle in Port Arthur, Texas. This book *"The Music of the Golden Calves: The Bride and Beat"* is available on **Amazon.com**, and I highly recommend it to sober minded Christians.

To those who are disgusted with the **Decibel Doctrine** and the new paths of worship that it breeds; I advise you to purchase the book for a directive and guide back to biblical paths of worship.

To those who have questioned this new doctrine of worship in Pentecost, purchase the book for help in identifying the deception wrought by rock concert decibels of music and beat.

To those who have embraced the **Decibel Doctrine** as biblical and are pleased with the results, purchase the book; hanging on your wall, it will double as both a dartboard and a mirror.

There is a most obvious absolute that went unnoticed that day by a majority of my church friends as they witnessed the violent rebuke of their former Pastor as the author inside of **The Yellow Envelope**. And that absolute is: there are only two sides to the war over worship, Good and Evil, Right and *Not-Right*.

Therefore, if the book titled, *"The Music of the Golden Calves: The Bride and the Beat"* is evil, then Elder Burr is evil, his doctrine on worship is contrary to God's pleasure, and he is a perverter of True worship.

If this book authored by Elder Murray E. Burr is Truth and not evil, then vice versa.

David Clark
05/2003

Reader:

Now you have a glimpse of the gamut of feelings that I experienced as an eyewitness to such violent travesty. Now you know why I felt like vomiting while in my office trying to vent onto paper my feelings with numb distaste the night my beloved Pastor was crucified in the Sanctuary. The catalyst of the whole spiritual trauma was protection and defense of the **Decibel Doctrine**.

The shallow and superficial say that this book launched a war over worship. But that is not true, for the war over worship is older than mankind. The learned understand that the **Decibel Doctrine** alluded to in this subject book is only a New-Age tactic in a very old war against Biblical Worship. So, the book inside of **The Yellow Envelope** did not launch a new war over worship; it simply exposed one-of-many pawns used by the dark-side to defy Biblical Worship. Unfortunately, and fortunately, I was there as a witness.

Here I Repeat Redundant Definitions of a Decibel Disciple:

One who believes the physiological reaction of the human body to extreme decibels of music and rhythm is Biblical Worship.

One who believes that God never found pleasure in man's worship until technology made extreme decibels of music possible in the 20th century A. D.

One who believes that physical movement to the point of sweating is "having Church."

One who believes true worship begins with speedy rhythm and ends in total exhaustion.

One who believes extreme volumes of music will "keep" the youth.

One who equates the volume of music with the presence of God.

One who refers to a church service which is void of extreme volumes of both music and drum beat as "dead" church. (blasphemous)

One who preponderates the power of his sound system in the sanctuary.

SELAH

I Witnessed This Biblical Scene Duplicated In My Home Church

And when the people saw that Moses delayed to come down out of the mount, the people gathered themselves together unto Aaron, and said unto him, Up, make us gods, which shall go before us; for as for this Moses, the man that brought us up out of the land of Egypt, we wot not what is become of him.

Exodus 32:1

Again, I use the phrase "in my small world." In my small world, I witnessed the duplication of Exodus 32:1 in my home church. In the absence of Pastor Murray E. Burr, the solid Biblical Worship he taught for forty-two years became meaningless, much too quickly.

In Exodus 32:1, God's people were intentionally willing to forget all the words of their leader Moses, the man of God, after he was absent for only forty days. But to the credit of the spiritual soundness of my Faith Tabernacle friends, for almost a year into the absence of Pastor Murry E. Burr, a man of God, they did remember his warnings about The Spirit of Serpent-Seed Music and the *Not-Right* worship that it forces.

The worship that God's people offered in the wilderness of Mount Sinai became like all other peoples in the land within forty days without their God-ordained Leader. Likewise, the worship offered by God's people in my home church in East Texas became like all other peoples in the land in the absence of their God-ordained Leader. But it took almost a year of violently forcing the **Decibel Doctrine** to re-train them in new worship.

I witnessed the power of the **Decibel Doctrine** all-too-quickly erase forty-two years of teaching out of the hearts of a very good people.

Again, I was there.

David Clark

Moral of this story to any retiring Pastor: Be very cautious who you trust in your absence, no matter how well the Church was taught in Biblical principles.

A Poem Dedicated to my Pastor

This poem was somehow an appeal of my sickened soul to my former teacher of Biblical Paths. It seems such a pathetic attempt to surmise such a pandemic of delusion that is forever settled in the world of religion.

This was written in 1998, three years after a Decibel Disciple was substituted as a pastor to replace Elder Murray E. Burr in Faith Tabernacle of Port Arthur, Texas. To remain ethical and obedient to the rule that forbade any contact with Elder Murray E. Burr, I waited until I left that assembly to share this poem with him.

David Clark
1998

Oh Fossil, Oh Fossil, "I wish I could say"

Oh Fossil, Oh Fossil
Your moaning is dear
And I wish I could say
There's no need to fear

Of Fossil, Oh Fossil
Your prophecy's so near
And I wish I could say

The spirit of serpent seed music
Will never find a home here

Oh Fossil, Oh Fossil
You love the sounds of Pentecost
And I wish I could say
The sounds you and your God love
Will never be forever lost

Oh Fossil, Oh Fossil
I know that it hurts
And I wish I could say
Our motto is not
"Crank up the music & let's have church"

Old Fossil, Old Fossil
Your paths are so old
And I wish I could say
Your old ways weren't dead
But the story's been told

Old Fossil, Old Fossil
The ways of worship are now new
And the new paths dare say
Chill out, Old Fossil
And let the music move you

Old Fossil, Old Fossil
A new way is there
And I am sorry to say
To really have church
The music must blare

Old Fossil, Old Fossil
I too remember back when
And I am sorry to say
The praise from our lips
Is now lost in the din

Old Fossil, Old Fossil
What a monument you've been
But now boldly they say
The volume of music
Is what stirs a soul from sin

Old Fossil, Old Fossil
I know what you see
But I am thankful to say
Instilled deep within me
The old paths will always be

Dear Fossil, Dear Fossil
The will of God I will seek
And I hope it helps to say
Against that spirit one day
I will speak, I will speak, I will speak

David Clark 1998

A Poem Dedicated to my Pastor's Wife

Hope to be Alive

I Have Hope to Be Alive,
When the Eastern Sky Does Part
A Hope That Helps Me Strive
A Hope Within My Heart

This Hope, That Day She Told,
The Reverent Wife of Elder Burr,
Stirred A Spark Within My Soul,
To Think, It Could Occur

If That Day My Flesh Should See,
Called Up From Life's Great Mire,
Please God, Let Me Be,
Alive With Holy Ghost and Fire

This poem was written to Sister Murray E. Burr after the death of her husband, my Pastor. In conversation she told me one day; "Brother Clark, I hope to be alive when the Lord returns." Her words prompted me to pen this simple poem for her.

David Clark

138

SECTION THREE

Allegories – Parables – Satire - Mockery

Daryl and Daryl Saw Jesus

One day every man will see Him. As we behold Him, every knee shall bow and every tongue confess. One day the redeemed will see Him on His throne and fall down and worship Him. As Jesus dwelt upon the earth, many saw Him, walked with Him, and even touched Him. Fortunate were they. Blessed and unique was their experience.

For almost 2000 years since then, no man has been honored with such a privileged encounter. That is until Daryl and Daryl saw Jesus in the year 2001.

A man's true self sometimes never manifests itself until ultimately tested. His inner being may lie dormant until circumstances demand the real man. A man is really a sum of what he has been taught, what he has learned, and what he has been fed; both spiritually as well as naturally. Like unto a young man who joins the Marine Corps is a "grunt," a wanna-be Marine, until he receives and survives training. It is training that makes him a Marine. But the success of training is not really known until the right scenario, the right environment, or the right situation demands performance of the real Marine. It is the inner man created and molded by training that passes the test. Likewise, is the training of a true worshipper.

Daryl and Daryl, longtime friends, had both been trained to worship. Both loved God and wanted to be true worshippers. They both understood that to bring pleasure unto God was the very purpose of creation. And one day, the conditions and the setting were right. On that day, the inner man was tested.

How effective was their training? A question to be assuredly answered that day. Both had been taught to worship.

Was the teaching and the training successful? When time instantly demanded true worship, what was really in these two men?

When the ultimate test presented itself, what was really within, came out.

The worship training of Daryl and Daryl manifested itself the day they saw Jesus.

****

Daryl drove a few country miles to see his best friend, Daryl. Parking outside the white picket fence, he honked and smiled at Daryl sitting on the covered porch. As Daryl stepped upon the front porch where he and Daryl would visit while drinking coffee, he jokingly said, "Well, the good-looking Daryl is now here. Shall we plan our next deer hunt?" Daryl stood up to shake Daryl's hand and retorted with a chuckle, "You're just jealous, I'll help you pray about that."

Instantly their laughter was cut short as they both saw Him. He was an unusual looking man and had appeared out of nowhere. His head and His hair were white like wool, as white as snow. His eyes were as a flame of fire, and it was as though He read the heart with just a glance. The aura of love that emanated from His very countenance seemed almost tangible. His spirit of love had the drawing power of a magnet, and Daryl and Daryl could actually feel it.

Simultaneously Daryl and Daryl first thought, "an Angel." But then Daryl and Daryl simultaneously saw the scars of Cavalry. Simultaneously, (you see Daryl and Daryl were a lot alike except in their training) Daryl and Daryl thought, "this cannot be." But then He softly spoke, "Fear not, it is I," and simultaneously, (they were nearly alike) Daryl and Daryl both recognized Him. Simultaneously (except for their training, they acted as twins) Daryl and Daryl breathed to each other: "That is Jesus!"

At first Daryl's mind panicked. His brain began to race, but could not process the information that it was being fed; Jesus…is…in my front yard, Jesus…is…standing in front of me…looking at me…. "For brain's sake what do I do?" thought Daryl? "Worship!" his recovering brain told him. "Reverence Him with worship." "Yes, that's it," whispered Daryl. "I must worship Him in spirit and in Truth. The Father seeketh such."

It was a crucial moment for Daryl; the ultimate test had come, and Daryl's training began to dominate his thought process. Years of training fast-forwarded through his mind as multiple flashbacks of his worship teacher's face flushed red with anger at church members who claimed the volume of music was hurting their ears. He could envision his Pastor screaming into an over amplified mike, "the Bible says worship Him with a loud noise." Flashbacks of countless Sunday night church services with no Word taught, only loud fast music to be heard as the worship teacher screamed "get in the aisle and worship." Flashbacks of an angry face as it screams, "Put cotton in your ears, we are not going to have dead church," "get in the aisle and dance" and much more.

All these and many more lessons from his trainer flashed through his mind in milliseconds. Words of the music director, "the volume of music brought revival." The words of the song leader, "We've never had a move of God in Faith Tabernacle without loud music." All of these flash-backs were recalled from years of teaching filed under "worship."

Principles of worship deeply rooted during years of training began to surface. Principles such as "you can't worship in the pew; you must get out in the aisle to worship." "You haven't really worshipped until you are wet with sweat." "All Apostolic worship should end in total exhaustion."

Automatically, Daryl knew what he must do; the inner man now had direction. As he turned to go into his house, he thought he saw Daryl fall down at the feet of Jesus in the yard. A very gentle tugging on his heart, that he had not felt in years, softly compelled him to "fall down and worship." "Bow before Him." "Speak to Him." "Tell Him you love Him." "Kneel at the feet of your Creator." "Humble yourself before your Creator."

He hesitated at this pricking of his heart, but only momentarily, for vivid was his memory of one of his trainers screaming from the pulpit, "I'm not going to let the Devil tell me how to worship." So, assuming it was the Devil trying to turn him against his training, he blotted out of his mind all lingering ancient words of "Old Path" Elders, and Daryl confidently continued his agenda demanded by his training.

Emerging from the screen door with a boom box (portable stereo with large speakers) and extension cord, Daryl had a this-is-gonna-be-good look on his face. A confident I-know-how-to-worship look. But to his dismay the CD in place was all "dead" church songs. Songs that made a person want to sing or lift their hands or kneel to God. Songs that might make the eyes a little misty if one thought on the words too long. What he needed and needed right now was real worship music, something loud and fast.

In desperation Daryl flipped the mode switch to FM, and immediately he smiled. The song playing was worldly rock-n-roll, but he had enjoyed this song many times and he knew that the remainder of the song was only instrumental with no ugly words, no words at all. So, confidently he thought: "that will work."

The bass guitar and drums began to dominate, and Daryl knew that the only ingredient missing now was volume. The power of his abnormally large boom box would rattle the neighbor's windows again, but today worship was more important than ever. Oh, how he wished that he could just snap his fingers and immediately have his church's sound system in his front yard. He could "really worship." But his boom box would have to do for the moment. With anxious fingers, Daryl turned the volume control toward maximum-move-of-God as he had watched the sound-man in his church do many times in training. Very quickly Daryl began to feel vibrations of worship in his feet.

He smiled as he momentarily envisioned his neighbor's face frowning through the window as his worship music rattled their windows one more time. He did not fear their interruption, for they had often confessed being scared of people who thrived on loud music. They thought such people to be volatile and quick to anger. "How silly," thought Daryl. That made him angry.

Daryl recalled the night in church that his trainer had said, "These new speakers will help keep our youth." Confidently, Daryl knew that he was a product of that doctrine. The **Decibel Doctrine** had made him a true worshipper and kept him. How silly of the old Elders to think contrary; he was irrefutable proof. He smirked as he remembered mocking church members who could not associate music volume with the manifest power of God. Some people are just unlearned. Wet blankets. Nudniks. His worship trainer had often said so.

It was time to worship, and he leaped high for joy. "Ouch!" exclaimed Daryl as his head hit a 2′ x 6′ porch rafter. He had forgotten the porch had a ceiling. Holding a hand to the swelling knot on top of his head, Daryl's feet began to move to the loud beat. Nothing was going to stop him from worshipping for this chance-of-a-lifetime moment. But his frantic feet movement jerked the extension cord from the electrical outlet. The loud music stopped, and Daryl's worship stopped (Just as in Church).

But Daryl quickly saw the problem, blamed it on the Devil, and bent over and plugged back into The Power. As he bent over to reconnect with power, he thought he heard his friend Daryl softly speaking in the distance, but his focus was on worship. He knew to keep his priorities focused at a time like this. He had been trained.

Quickly his feet began to once again match the beat of the drums. The tempo of the beat accelerated, but Daryl easily kept up, smiling as he remembered words of one of his trainers, the music director; "We now have a new beat." "New beat," meaning faster and more aggressive. "Now have" meaning now that the previous Pastor of 42 years, Elder Burr, a seeker of "Old Paths," is now gone and the progress of worship is no longer hindered.

To Daryl's dismay, he realized that he was not sweating. The day was cool; the sun had barely been able to thaw the frost in the front yard. Run, "take-a-lap" they called it in Sanctuary-Worship training. That would make him sweat. Daryl's boom box was not loud enough to make him feel like running, but he would run anyway because today was a special day for special worship. So back and forth he ran the length of the front porch, slower than in Church for there was no wall to bounce off of to control his momentum.

Soon, Daryl was wet with sweat, nearing exhaustion, and he thought to himself: "mission accomplished"! He turned to see if Jesus was pleased. But there was no Jesus standing near as moments ago. The presence of God departed without him even noticing. Even his friend Daryl had gone away. Though physically exhausted, Daryl's feet kept trying to move to the beat, so he turned the music volume down, and he was able to stand still.

Finally able to stand still, Daryl looked toward an "old path" that wound through a slightly treed meadow and saw two men. Two men casually walking farther and farther away from him, arm in arm, talking and seeking each other's face. The two men seemed to find pleasure in each other's company. One was a dark-haired man, much like his friend Daryl, the other had hair like wool, as white as snow.

Daryl and Daryl were so much alike. "Almost twins" their friends called them. Best of friends, almost two-peas-in-a-pod. The only difference between Daryl and Daryl was their worship training. A Decibel Disciple trained Daryl while an Elder of Biblical "Old Paths" trained Daryl.

David Clark
11/14/02

The Elijah Challenge

There is another particular sign that will never follow the *Not-Right* practice of the **Decibel Doctrine**. That sign is the "Elijah Challenge" as found in I Kings 18:21-39. False prophets of the 21st century will never challenge a prophet of God as to whether or not their worship is biblical, and/or, will be validated with a response from the God of Abraham, Isaac, and Jacob.

This Old Testament scene is where Elijah challenged the false prophets of Baal in an effort to demonstrate that only Jehovah God could answer by fire and that Baal was a false god.

One very important reason that New Age Decibel Disciples will never dare, nor qualify to duplicate the "Elijah Challenge" is because Elijah understood the value of altars. Elijah's priority in preparation to call on his God was to first rebuild the altar of the Lord that was broken down. Today's Decibel Disciples despise altars; calling them "mourner's benches," removing them from the sanctuary, referring to them as "in the way." Decibel Disciples are fully aware that altars in a church setting are not user-friendly to physical motion forced by loud music and loud beat. Therefore, they consider altars where saints and sinners repent and weep and worship before God, as an interference to "their worship." And it is.

Decibel Disciples consider the approach to God through humbleness and contrition and reverence at an altar as non-exciting and boring. In summation, altars are only a nuisance to those who embrace the **Decibel Doctrine**.

Just for fun though, let us imagine the scenario of false prophets of the **Decibel Doctrine Brotherhood** contending with a twenty-first century Elijah over the worship that should be offered to the One True God. It would be fair to allow the same ratio of false prophets to True Prophets found in the original "Elijah Challenge"; 850 false prophets/1 True Prophet.

The Challenge?

Will God respond to the oblations of super loud banging music and the physical motion it produces? Or will God respond to a few words prayed in humbleness in the presence of an altar. Is the worship forever sought by the Creator still the Hebrew word pronounced *Sha-khaw'* in the Old Testament and the Greek word pronounced *Pros-koo-neh'-o* in the New Testament? Let God decide what He wants.

First of all, on the light side, any entrepreneur in the crowd would request all concession rights to sell ear plugs, knowing the profit of one "worship" service led by a Decibel Disciple would bring ample monies for retirement.

Can you envision the intense focus of those 850 Decibel Disciples as they began to truck in more and more equipment? It would take days and more days to get all the necessary equipment together to accumulate the "power" to worship their god.

Simultaneously, the **Decibel Doctrine** Pastor would be studying his holy script for instructions in serious "worship." The cover of his holy script would read: *Guide to Sound Systems for Worship DDV*. Meanwhile the man of God whom they have challenged, a follower of the "old paths," would be peacefully strolling as he hummed a song of prayer to his God.

When their leader of "worship," the **Decibel Doctrine** soundman, had all volume controls set on "maximum move of our God," the Decibel Disciples' efforts to call down fire would cause total exhaustion of all "worshippers." Physical exhaustion from leaping, and running, and even jumping on the altar that they despise. Finally, now wet with sweat, legs weak from physical exertion, and knots on foreheads from uncontrolled collisions with brethren-of-like-precious-faith, all those who offered *Not-Right* worship would stand still when the beat stopped. Then their **Decibel Doctrine** Pastor says, "Well done, thou good and faithful servants."

The crescendo of the soundman's efforts to "make it happen" would fade into thunderous echoes as sound waves bounced off of far-away mountains and ricocheted through distant valleys. The ground would slowly stop vibrating, the dust would silently settle, and leaves that had been dislodged from violent sound waves would silently float to the ground. The blinking light flashing "STRANGE FIRE" would dim away as their "worship system" once again became lifeless. Nature would cautiously begin to relax.

The following silence would be astronomical in comparison, only to be broken by an Elijah-like voice: "Oh God. There is no God like You." Turning toward the voice, we would see a rugged old man bending over an altar to ease the pain in his prayer-worn knees. Again, he would offer words of praise; "I love you Jesus, You alone are my Lord and Creator," without lifting up his head. Words that reach into the heavens and softly find the ear of God.

Then as he slowly lifts his hands toward heaven to honor and worship his creator, his coarse voice asks, "Where is the God of Elijah?"

And the fire falls.

****

In writing this scenario, a question arose. Why did Elijah slay all the false Prophets? They had just received irrefutable proof that Elijah's God was the True God. Was that not sufficient to convert them?

The answer is simple and yet profound; **it was their inability to repent that cost them their life.** God knew that they could not repent of *Not-Right* worship and lead the people in *Right* Worship.

It appears to me again, that embracers of the **Decibel Doctrine** are incapable of repenting.

A sign that follows *Not-Right* worship.

David Clark
2018

Who's Yo Momma?

It Does Make a Difference

Unknowingly, little Johnny was fooling with Mother Nature. Pulling the still warm egg from his pocket, Johnny's small hand slipped it under the fussing red chicken hen setting her nest of eggs. Distracted by frantic quacking, the young boy looked toward the pond to see a fretting mallard hen. The momma duck was searching the very same nest where Johnny had just found and removed an egg that he felt needed a momma chicken.

Little Johnny changed the natural course of nature, unaware. Little Johnny had innocently changed God's design, God's plan, into something that was contrary to Mother Nature. He changed a naturally good thing into something it was not meant to be. He made a right thing not right with his whimsical better idea. With the works of his own hands, Little Johnny changed the God-ordained destiny of a baby duck named Pato.

Likewise, New Age Pentecost changes the natural ways of God-ordained worship with their better ideas. Blinded by deception as peer pressure overrides Holy Scripture. And today, the works of men's hands are swiftly changing the God-ordained destiny of many Christian Patos. They know not that when "YOUR WORSHIP ISN'T RIGHT – YOU AREN'T RIGHT."

In natural course the duck egg hatched simultaneously with the chicken eggs. Pato was the name of the baby duck. At birth (I need to use this terminology) Pato smelled chicken, he heard chicken, he felt chicken, he saw chicken. Naturally, chicken became his security. Naturally, chicken became Pato's leader, his teacher, his source of life and safety. Naturally, the red chicken hen became his momma. But what naturally evolved was unnatural to God-ordained nature.

Momma chicken's cluck told Pato when to eat, when to play, and when to hide. Pato did not have to constantly watch momma chicken for guidance because his ears were ever in tune to momma. Pato had naturally learned to totally trust the sounds of his unnatural momma.

One day the big bad wolf came to the farm yard looking for supper. The farm ducks were near the pond, nibbling on tender sprouts of grass while momma chicken and her young ones were drinking water from the pond. As the big bad wolf began to slink toward the pond, the ducks and momma chicken all saw him, and suddenly there was pandemonium. In a flutter of wings, the ducks quickly escaped to the water while momma chicken went squawking and running for her life.

Pato surprisingly found himself in the pond with the ducks. Floating on water for the first time in his life. Instinctively, without thinking, Pato had naturally fled to the safety of the pond. The water felt naturally safe, but the surrounding cacophony of sound frightened him. That noise disoriented him. All he could hear was quacking. Quacking-Quacking-Quacking. The sound that real ducks naturally make was flooding his ears, inundating his very being. "Where is my momma?" thought Pato, "I want my momma."

Faintly over the din of quacking ducks, he heard the sounds of momma chicken and Pato naturally did what was contrary to nature; he left the safety of the pond and began to run to momma. But he could not run like a chicken because he was a duck. Pato, the baby duckling could swim well by God's ordained design, but on land he could only waddle. And as Pato waddled with all his might in search of his unnatural momma; his real mother according to God's design, watched from the safety of the pond as Pato became an easy meal for the hungry wolf.

Little Johnny saw it all, but never fully comprehended with understanding. There was no Prophet Nathan to point a finger and say, "Thou art the man." Ignorantly blind to truth, Little Johnny thought "it's all your fault Pato, you should have stayed with MOMMA."

Similar is the deception taught by a Decibel Disciple. For years he leads a people with extreme decibels of music and rhythm. For years the adrenaline-producing explosive decibels and irresistible motion commanded by the beat in the Sanctuary is presented as their momma, their protector and giver-of-life. The sheep are taught to feel safe and secure in an atmosphere of sanctuary ecstasy and thunder.

And as newborns, many spiritually hungry men receive the Born-Again experience of the Holy Ghost while inundated with the sounds produced by the **Decibel Doctrine**. The fruit of the **Decibel Doctrine** naturally becomes their unnatural momma.

Then the day of danger comes and to their demise, they naturally look for a momma that is not God-Natural. They cannot hear momma, they cannot feel momma. "Where is that protecting power?" they cry, "where is that power of thundering sound that secures me?" But the man with the keys, the Decibel Disciple's right-hand man (the sound man) is not available. The sheep fall prey, and the Decibel Disciple wags his head and says, "shame, shame, shame, it's all your fault."

Almost 2000 years ago, mankind received the Born-Again experience in an Upper

Room in Jerusalem as God poured out His Spirit upon men. A spiritual birth that starts a new Born-Again life. The Bible describes the environment of their birth that day as prayer and supplication. The sounds of prayer became their "momma" on the Day of Pentecost. They naturally came to feel secure and safe surrounded by those sounds. The sounds of prayer and supplication became their source of life, strength, and direction. It was God's ordained design, and it is only natural for Born-Again Christians to seek this sound and feel at home with this sound.

Over 100 years ago there was another historical outpouring of this same Holy Ghost documented in Los Angeles, California. This historic revival, called the Azusa Street Revival, started on April 9th, 1906. Because of its resemblance to the Day of Pentecost in the second chapter of the book of Acts, one might call it Upper Room II. Historical facts of this outpouring in early 1900's make it very plain that the environment of these new births was identical to the Upper Room in Jerusalem nearly 1900 years prior. Our God who never changes, chose the same birthing environment in 1906 A.D. that He chose in 33 A.D.; prayer and supplication.

To those born again in 1906, the sounds of prayer and supplication became their security, their strength, their source of life; those sounds became their momma. That is God's design; that is God-Natural.

History documents that this World-Renown Revival in 1906 did not have music to make-it-happen. Testimonies from this large group of Born-Again believers were synonymous; All agreed: "We felt no need for music."

I still remember the voices of people praying for me as I sought this New Birth experience. By this time mankind had added music to the environment of being Born Again. Soft melodious music that could be heard in the background during prayer. The sound of people praying was always louder than the music in those days.

The night God so mercifully filled me with the Holy Ghost, all the musicians had gone home. The sounds heard during my new birth were prayer and supplication. The sound of prayer and supplication became my momma. I am at peace around it. I am secure around it. That sound reminds me of my New Birth. It reminds me of the Pentecostal experience. The month prior, my wife had received the Holy Ghost in a prayer meeting with no music. The sounds of prayer and supplication became her momma also. And in times of dire need, my wife and I both find safety in that momma.

But mankind has never ceased changing the God-Natural birthing environment.

Technology, electronics, and little Johnny's ignorant blindness has turned the birthing environment into something the original 120 in the Upper Room in Jerusalem would not even recognize. Today the sound of prayer and supplication is completely overwhelmed and obliterated by rock concert decibel music around the altars. Altar services today are a bedlam of decibels and rhythm. The bass guitar vibrates the seekers chest, the drums are always an obvious favorite of the head-bobbing sound man, and the artificial volume of the microphones numb any unprotected ears. In order to be heard over the music, friends must scream their words of encouragement into the ears of the one seeking the gift of the Holy Ghost.

Yet God honors His Word. He honors a hungry heart no matter how obnoxious the music. The Holy Ghost is still a promise, no matter how foreign or unnatural the hands of man make the environment. And perverse to what is spiritually natural, we now often "see them speak in tongues" instead of "hear them speak in tongues" as God gives the utterance. "Hearing them speak in tongues" is Biblically edified and spiritually natural, while "seeing them speak in tongues" is not.

This 2000-year-old Born-Again experience creates a new life, and the sounds of the birthing room naturally became the newborn's momma. Today's New Age sounds in the birthing room are diversely contrary to God's design. The dominating beat of the drum, the roar of an over amplified organ, the body tingling vibrations of the bass speakers, the ear-piercing volume of an electronic keyboard, and of course, the multiple praise singer voices artificially amplified to a point of distortion to overcome the volume of music; all accumulate into a din of synthetic sounds that naturally become the newborn's unnatural momma. The physiological effect of the extreme volumes that can be felt physically, emotionally, and mentally bond the newborn with its momma.

In New Age Pentecostal protocol, the newborn receives a birthmark from its very present and sensational momma. The feeling-secure-in-these-sounds, the trusting-in-these-sounds, the searching-for-love-in-these-sounds; is the natural birthmark placed upon the newborn. The **Decibel Doctrine** produces unnatural sounds that naturally become the newborn's momma. And it is naturally very unnatural. It is not God's design. Not even close.

The original 120 men and women in the Upper Room of Jerusalem tarried with prayer and supplication for ten days as they waited for the Comforter (Holy Ghost). What if some of the Disciples from the Upper Room should witness a New Age Pentecostal altar service of today; where the spirit of the **Decibel Doctrine** dominates? Just what if?

152

They would find all prayer and supplication drowned out by excessively loud throbbing music. The disciples from the Upper Room would not be able to hear their spiritual momma. Would they fear the absence of their natural spiritual momma? Would their spirit cry out, "I want my momma?" Would their spirit question today's ever-so-popular new momma? Would they confess: "we don't feel comfortable here with your momma." "The truth-be-known, your momma is a little spooky."

What if a Born-Again New Age Pentecostal could experience the original sounds of the Upper Room 2000-plus years ago? Or, what would they feel if they went back in time only 100-plus years to Azusa Street or Topeka, Kansas and tarried with them at altars of prayer? No loud music, no music at all, just the sound of prayer and supplication.

Would this present generation of Pentecostals feel uneasy? Would they feel frightened and insecure without their momma? Would they cry, "I want my momma"? Would they be bored with the ancient momma of old-path Pentecost and go frantically searching for the beat and the volume? Would they flee the pond of safety in search of a spiritually artificial, unnatural momma?

John wrote of sounds he heard in Heaven. Many voices, multitudes of voices. So many voices in unison that the sound was likened unto the roar of many waters as in waterfalls or rushing waters or great thunder.

John heard sounds that come out of man's mouth as does prayer and supplication. Natural sounds. Obviously, many loud voices were heard by John that day in heaven… naturally. No artificial volumes.

Heaven; a place where Apostle John wrote that the voice of the harpers can be heard over their harps, naturally.

In such an antique environment as John described, would New Age Pentecostals feel nervous and insecure? Would they want to leave the safety of the pond in search of the momma (environment) that birthed them?

Feeling out of place in heaven, would they cry, "I want my momma"? Because of their birthing environment, because of their birth mark, would they naturally seek that which is unnatural?

Who is Yo Momma? It does make a difference.

The cluck of chicken hen told Pato, the newborn, when to eat, when to play, when to hide, and when to run.

That sound of his unnatural momma, naturally controlled him from birth and cost him his life.

Today - Extreme volumes of music tell New Age Pentecostal Newborns ditto, ditto, ditto.

The **Decibel Doctrine** is their Mother Dear. Naturally Unnatural

New Age Pentecostal motto:

IF IT AIN'T LOUD, IT AIN'T MY MOMMA!

David Clark
9/16/02

Silent Laughter on a Normal Sunday Night, and All is Well

The menu read, "Welcome to Mamacitas," one of the finest Mexican food restaurants in Kerrville, Texas.

It was a "**normal Sunday night**" in this West Texas town that sat on the south side of Interstate 10. The dining elder ministers from out-of-town saw two young men enter the front door. Clean cut teenagers, short and neat haircuts that did not copy the trends of Hollywood. Their white dress shirts were clean and buttoned and tucked in. Their full- length pants were neither immodestly tight nor trendy baggy. Apostolic boys in modest apparel.

The entrance of the young Apostolic men seemed quite early in the night to have been dismissed from an evening church service, so the eldest of the out-of-town ministers questioned the length of their Sunday night service. The young men replied in unison; "He shouted us and let us go."

"He shouted us and let us go." The summation of a "**normal Sunday night.**" An answer that required no hesitation or thought because it was a "normal Sunday night." A very frequent occurrence, a norm. So common, that they answered simultaneously: "He shouted us and let us go."

It is of interest that the young men knew what really happened. Less perceptive young men would have said, "They cranked up the music (both in volume and rhythm) and the power of God took over." Obviously aware of what really happened, these young men knew that "**He** shouted us and let us go." "He" meaning the Pastor, not God, nor God's Word.

What did the Pastor do? "Shouted us." Not the Biblical "shout" that comes out of the mouth, but rather the Twenty-first century physical frenzy, inaccurately called "shout" that is spontaneously demanded by extreme volumes of music and rhythm. A "shout" that is so instantaneous that it takes hardly any time at all to "have church," especially on a "**normal Sunday night.**"

Please note the phrase: "He shouted us." It explains who did it and what he did, but not HOW he did it. Since the setting is God's Sanctuary and the purpose is to please God, I am sure that it was prayed down or preached down. "Yeah wight," said the little boy. If it was a "**normal Sunday night,**" "it" was done with no Word of God at all. But rather large speakers were used to produce chest-vibrating volume and breath-taking rhythm. The power of God was not the catalyst that Sunday night, but rather, the proven power of New Age Pentecostal sound systems.

Long ago, Worshippers of Rock and Roll Music discovered what science has since then proven over and over; if the music is loud enough, and fast enough, for long enough, there will be a physical reaction of the human body. Only a conscious effort can control the adrenaline rush produced by the physiological reaction of the human body to extreme decibels and rabid-rapid-rhythm.

No doubt, within this Sunday night setting, the echoes of time reverberated frequent words preached over and over: "you can't worship in the pew, get out in the aisle and do something," "you haven't worshipped God until you are wet with sweat," "the volume of our music brought revival," "these additional speakers will help us keep our youth."

Very likely writings like *Music of The Golden Calves, Serpent Seed Music*, and *Strange Fire* (Author being Elder M.E. Burr), have been criticized from the pulpit by the one who shouts-them-and-lets-them-go in Kerrville, Texas. It is public knowledge that the author of such Godly-Accurate writings has been rebuked by this subject Pastorship in Kerrville, Texas, with these words; QUOTE – "M.E. Burr don't even know the meaning of worship!"

So, it was just another "**normal Sunday night**," and "he that shouts them" observed the music-induced physical motion and beads of perspiration upon the faces, and satisfied, he thought: "another **normal Sunday night, and all is well.**" So, he "let them go" back into the spiritual war against the world, with no strength from the Word of God. "He that shouts them" sent the children of God to bed hungry. Hungry for the Word of God.

Observing the fruit of the **Decibel Doctrine** throughout the land of Apostolic Brotherhood, I have come to realize that some pastors are missing cowboy-wisdom. A real cowboy respects even his horse enough to not "let him go to bed" hungry and wet with sweat.

The anointed Cherub of great beauty and brightness was there watching the Flock that night. Sunday night was his favorite; for minimal was the risk that he would encounter his most formidable enemy, the Word of God. The enemy against whom he cannot stand. The same enemy that has prophesied his future to a bottomless pit of eternal flames and torment. The enemy that is sharper than any two-edged sword. If this anointed cherub of great beauty and brightness had his way, this Church Service would be a "**normal Sunday night.**" And God's Word that pierces him and divides asunder even his joints and marrow by its mere presence, would be counted absent.

Yes, the anointed Cherub, Lucifer himself was there, confidently watching and determined. No less determined than thousands of years ago when he first swore to exalt his throne (covering) above the stars of God and to sit upon the mount of the congregation, (Isaiah 14:13).

One third of the Heavenly Host was presently at his command this Sunday night. For years this host of angels-gone-bad had run messages of deceit for the one they worshipped. Subliminal messages often orchestrating a "**normal Sunday night**." A multitude of innovative contemporary instructions in these last days like unto as follows:

1.) The decibels of music MUST create vibrations of a magnitude that can be physically felt by the flesh.

2.) The drums MUST dominate not only in volume, but also in sensation to the flesh.

It was a "**normal Sunday night.**" Not normal in comparison to Biblical Apostolic Sanctuary Sundays, but normal to previous Sunday nights in Kerrville, Texas, with the one that "shouts them and lets them go."

The prince of the power of the air observed this subject Sunday Night church service in humor as the last runner of the fallen angels delivered one of his favorite messages into the ear of the Pastor who shouts-them-and-lets-them-go; "Tell the sheep that true Apostolic worship ends in total exhaustion."

This angel called Lucifer with the God-given ability to "entwine as a screen and cover over" had watched long enough. It was his turn and he was the master of deception. It was time to entwine, it was time to screen and cover over, and it was time to camouflage and deceive. He choked back laughter as he invisibly approached the Pastor who shouts-them-and-lets-them-go. "Am I not prince over the power of the air?" he thought to himself as his smiling lips whispered into the ear of the Pastor who shouts-them-and-lets-them-go: "Tell the sheep that the vibrating sensation in the air that tingles their flesh is the present power of their God, and all is well."

No longer could the one of beauty and brightness contain himself. Chilling laughter erupted from his wicked mouth, uncontrollable joyful laughter of intense gaiety. Contagious in its fervor, the eerie sounds of glee spread throughout his submissive subjects known as fallen angels. And as they all momentarily forgot the pit reserved for them, their celebrant raucous laughter was accompanied with "high fives" to each other as they chanted to the worship beat that was dominating the atmosphere and vibrating the wall, the pews, and the people. Their chant was more than chilling; "All is well!" – "All is well!" – "All is well!"

However, the din of laughter was unheard by human ears for it existed only in the spiritual realm. Haunting echoes of vengeful laughter reverberated throughout the kingdom of the prince of the power of the air. Echoes that mingled and coincided with those from last Sunday night and the Sunday night before and the one before. Even if the accumulated laughter of one third of the original Heavenly host could match the electronic volume of music on a "normal Sunday night," it would have yet remained audibly silent. Audible only to the spiritual realm.

Victorious, celebrant mocking laughter, silently dominating the spiritual realm. The spiritual realm, where the war over worship started in the beginning and continues today.

Thus, came the title of this article:

SILENT LAUGHTER ON A NORMAL SUNDAY NIGHT, AND ALL IS WELL.

David Clark
1/6/03

A Decibel Disciple in Heaven??

I ask the reader to fantasize with me for a moment. Perchance a Decibel Disciple should slip into heaven? Of course, his power (sound system) would accompany him; for the two are inseparable. And of course, he would not want to be in Heaven without his worship.

Help me think; where would his assigned mansion be located? How far from the Lord would one place the mansion of a *Not-Right* worshipper who uses man-made technology to drown out the voice of the bride and the praises of the redeemed?

Are the dimensions of heaven described by John in the book of Revelation even sufficient in magnitude to safely distance a Decibel Disciple away from the throne? Upon whom would the lot fall to be his neighbor?

Questions that need not answers, no not ever. But anyway, let our imagination fantasize such a dilemma.

It sounds ugly to say that it would be heaven and hell. So, I will replace the words "Heaven" and "Hell" with "Bliss" and "Anguish," lest I understate the extremes of either. It would be "Bliss" to the Decibel Disciple who gets to keep his power, and "Anguish" for his neighbor who has to wait for a power outage to enjoy the peace of communing with his Lord whom he loves.

Just the mere thought of suffering the *Not-Right* worship practiced by a Decibel Disciple in heaven with me for eternity makes me wish Purgatory was real…, well…not really, but kind of.

What a wild dream! I mean, what a far-fetched nightmare. What an impossible perchance.

Decibel Disciples always strive for the pre-eminence of the airways. Their power, when cranked up, always dominates and devours the praise of the redeemed. And is inescapable. As on earth, their spirit and agenda would clash, literally, with the spirit of the Bride of Christ in Heaven.

So, the sane would agree it to be an understatement to declare the mere thought of a Decibel Disciple in heaven as ludicrous and preposterous; surely even a little on the scary side.

Picture this dialogue in Heaven:

God, frowning – "Gabriel, why are the pearly gates vibrating? Go find the source before I have to rehang the stars."

Gabriel, panting from his trip far from the presence of God – "That is Jubal, the great, great, great, great grandson of Cain the first *Not-Right* worshipper. You-know-who has given Jubal a man-made thing called a sound system. Jubal is wearing a name tag that says *Decibel Disciple*, and a hat that says *Love is Loud*, and a T-shirt that says *Dedicated to the One I Love.*

God, fingers in ears – "why is his music so loud!?"

Gabriel, avoids hurting his Master – "you would not believe it if I told you."

> *The Lord is not slack concerning his promise, as some men count slackness; but is longsuffering to us-ward, not willing that any should perish, but that all should come to repentance.*
> **2 Peter 3:9**

Our longsuffering God will forgive even Decibel Disciples, IF…, IF…, they repent of *Not-Right* worship.

However, I once was young and now I am old, AND, I have never met an EX-Decibel-Disciple.

Selah.

David Clark
August 2019

Saved From the African Siguco

This article is lengthy and will address documented testimonies of individual Christians who found Truth in Africa. The title of the book from which I will quote is *God Delivered Me*. *God Delivered Me* is a suggested reading that will help enlighten the reader to the power of *Not-Right* worship in any country. In it you will find Twenty First Century Pentecostals of America, of whom I am a part and whom I love.

I am thankful to God that the publisher of this subject book has granted me permission to quote text of which all Christians should take notice. The main focal point of this article is the **Siguco** from which these African Christians were delivered. The reader will discover that in America we practice an American Style of the **African Siguco**.

African Siguco?? Just what per say might that be?

I will begin with what the **African Siguco** is not. It is not a deadly virus or disease, it is not a clawed predator that seeks human flesh under the cover of darkness, it is not a slithering reptile with venom equal to the Black Mamba. It is much more devastating and detrimental to a man than any enemy of the flesh. It actually seeks the soul of its victim.

The **African Siguco** is subtle, it is delusive, it is a deceptively camouflaged snare set for the unaware. It appeals to the flesh, while giving false preeminence to God. Its promoter is a deceitful crafty liar, a fallen angel with God-given anointing to cover over, to conceal, and to overwhelm. (Lucifer's anointing and God-given abilities are found in study of "anointing," "covering," and "throne" in Ezekiel 28:14-16 and Isaiah 14:13).

Assuredly, only God can deliver from the African Siguco. It is a religious practice.

I want to first emphasize and direct the reader's focus to the title chosen by the author to identify his book containing testimonies of African Pentecostals: *God Delivered Me*. These testimonies are from people who God graciously led to Truth, so the title could have been "I Found Truth," or "I Found The True Church," OR "I Found True Worship." But the title, *God Delivered Me* appropriately emphasizes that these witnesses were delivered and saved **FROM SOMETHING that at one time CONTROLLED them and HELD THEM CAPTIVE inside of their religion.**

Saved from the wages of sin of course, as are all of us. But even more so, they were saved from a religious ritual/practice that is not found in the Bible. A religion whose followers were totally dedicated to that ritual/practice, while their deception by this ritual/practice was equal to their dedication. Their religion "worshipped" God by means of this ritual/practice to which they were dedicated and addicted.

In fact, this so called "worship" was the foundation and focal point of every church assembling. This religion was so confident in its rituals/practices that when a friend or loved one left these rituals/practices, there was much contention and banishment among families and friends. Any man who refused to practice their method of "worship" was judged as ungodly. Their method of "worship" was a "test of fellowship." This African church persecuted and shunned any brother who considered their method of "worship" as non-biblical.

I can testify to witnessing and suffering this same practice among the religious in America.

The real-life testimonies recorded within this article paint a picture of a religion and its rituals/practices of "worship" that these Saints are grateful to be delivered from. And they are thankful to God. In accordance with the title *God Delivered Me*, these documentations will describe from what God delivered these precious sincere people: the **African Siguco**.

The name of the religion that the following witnesses were delivered from is ZIONISM. (Not to be confused with the world-wide Jewish movement also known as Zionism.)

According to the author of *God Delivered Me*, **this sect of religion is a mixture of Christianity, Muti, and ancestor worship.** Muti means "medicine" and is generally used when referring to witchcraft. The word "JUJU" is sometimes used interchangeable with the word Muti, which also refers to the African practice of witchcraft. The practice of ancestor worship is a known form of idolatry.

So, this African Zionism is a practice of Christianity, Witchcraft, and Idolatry.

And, it is the method of "worship" practiced by such a religion that these witnesses were thankful to be delivered from.

Now we all know that the name of a religion, or the name of a church fellowship, or the name of a church building, is man-made. These man-made names do not save us, nor do they identify with any accuracy the type or manner of a church. For example, many churches today claim to be Pentecostal, but their practices and lifestyles separate them from Biblical Apostolic Pentecost.

It is the *practices* of a religion, or a fellowship, or a church, that constitute what it is. Whether it is a church of God or a church of man is determined by its practices. Not by the chartered name. Practices identify a religion or a church; its name does not. Therefore, the evil from which the following witnesses were delivered is the *practices* of Zionism, not the name of the religion.

These witnesses were delivered from a religion that practiced a mixture of Christianity, Witchcraft, and Idolatry. And every assembling of this subject Zionist Church in Africa manifested and exemplified **a portion of Christianity**, **a portion of Witchcraft**, and **a portion of Idolatry**; all under the pretense of being Godly.

So, what are the practices of a religion that mixes Christianity, Witchcraft, and Idolatry?

The author of *God Delivered Me* allows witnesses and personal testimonies to answer this question and convey to the reader manifestations of such a mixture.

Obviously, Zionists believe that Jesus was the awaited Christ. That He was crucified, buried, and resurrected. The subject book makes it very plain that they believe that baptism by immersion in water was essential and that they taught about receiving the Holy Ghost. So, I think that one could safely say they are a Christian church. And if they receive the same Holy Ghost that was described in the Bible as poured out on the Day of Pentecost, then they are Pentecostal in experience.

And surely, they believe in an eternal God that can give eternal life, else why would they be so consistent and faithful in their rituals/practices which they believe brings them favor from their God?

So, just what kind of a church species, or "Heinz 57," would be generated by such a mixture as Christianity, Witchcraft, and Idolatry? What kind of a strange duck would this mixture breed? What mutation of Biblical Truth would be birthed by adding Witchcraft and Idolatry to Christianity? If such an ungodly blend was thoroughly mixed together, what mutation would evolve and be manifested?

The answer is in their practices. How would such a mix-breed species conduct a church service? What would be the characteristics of a church meeting? For what purpose would they assemble? What would be their primary focus? What would a visitor see and witness? How would a visitor describe his experience in a church service with the assembling of such a mutation?

The answer to these questions is in the mind and memories of these witnesses. Time and limits no doubt restricted the author of *God Delivered Me* to compile and convey only the most visible and most obvious practices of Zionists in Africa.

When asked "tell me about Zionist church services," the witnesses conveyed the most dominant rituals/practices, the most distinctive rituals/practices, the most consistent rituals/practices, and the most manifest rituals/practices.

As these witnesses testify, they are describing "What God Delivered Them From."

Quote from *God Delivered Me*:

"In the Zionist church, it is sometimes necessary to undergo the holy ritual of "siguco." "Siguco" is a kind of activity during a Zionist church service in which the male section of the assembly will dance ecstatically to a song moving around a pole. This movement starts at a relatively slow pace, but gradually increases until the men are moving so fast their feet do not seem to be touching the ground, this can last for hours. The "siguco" forms the basis of nearly every Zionist church service, and preaching is often suspended to give time to the 'siguco'."

There is nothing mystical about the pole around which they dance ecstatically to a song. It is merely an object of boundary since most of their church meetings are out under the stars. Common sense tells us that if vigorous physical movement continues in a single direction, the "mover" will find himself farther and farther away from his original point of movement. Considering that the motion practiced in "**Siguco**" is very speedy and can last for hours, the participant of "**Siguco**" could find himself hours away from the assembly of his friends if he did not move in a circle.

Many assemblies in American Churches use 4 walls to contain their **Siguco**, (ecstatic movement to hyper-rhythmic music) and now often utilize the space between the front pew and the platform. In most 21st Century American Pentecostal churches that perform the **Siguco**, the designated space near the platform is preferred because that location is closest to the only instrument that can initiate the necessary ecstasy, and accelerate the rhythm to "speedy," and maintain it for hours…. the drums. Without the beat of the drum, there can be no **Siguco**. Neither in Africa, nor in America.

Today, a very common sign among American churches that practice **Siguco** in the space between the front pew and the platform, is the absence of altars. In this sacred space, from which altars at one time beckoned man's soul to kneel and pray to his Creator, the flooring is worn from aggressive physical movement.

Long ago, when this sacred space honored altars, stains from tears of thanksgiving, worship, reverence, love, and repentance could be seen. Today, the floor is stained from the sweat of human bodies as they fulfill the command to "worship,"… **African Siguco** style.

The ancient "old-path" altars which came to be considered as unnecessary, were necessarily removed to make room for the **African Siguco**. (If Jesus delays His second coming long enough to allow the younger generation to read this article, to them I say: "YES, believe it or not, there was once altars in our Pentecostal churches where saints and sinners knelt in submission before their God.")

Might I ask the reader, how many times have you heard songs in American churches that started at a normal rhythm with which the words were intelligible; only to experience an incremental increase in rhythm to a point at which the words become meaningless and unintelligible? At that point of accelerated rhythm, the vocals lose their meaning and harmony, and become a part of the beat.

Meaningful words which are the building blocks of every Biblical song, can quickly become a part of the syncopation instead of the thought process. The emotion stirred by the thought process of beautiful heart-felt words is overcome by the physiological response of the human body to rhythm. And of course, the physiological effect of the beat begins to manifest; physical movement of the "worshippers" accelerates to match the frenzy of the "new" beat. In America, this desired effect is enhanced and magnified by extreme volume, because we have the money to buy it.

I am partnered with normal-decent-common-sense in assured agreement that American New Age Pentecost has traded much for ecstatic movement to incessant speedy beats-of-the-drum in the Sanctuary. Conversely, they say "Nay", we have gained much. Blinded by deception, they NOW say "Our church services NOW have life, and our God is NOW impressed with the way we worship."

And like unto the African Zionist Church, New Age Pentecostal churches in America call this beat-induced motion/commotion…."worship."

Poor God.

Quote of Sister Gladys Diamini: *"Before being baptized, I was told a 'siguco' had to be performed for me. The "siguco," they told me, was necessary to help drive out all the dirty spirits which possessed me before I became a child of God; so it was done."*

Please understand that Sister Gladys humbly submitted to that practice because she is a sheep; a submissive, trusting saint. The leadership of this Zionist church, (part Christianity, part Witchcraft, and part Idolatry), told her that the "siguco" was a necessary part of her salvation. And she believed them because she is a sheep.

False prophets have proven time and time again that people will believe whatever is taught, if repeated over and over. She was told that this physical movement to the beat had power to cleanse her. The "siguco" was her protection. This was her spiritual help. This physically ecstatic performance would make her spiritually pure.

To the reader, how many times have you heard "physical response to loud fast music" in American churches touted as a show of spirituality? A sign that all is well? An exhibition of holiness?

Continued quote of Sister Gladys Diamini --- *"The purification ceremony itself involved the routine of singing, dancing, and jumping in ecstasy as the spirits overwhelmed each of us."*

Please note three points:

1. Physical movement wrought purification.

2. The ecstatic physical movement is referred to as a routine.

3. There was a plurality of spirits involved.

Just like in my country of America.

Quote of Sister Hettie Khonangani Nkosi: *"On the other hand, we used to enjoy the activity found in the Zionist Church. Everything they did there was very active and had some liveliness to it. I used to also enjoy the prophetic outbursts which are characteristic of every normal Zionist service. I must say that our interests at that time were not genuinely spiritual, we just enjoyed the few lively activities and the show that occurred. Perhaps an even stronger reason I went to church at all is that most members of my family were going to the Zionist Church."*

I do not want to discredit the anointed exuberant display of emotion when a Holy Ghost filled saint is excited about what their God has done for them. However, I do want to repudiate today's **Decibel Doctrine** that associates physical movement with spirituality, and equates physical motion to Biblical worship. I also repudiate the belief system that spiritually credits the volume of their powerful sound systems.

Please Note: Sister Hettie was not interested in spirituality; she attended church for her family and for amusement. So, it was her flesh that enjoyed the lively action, and it was her intellect that rightly acknowledged the lively action as an ostentatious man-made show.

Continued quote of Sister Hettie: *"I later got disappointed with the Zionist Church when the prophets would no longer pray for us without a charge."*

I heard of a Pastor in Port Arthur, Texas, United States of America, that would not go pray for someone who did not pay him tithes. Publicly known as a bona fide Decibel Disciple.

Quote of Brother Moses Kiyane Mtshali: *"In the Zionist Church, the Bible is not well explained, due to a number of factors. First and foremost, the Bible and preaching are not central to a normal Zionist service."*

In other words, their **normal religious service does not focus on the Word of God**. So, a church that is part Christianity, part Witchcraft, and part Idolatry, is **void of the "Teaching Priest." No preaching - no teaching - no Word of God** is **The Norm**. One can reasonably presume that the first half of II Samuel 6:14 *"David danced before the Lord with all his might"* was passionately screamed out in every Zionist Church service; along with American Pentecostal catch phrases such as "Let's have church around here," or "Are there any worshippers in the house?" or "Let's get crazy for Jesus!" Obviously in demonstration of the **Siguco**, physical motion usually took over the service, and there was no time for preaching.

My toes and fingers are not enough digits to count the times I have heard in America; "God just took over, and we had a runaway service without the Word of God."

Like unto many 21st century Pentecostal churches in America; the norm and central focus and primarily-pushed-priority in African Zionist Church services is ecstatic physical motion inspired by the beat. The preaching of the Word of God struggles for a position of priority, **often being totally occluded**; literally barred from preeminence. In America, where adequate money is available, our Sanctuary Sound Systems ramp up this resistance to Word-of-God-Time; justification of which is signified by profound Pastoral declarations such as: "Saints can only endure 15-20 minutes of preaching."

Continued quote of Brother Moses: *The 'siguco' is thus the most important part of a Zionist service. There can be no Zionist service without the 'siguco'; it forms the basis of a Zionist Church service. Preaching can even be suspended or given very, very little time rather than miss the 'siguco'. It is said there can be no revelations without the 'siguco'. The prophets will often be shown who is sick among the brethren during the 'siguco'."*

In this church that practices Christianity, Witchcraft, and Idolatry, they dance ecstatically to rhythmic music **in every service**. The **ecstatic dance at frenzied speeds can last for hours**. (We have all seen it in America) The "**Siguco**" takes

167

preeminence over all else, including the Word of God.

As an American Christian in the 21st century, I have witnessed many sessions of the "**Siguco**" in Pentecostal churches in America. In a church service in the state of Louisiana, I witnessed men form a circle by embracing each other arm in arm together. This circle of men formed a boundary within which one or two men at a time entered the circle and performed a very ecstatic physical demonstration during which they move so fast "that their feet did not appear to be touching the ground."

Of course, the atmosphere was smothered by extreme volumes of music supported by a bone-tingling drum beat. As the participants got tired and wet with sweat, they allowed others to enter the circle and replace the sweaty participants and the "**Siguco**" continued. Only drums with the right beat can keep this American "**Siguco**" session going, sometimes for hours; while the Word of God and His preacher remain silent.

And the final synopsis of the shallow is: "God took control of the service, and the preacher didn't even get to preach, Hallelujah!"

<u>Continued quote of Brother Moses</u>: *"The baptism is itself a strange activity. The candidate is violently immersed in the water during the session. The event is so violent, the candidate almost incurs an accident in the water."*

Webster's definition of violent: *"marked by extreme force or sudden intense activity, notably furious or vehement, excited or mentally disordered to the point of loss of self-control."*

Have we not all seen violent improper assistance to seekers of the Holy Ghost? Sometimes they are pushed back and forth. Sometimes shaken. Sometimes ran around the church.

This violence never manifests itself in a prayer meeting. But is most consistent with altar-call services dominated by rock concert volume music and drums.

How is it that we descended to a depth of calling sudden intense activity "worship"?

Have we not noticed that promoters of *Not Right* worship often lose control of their anger and become violent in the pulpit when their worship is resisted by the sheep?

Can the spirit of Biblical Apostles even remotely walk in concordance with the violent spirit of a Decibel Disciple?

****

I had the privilege and honor to visit several Apostolic churches in Tanzania, Africa. The practice of praise and worship that I witnessed in Tanzania was nothing like the quotes of witnesses in *God Delivered Me* concerning the Zionist Church in Africa.

Much to the contrary. The practices in the Tanzania church services consumed me with a fervent love for God. Every practice that I witnessed in the Sanctuary portrayed a people hungry for God, in love with God, and in reverence to God. What I witnessed among the saints in Tanzania Pentecostal Apostolic church services changed my life. Though it has been 5 years ago at the initial starting of this collection of articles, what I felt in their services still draws me.

I will never forget the sound of their voices simultaneously singing and praising God. The voices of all the congregation could be heard singing, praying, and praising. The sound of their praise was not drowned out by amplified volumes of music as we practice in America, nor were their voices overcome by a select few with cranked-up microphones as in America.

My favorite "church service" or experience during two weeks in Tanzania was singing to God while camped in the jungle of the Serengeti Plains. On two occasions, five native men from the missionary's church gathered around our camp fire and began to sing toward the heavens, praising God for almost an hour. One of these two times, they used musical instruments; an accordion and soft drink glass bottles filled to different levels with water and tapped with a metal spoon. Rhythm was kept with an empty 5-gallon plastic square water jug. One corner of the jug was bumped on the hard ground for sound, and the side of the jug was tapped with a small limb cut from a bush. The experience was soul rending. It was as though these men were in the courts of their God, and out of their mouths flowed the abundance of their heart as they praised their Lord on His throne.

I think back to these nights and wonder if the wild animals in the jungle felt a peaceful touch of heaven during these sacrifices of praise. What I witnessed and felt as these men praised their God with song in our camp on the Serengeti Plains was diversely contrary to our American-way of extreme electronic decibels.

So, by personal experience, I know that all African churches are not as described by the witnesses in *God Delivered Me*. The author of *God Delivered Me* wrote that these African witnesses later found and attended United Pentecostal Church assemblies that were Biblical and much different from what they were delivered from.

****

<u>For humor's sake…</u>

What if a Decibel Disciple was allowed to demonstrate his "worship" in the jungle on the Serengeti Plains; around that same camp fire where my heart was strongly touched by true praise? What would heaven witness as a Decibel Disciple did his "thang" and worshipped his god?

He would require powerful generators to produce his "powerful worship," and trucks and trailers to haul large speakers, and of course, a lukewarm sound-man to crank it up. While the electrician made the last connection that would empower the control knobs of the Decibel Disciple's source of power, the **Decibel Doctrine Lover** would impatiently pace back and forth murmuring "I can't wait to show this Land of Africa how to worship!" And when The Power was alive and at his fingertips, the Decibel Disciple would rudely shatter the harmony of nature shared by jungle life on the Serengeti Plains since creation.

Would the wild animals run away, or would they begin to devour each other as laboratory rats have been documented to do when subjected to "rock" music?

Surely the families in Maasai huts miles away, would be troubled by the pestilent noise. Though Maasai warriors are brave and fear no sound in the jungle except the roar of a dominant male lion hunting at night; would heaven witness the look of fear as brave Maasai warriors hid behind Acacia trees and peered out from behind much cover with spear in hand? Each one whispering to their fellow warrior in their native Swahili language: "by the size of his roar, that is a big, big monster."

If the **Decibel Doctrine** Worship was directed toward heaven, could God stay on His throne, or would He quickly leave His courts in search of a Garden of Eden atmosphere????

What I do know for sure is that the Decibel Disciple would be wet with sweat from responding to his self-induced ecstasy. I do also know that he would rebuke (and hate) anyone who could not believe that the feeling produced by his sound system was the true power of God.

Have we American Pentecostals not idolized the beat and electronic volume to a point that we call church "dead" without it? Surely, even the casual observer can testify that extreme volume and beat is the preeminent practice of today's Pentecostal church culture in America because we love it and can afford it.

We Pentecostals believe that Jesus was everything He said He was, and that Jesus was everything that Old Testament prophecy said He was. This belief separates us from most Christian religions. But, the addiction to extreme volume and ecstatic beat as a form of worship unites us with practices predominant in the

African Zionist church and unites us with the common core of most Charismatic Christian religions.

Do we not practice the same **Siguco** that witchcraft promotes as their spiritual power? Is ecstatic movement to a fast and loud beat not a necessary part of almost every American Pentecostal church service in this day of electronic technology? Do we not often allow and even prefer the **Siguco** to take preeminence over the preached Word of God and boast about it?

Have we American Pentecostals not allowed the **Siguco** to become the central part of our services even to the point of accrediting it as a test-of-fellowship or a gauge-of-spirituality?

I thank God that not all of American Pentecostal churches are as described in this article. But the percentage that do so are increasing exponentially as the **Decibel Doctrine** is becoming a meme among New Age American Christian Churches.

Question to the reader --- If Sister Gladys and Sister Hettie and Brother Moses visited a Twenty-first Century Apostolic Pentecostal Church service in America on a Sunday night and they were invited to come again, would their comment be: **"God delivered me from that"**?

To those who have stood and asked for the old paths, I bid you God speed.

You are few, but you are the chosen.

David Clark
January 21, 2004

****

Let the records state that as I expose a false direction of "worship" witnessed among my Pentecostal peers, I find among them the best of the best, and I do love them. Their Doctrine of Salvation is Biblical, while their **Decibel Doctrine** of Worship is not. And I do believe the Bible proves that **When Your Worship Isn't Right – You Aren't Right**.

What is wrong with The Spirit of God taking over a church service without the Word of God??

Nothing; if it is God who takes over. Whatever God chooses to do is always best.

What is wrong with God taking over a church service during Prayer or Preaching??

I say, Nothing, IF it is God who takes over.

Decibel Discipled Sheep say: Boringly Impossible.

A Decibel Shepherd

Before his kingship, David was a shepherd boy. A shepherd herds sheep in pastures of safety and nourishment. So, as a maturing lad, David tended and herded his Father's sheep.

David spent many long days and long nights on hillsides watching his Father's sheep. He was a shepherd at heart. And more importantly, he was a man "after God's own heart."

...I have found David the son of Jesse, a man after mine own heart...
Acts 13:22

David's skill upon his harp coupled with his love of God produced sounds of praise that soothed and comforted the sheep as they bedded down with heaven as their canopy. It is probably not by chance that the harp is the only instrument referred to in the Bible as being in Heaven.

*And I heard a voice from heaven, as the voice of many waters, and as the voice of a great thunder: and I heard the voice of **harpers harping with their harps***:
Revelation 14:2

So, the sheep under the WATCH of David the Shepherd, found heaven-on-earth peace. How pleasant must have been the sound that drifted down to the sheep as David sang and plucked the strings of his harp. With a little imagination, we can hear the sheep softly bleating: "SHALOM," on the hillside with David being their Shepherd.

Allow me to say that it was David's care of the sheep and his pleasantly peaceful praise that won God's heart.

I recently heard of a Pastor who said "David liked loud music," as a justification for his painfully loud sound system. Everybody knows that statement is a validated cop-out by a loud-loving Pastor void of understanding.

But, what if? Just what if David preferred loud music as some Pastors preach? Suppose David was a mutation-mix of Shepherd and Decibel Disciple? He would be known as a **Decibel Shepherd.**

And even more un-nerving; what if Twentieth Century Sound System Technology had been available in the days of David?

Everyone knows that soft pleasant melodious music is soothing and calming. Everyone knows that extreme volumes and aggressive beats do the very opposite. So, the scene of David peaceably tending the sheep on the hillside would have to be re-written, if David was a **Decibel Shepherd.**

Time would take its toll. In time, those sheep that endured the WATCH of David-the-Decibel-Shepherd would become spiritually gaunt, just like their Shepherd and Watchman on the Wall.

The sheep would be constantly herded here and herded there and herded round and round, without allowing time to feed. (As in a **Decibel Doctrine** church where physical movement replaces the fed Word of God)

Never again would the sheep bleat "SHALOM." In fact, the peaceful bleating of the sheep (fruit of the lips) would become only a pleasant memory to the hillsides. Never to be heard again, to the delight of the **Decibel Shepherd**.

The Old Path that promises *ye shall find rest for your souls* (Jeremiah 6:16) would become a very faint lingering memory. Replaced with today's Cutting-Edge New-Age Paths of Ecstasy.

No rest for the sheep. David the Decibel Shepherd would play very loudly (of course without the inadequate harp), utilizing the secret of the beat: *I'm gonna dance-dance-dance-dance all night all night.* Tending (exercising) the sheep nightly.

In time the shepherds in yonder hills would quit preparing for rain when they heard thunder rolling through the valley. Eventually learning; it's just David the Decibel Shepherd and his sound system tending the sheep.

In time, SOME sheep would get tired of hearing: "This loud music will keep your baby lambs."

In time, SOME sheep would escape at the cost of persecution to save their families.

In time, those sheep that thought they could survive the WATCH of the **Decibel Shepherd** would become much like their new shepherd; irritable, quick to anger, gaunt, and wet with sweat, and in love with the power of their Loud Music.

Unconsciously deceived and mutated in their spirit.

May God help innocent, humble, gullible, trusting sheep.

What if David had been a Decibel Shepherd?

Assuredly, He would NOT have been found as a man after God's own heart.

David Clark
God help me to be a Word-Instructed Shepherd.

The Wonderful Wizard of Oz

The Wonderful Wizard of Oz is an American children's novel written by author L. Frank Baum and illustrated by W. W. Denslow, originally published by the George M. Hill Company in Chicago on May 17, 1900.

In January 1901, George M. Hill Company completed printing the first edition, a total of 10,000 copies, which quickly sold out. *The Wonderful Wizard of Oz* sold three million copies by the time it entered the public domain in 1956.

It has since been reprinted on numerous occasions, most often under the title *The Wizard of Oz*, which is the title of the popular 1902 Broadway musical as well as the iconic 1939 musical film adaptation.

The novel is one of the best-known stories in American literature and has been widely translated. The Library of Congress has declared it "America's greatest and best-loved homegrown fairytale."

The main character, Dorothy, and her pet dog named Toto, are swept away from a farm in Kansas by a tornado, to a magical land of Oz. She desires to go back home, but is helpless to do so. Then she is told that there is a Wizard in Oz who has magical power, and he would be her only hope to get back home. The plot of the story is of her journey to find the Wizard of Oz and her experiences along the way.

Her quest to get help from the Wizard of Oz is accompanied by newly met friends; the Scarecrow who wants a brain, the Tin Woodman who wants a heart, and the Cowardly Lion who wants courage. The Wizard of Oz is purported to have the power to help Dorothy get back home and supply her friends with their needs and wants.

Dorothy and her friends travel to the Emerald City in the land of Oz where it is said that the Wizard of Oz sits upon his throne. The reputation of the Wizard of Oz demanded that he be approached with much fear, and his intimidating presence was renowned in the land of Oz. So, their search for the Wizard was done with caution and fear.

When finally entering the throne room of the Wizard of Oz within the Emerald City, the Wizard of Oz magically reveals himself to the four trembling abject beings. To Dorothy, the Wizard showed himself as a giant head upon a marble throne; to the Scarecrow, the Wizard made himself appear as a lovely lady in silk; to the Tin Woodman, the Wizard portrayed himself as a terrible beast; and to the Cowardly Lion, the Wizard made himself appear as a ball of fire.

His voice was booming and powerfully frightening and intimidating. Thunder roared, and lightning flashed when the Wizard spoke. Dorothy and her friends stood trembling in the throne room as that powerful voice agreed to use his power help her get back home and to supply the needs of her friends; only if they would kill the Wicked Witch of the West.

The story goes that they managed to destroy the Wicked Witch of the West and made their way back to the throne room again to approach the highly feared Wizard of Oz. As before, the real Wizard remained hidden, but his power was felt in his voice as it thundered and shook the throne room. They flinched and trembled at the power of his voice and stood weak-kneed waiting for instructions.

In the midst of such a fearful display of intimidating power, Dorothy's pet dog Toto, accidentally knocked over a cloth screen in a corner of the throne room. The real Wizard, who had been hiding behind the screen, was revealed. The real Wizard was no more than a common man who had been portraying himself as powerful via special effects from his hand-made sound-system.

Immediately upon discovery, the not-so-powerful Wizard began to confess and timidly explain that "he is humbug - an ordinary old man who had come to Oz by chance from Omaha in a hot air balloon." His reputation as a demigod dwindled and pined away to humbug.

In REALITY, he was just an ordinary old man who used a sound system for SPECIAL EFFECTS. While hiding behind a screen, he was able to manipulate his hand-engineered sound system to portray himself to others as having supernatural power that merited fear.

His power was only superficial; simply special-effects. His purported power was superficial sensationalism accomplished by technology.

He was not a "Wonderful" Wizard. But he was a wizard like unto Simon the Sorcerer in the Eighth chapter of Acts who convinced the people of Samaria that he himself was some GREAT ONE.

The Wizard of Oz is a type and shadow of today's **Decibel Doctrine** Disciples. Without their sound systems and special effects and sensationalism, they are mere "humbugs – who got where they are, using hot air."

A Decibel Disciple loses his "anointing," when stripped of his sensationalism. If technology should fail to maintain the magic of extreme volumes during a church service, he becomes powerless.

Think it not strange when a preacher is preaching, and though the power of the sound-system is thunderous to the point of vibrating the windows and loud enough to reach the people in the parking lot outside; he tells the sound man: "MAKE MY MONITORS HOT, I WANT TO HEAR MYSELF."

The purported power of The Wizard of Oz was longtime insinuated to be beyond that of any mortal man. And today, like unto the Wizard of Oz, some New-Age preachers use the façade of sensationalism, which SPELLBINDS many saints with awe; but it is not power from above. Just like the Wizard of Oz, they have gizmos, and gadgets, and technology, and tricks, and hand-crafted inventions and maneuvers that can create the "**AWE**" factor with fear.

I think it fair to say that the dwindling and pining away of the Wizard of Oz, after the source of his power was exposed by Toto, is comparable to today's Decibel Disciple experiencing an electrical power outage. His purported power becomes equal to that of a deflated blowup mannequin of Superman.

Surely, even the lukewarm can see that.

David Clark

Worshipping the King of the Jews

Now when Jesus was born in Bethlehem of Judaea in the days of Herod the king, behold, there came wise men from the east to Jerusalem,
2 Saying, Where is he that is born King of the Jews? for we have seen his star in the east, and are come to worship him.
Matthew 2:1-2

This Jesus was not just any baby.

Isaiah wrote of him:

For unto us a child is born, unto us a son is given: and the government shall be upon his shoulder: and his name shall be called Wonderful, Counseller, The mighty God, The everlasting Father, The Prince of Peace.
Isaiah 9:6

Apostle Paul called him God.

And without controversy great is the mystery of godliness: God was manifest in the flesh, justified in the Spirit, seen of angels, preached unto the Gentiles, believed on in the world, received up into glory.
1 Timothy 3:16

John called him The Creator.

He was in the world, and the world was made by him, and the world knew him not.
John 1:10

Jesus identifies Himself to John as the "All-Ruling Absolute Universal Sovereign God."

I am Alpha and Omega, the beginning and the ending, saith the Lord, which is, and which was, and which is to come, the Almighty.
Revelation 1:8

The wise men referred to him as being born King of the Jews.

And they acknowledged having seen a star in the east that supernaturally announced – ONE WORTHY of WORSHIP.

I have used scripture to make it clear in the mind of the reader that this journey to worship Jesus was possibly the most important mission ever endeavored by these wise men. This was a sacred mission challenging these wise men to be reverent to the deity of Jesus.

I love this story, but I am writing articles on the subject called the **Decibel Doctrine.**

So, imagine with me please. What if one of the wise men bearing gifts to the King of the Jews was a Decibel Disciple? We shall name him Brother DD.

The Word of God described what History witnessed that day;

> *And when they were come into the house, they saw the young child with Mary his mother, and fell down, and worshipped him: and when they had opened their treasures, they presented unto him gifts; gold, and frankincense, and myrrh.*
>
> **Matthew 2:11**

While the real wise men humbly bowed down and biblically worshipped the King of the Jews, it would be only fitting for Brother DD to stand erect, chewing gum, bobbing his head to yesterday's upbeat Christian rock song still throbbing through his brain. And possibly mumbling, "Boy, these guys are boring me; is this an antique show or what?"

After the real wise men had worshipped Jesus (God manifest in the flesh) and then offered precious gifts, maybe Brother DD said: "My turn, everybody stand back, I want to worship Him and offer MY treasure." And he began to unwrap the gift that he had borne in search of the King of the Jews. Excited about the gift of worship he was about to offer to the King of the Jews, his adrenaline began to flow (just like at his church), his heart rate increased (just like at his church), his forehead became damp with perspiration, (just like at his church) and he could feel the spirit that often moved him, racing through his veins (just like at his church).

Laid at the feet of the King of the Jews, Brother DD's gift drew the attention of every eye in the room. Joseph, Mary, and the real wise men quizzically stared at the gift. Their expressions silently asked "What, pray tell, is that?"

Joseph asked, "What are you offering the Son of God?"

Then Mary asked, "What are you offering my son, Jesus?"

The wise men asked, "What are you offering the King of the Jews?"

Brother DD proudly replied, "A drum!"

The real wise men, and Joseph, and Mary simultaneously spoke: "Tabrets we know, tambourines we know, and cymbals we know, but what is a drum, and what do you do with it?"

Brother DD knew that his offering to the King of the Jews had the power to take preeminence over all the other offerings. Especially over non-exciting humble worship with a bowed down face or bended knee. So, he arrogantly replied, "You beat it." "Beat it?" they all asked in unison.

"Yes, watch," answered Brother DD. So, he began to beat it, and beat it, and got inspired and beat it some more (just like at his church), and got anointed and beat it some more (just like at his church), and got lost in his offering as the fervent beating grew in power (just like at his church). When he came to himself, he was disappointed to see everyone flinching with their hands over their ears, as though they were not excited about his offering of worship. Only baby Jesus did not cover his ears; he just cried like any little baby does when frightened.

Brother DD got mad when he saw their response to his superior offering of worship. The same mad anger displayed by Cain when his offering was rejected by God. And like Cain, the Brother DD that crept in unaware among the real wise men, refused to change his offering of worship and walked away from the presence of God.

But in time, centuries of time; Brother DD's mad was made glad when he proved to his peers that "his worship" could draw a crowd and take preeminence over the airways. His mad was made glad as he witnessed his seed, 21st Century Decibel Disciple Juniors, proclaim the necessity of the beating drum in praise and worship and offerings to God. And today his mad is made glad unto perfection as he hears 21st Century Pastors say from the pulpit; "**a drum will do things for you that a prayer meeting cannot. Just beat it, just beat it**."

We witness this timeless spirit manifest itself today as we hear Christians proudly say, "Wow, did we ever have church last night. It was a runaway service. Our worship (frantic bedlam in response to the drum) took preeminence over the Word of God."

And while we are imagining a Decibel Disciple among the real wise men in the presence of the baby named Jesus, maybe his departing words were prophetic: "**You ain't heard nothing yet; wait until the descendants of Cain invent electronic technology to amplify my drum**."

David Clark
3-7-18

The favorite offering of a Decibel Disciple is the beat.

And then he refers to the beat and the accompanying physical response as:

Worship

Of

The King of Kings

Remove Not the Ancient Landmarks

Remove not the ancient landmark, which thy fathers have set.
Proverbs 22:28

Our America is a Nation established "Under God" by our American Forefathers. My American contemporaries and I can take no credit, but rather are blessed to enjoy what our Forefathers established.

The Preamble is an introduction to The United States Constitution; the foundation upon which our American Forefathers safely and securely built the country that Americans love.

The Preamble was written in the summer of 1787 by men who loved America and sought its welfare. This fifty-two-word document clearly communicates the intentions of the Authors and Forefathers who framed The United States Constitution.

The Preamble: *"We the People of the United States, in Order to form a more perfect Union, establish Justice, insure domestic Tranquility, provide for the common Defense, promote the general Welfare, and secure the Blessings of Liberty to ourselves and our Posterity, do ordain and establish this Constitution for the United States of America."*

Every human who participates in the freedom and security afforded by our America, owes much honor and respect to our Forefathers. The Forefathers of America were Patrons of our country, and they wisely left in place Ancient Landmarks that ensured the survival of the American people. Namely; THE CONSTITUTION OF THE UNITED STATES OF AMERICA.

Likewise, Christianity has Landmarks set by Forefathers. Prophets of the Old Testament set Ancient Landmarks of Monotheism and the ways and attributes of the One True God. The New Testament Apostles set Ancient Landmarks and absolutes for the followers of Jesus Christ.

The descriptive word "Ancient" alludes to the secular time of their setting and does not hint that those Ancient Landmarks are outdated. Ancient, but relevant, AND necessary for today's Christian.

The Bible conveys Ancient Landmarks and Ancient Absolutes that protect and guide any Christian today who honors the efforts of our Godly Forefathers. Ancient Landmarks apply to the current needs of today's Christian because Time does not minimize the necessity of Ancient Landmarks even for contemporary Christianity.

Biblical Ancient Landmarks are timeless in their good.

So, we thank God for Ancient Landmarks established by our God-fearing Forefathers. One of which is the late Reverend V.A. Guidroz. He was an honored Forefather in the Pentecostal Fellowship whom I love and respect. This God-Ordained Patron of the Apostolic Faith is the subject Forefather of this article.

Remove Not Ancient Landmarks Set by Forefathers

Our UPCI organization has a wonderful facility in Lufkin, Texas, with a magnificent Tabernacle where God-anointed Biblical preaching and teaching takes place. Centering the front approach to this magnificent sanctuary, there is a stone memorial as part of the beautifully landscaped entrance. That stone memorial is a bust of an honorable servant of God by the name of Reverend V.A. Guidroz.

It was upon this man's leadership and upon this man's precepts that these edifices and campgrounds and general assemblies were established. It was an honorable act to dedicate this magnificent Tabernacle to this man of God. He was undeniably the Forefather of many Ancient Landmarks in the Pentecostal Movement. And while viewing this stone memorial bust, I did observe that it was planted solidly into cement as though it was meant to be permanent.

I am told by senior Pastors that this man of God, was "death on drums." Meaning he would not allow them to be used in worship services within the UPCI Campground Tabernacle in Lufkin, Texas. I myself heard this Forefather (on cassette tape) preach and warn against hidden dangers of emphasizing the beat. I think the title of the sermon was "Marching to Hell."

I could feel his anointing as he pled with a burden for the church to stop the then-present (1980's) trend of Pentecostal music that received its anointing from the drums. This revered man of God, this true servant of God, considered the beat of the drum incapable of enhancing the sacrifice of praise offered to his God.

His preaching revealed a fear that the infectious adrenaline produced by emphatic focus on the beat would be mistaken for the presence of his God. Fear and concern that the physical movement demanded by extreme rhythm would one day be mistaken for worship of his God. His God-ordained intuition and wisdom caused him to fear that the beat would so dominate and lift itself up to such an elevated preeminence, that sincere God-loving Pastors would one day succumb (degenerate) to the delusive conclusion that a church service without drums is dead.

In our New Age of Pentecost, I have personally witnessed it said; "it is the drums that keep a Church service going," and "volume and beat bring life into a church service."

Questions concerning our honorable Forefather, Reverend V.A. Guidroz:

Was this man of God wrong?

Did he misunderstand the God that he served?

Was his gift of discernment tinker-toy quality?

Have we proven his precepts and principles and convictions boringly ancient and unimportant?

Have we as a religious movement proven him wrong?

I wonder about the Old Paths and Ancient Landmarks that Reverend V.A. Guidroz embraced; **were they personally his, OR were they also his God's?**

One Camp Meeting night I exited this Lufkin Campground Tabernacle as soon as I realized the preliminary hour of praise would fulfill the new trends of obnoxiously loud music. As I escaped the Sanctuary, I found myself pondering the granite memorial of Reverend V.A. Guidroz in the outside courtyard.

While considering the face of this honored Forefather etched into this granite memorial, I could hear the fruit of the focused fingers of the sound man as he used man-made technology to force extreme power into the airways. The dominating sound in that fruit, the dominating instrument that seems to declare "I will lift myself up," "I will ascend above the mount of the congregation," "I will exalt myself as the prince of the power of the air," was of course, the drum.

The beating of the drums is a *persistent* effort in Pentecost today that can only be matched in *persistency* by the God-created force called gravity, which is perpetually *persistent*. The beating of drums has become Omnipresent in New-Age Worship.

Physics and science have proven over and over that the only way to increase the physiological effect of the beat upon the human body is to amplify it. It is no secret. Proven and natural, the greater the decibels with which the beat is delivered to the human body, the greater the physiological effect.

Pondering the fixed gaze of the stone bust that night in Lufkin, I could not help but wonder as the Sanctuary thundered and rocked; "What if those eyes of stone became flesh?" Would they narrow in anger at the enemy of biblical worship, or would resignation to defeat cause those eyes to become fountains of tears? What if the God of heaven gave a voice to that mouth of stone, and the man of God spoke one more time with uncanny anointing; could those spirit-filled words even be heard over the sound-man's anointing?

In summation, has our Forefather, the servant of God named Reverend V.A. Guidroz, been proven right or proven wrong?

What if the concrete chains that hold this granite bust in place were dissolved, setting this honored Forefather free? Would he flee the grounds of the Tabernacle to roam the old paths with his ancient God?

If aware in any earthly sense today, does this man of God wish from heaven above that his guidelines, his precepts, his revelations, and his Ancient Landmarks would have been set in concrete for a memorial, instead of his bust and face?

The bust of Reverend V.A. Guidroz was respectfully placed in the decorative courtyard at the front entrance of the Tabernacle sanctuary to honor him as a Forefather. A memorial to recall memories. A memorial to maintain memory of him; his facial structure, his demeanor, his anointing, his name, and those prominent glasses…. BUT NOT his Ancient Landmarks.

Remove not the ancient landmark, which thy fathers have set.
Proverbs 22:28

David Clark

Where is the Voice of My Children?

He walked through the large double glass doors and stepped into His house. With anticipation He passed through the sanctuary doors into the presence of His sons and daughters.

His heart abounded with a love much greater than any Father could ever know. It was a lonesome love, for it would be years before all His children on Earth could be with Him. Slowly, the look of anxious anticipation upon His face began to fade into a less hopeful, almost inquisitive appearance. His countenance saddened as He questioned in His heart, "**Where is the voice of my children**?"

Those who know Him as a jealous father might have expected to see anger, but anger did not come. Only in His eyes could one read the emotions of His heart. Instead of anger, there remained the longing look of a desire to hear His name called by the ones He loved. Seeking His name, He stood. Seeking His name, He listened. Nowhere could He hear His name, nor could He hear, "I Love You." Nowhere did He hear, "I Thank You," "I Need You," or "Lord, I Bless Your Name." Momentarily He pondered, "Do they even remember me?"

Suddenly with a loud voice of authority, He began to speak: "It is I. I am your Father. You are my children. I am the one who suffered on Calvary and shed my blood so that you may have remission of sins. I am the one who has prepared a place for you so that where I am, there you may be also. I purchased you with my blood. I died for you. Where is the sacrifice of praise, the fruit of your lips giving thanks to my name?"

"I am Alpha and Omega, the Ancient of Days, the One True God. I am your Creator. You are a supernatural creation for my glory, for my namesake. I seek worship. I seek praise."

"I see your efforts. I see your uplifted hands, your exuberance, your joyful clapping of hands, your bended knees, and your tears. It is all good, but I cannot hear your words of praise. Where is the fruit of your lips, the sacrifice of praise? Oh, how I long to commune with my people and hear the voice of those called by my name."

But His plea was not heard. His voice was also lost in the din with the voice of His children. The only voices heard were the few voices electronically amplified to rock-concert decibels as they sang, "Crank up the music and let's have church." At the word "church," Jesus reflects and whispers to Himself: "These called-out ones are my church, my chosen Bride. Exactly what do they mean when they sing, - let's have church?"

As He observes the most powerful sound system that money can buy, and huge omnipotent electronic speakers hanging from the ceiling and on the walls and on the floor and on the platform; He begins to understand. Then He knew why the organ was now a roar, and the piano was a banging jangle, and the lead guitar produced an intrusive shattering decibel, and the base guitar vibrated all bodies and all furniture with rhythm, and the drums raced to dominate the airways.

The answer is simple. My adversary Satan, who remembers the sounds of praise and worship in Heaven, hates the sounds of praise and worship from God's creation.

As He turned to leave His house and children, the force of the music tingles at the large scar in His side. But before He leaves the Sanctuary, the God of mercy shows mercy. He heals the sick because of His stripes; He stirs the sinner because it is His will that all men come to repentance; He fills the thirsty with His spirit because it is a promise; NOT because the volume of the music is cranked up by the works of man's hand.

As He exits his children's room, He passes unnoticed by the soundman, who is habitually focused on his duty to "make-it-happen." While passing by this head-bobbing soundman, Jesus is tempted to scream out, "You little speck of dust, who do you think you are to completely drown out the voice of my children as they give glory to their Creator?" But, remembering the responsibility is not His, the disappointed father holds his peace.

As Jesus walks out of His house and then through the exterior glass doors in which He had entered, the vibrations of the soundman's effort to "have church" could still be felt. Walking slowly away from His house, He could still hear the premeditated purpose of the sound system as it pumps synthetic praise through a wooden wall and a brick wall.

It seemed to Him only yesterday, the sounds of worship and praise two thousand years ago were so different. The sounds of adoration echoing through the Upper Room as His children prayed, were still so pleasant to His ear.

"Where is the voice of my children? Do they not know that it was I who shook the place in Acts 4:31; only because they prayed where they were assembled, and I heard their voice?"

"Do they not understand that tomorrow Revelation 5:11-12 will be here? Many voices will say with a loud voice 'worthy is the lamb'. Soon and very soon, I will hear the voice of my children again. As in Revelation 19:1, a great voice of much people will say, 'Alleluia' unto me and I will hear the sacrifice of praise, the fruit of their lips."

"As in the beginning, so will the end be."

Jesus continued walking on Earth, from Sanctuary to Sanctuary in search of old-path Pentecostal sounds of praise. And finding none, he uttered words that chill: "Where art thou O watchman, what of the night?"

David Clark
March 4 1999

A Type and Shadow from the Old Testament

Moses delivered God's message to Pharaoh; *Let my people go that they may serve me.*

God's heartbeat – But man interferes.

Today, the voice of that same God is silenced in His Sanctuary amidst the delusive volumes of the **Decibel Doctrine.**

Today, if heard, that same voice is saying;

Let my people go that they may offer the sacrifice of praise to Me continually, that is the fruit of their lips giving thanks to My Name.
Hebrews 13:15

God's heartbeat – But man interferes.

Tar Baby

Please allow me to go back to my childhood days and have some fun.

It is told that a long, long, time ago, there was a good rabbit named Brer Rabbit.

This one called Brer Rabbit had an enemy known as Brer Fox, that roamed to and fro, seeking how he might devour Brer Rabbit. Brer Fox, the enemy of any good rabbit, desired to consume Brer Rabbit as a satisfying meal. But all endeavors to trick and trap Brer Rabbit only failed continually. Even in all his subtlety and craftiness, Brer Fox was unable to snare and take Brer Rabbit to devour him.

There seemed to be an invisible hedge of protection around Brer Rabbit. It seemed to be a hedge-of-common-sense that kept Brer Rabbit from the deceitful efforts of Brer Fox.

But one day Brer Fox tried something new. Something that he had never even thought of before, until…., "whatever" put the thought in his mind. He grinned as he could feel his spirit being led by…, "whatever," to create this new invention. Brer Fox's consistent failures made him willing to try anything to "make it happen." Whatever was prompting him did not matter to a subtle fox, if "it worked." Following the instructions of this new spiritual assistance, or "whatever," Brer Fox mixed turpentine with tar and craftily formed a manikin.

"Now what?" thought Brer Fox in his mind as he stared blankly at the black and sticky new innovative creation made by his own hands. The dark side, the "whatever," still assisted him and answered that question. "Stir up Brer Rabbit's emotions. Stir up his emotions to a level that he will leave the protecting hedge-of-common-sense, and he will become snared and taken at your will."

In this story told long ago, the new invention was named Tar Baby. The wily inventor, the "whatever," led Brer Fox to place the Tar Baby where Brer Rabbit could not resist testing it. The introduction of the new invention into Brer Rabbit's life quickly led Brer Rabbit beyond the boundary of the protecting hedge-of-common-sense and led him into a fit of beyond-common-sense emotion.

It is told in this fable that Brer Rabbit attempted conversation with the Tar Baby, and got angry because the Tar Baby would not speak nor respond.

So, unable to control his anger, Brer Rabbit tested the new invention with a left jab and promptly stuck his paw in the tar. He then punched with his right paw which also became stuck and non-retrievable.

Under the influence of beyond-common-sense emotion, the good rabbit then tested this new invention with both of his back feet. Now all four paws were stuck to the new invention and became non-retrievable. So, the beyond-common-sense emotion stirred up by the new invention lead Brer Rabbit into captivity. Ensnared in the first "testing" and totally held captive under the influence of this new thing.

The snare designed by "whatever" was like unto a "new path" to Brer Rabbit. Tar Baby was enticing, yet harmless to Brer Rabbit as long as he walked the "Old Path" in which he had found peace and protection by a hedge-of-common-sense all of his life.

The Dark Silent Spiritual "whatever" chuckled to Brer Fox: "It works." "Offer a curious New Path to man, and he will test it."

The summation of the demise of Brer Rabbit was that he found himself deceived, yet incapable of letting go or turning back. (Here I remind the reader that two of the signs that follow *Not-Right* worship as described in Cain's life are *Anger* and the *Inability to Turn Around*.)

And by analogy, childish analogy, such is the demise of good men who test the power of 21st century new inventions of technology that promise foundation-shaking power in the Sanctuary. I am specifically speaking of the power of extreme decibels of music produced from new and improved omnipotent sound systems. I am not referring to the basic functional purpose of sound systems to enable audibility, but the testing of higher levels of decibels for their special effects on people.

At first curious glimpse and testing, the spirit of a good man rejects the experienced emotion as a stirring of the flesh by "whatever." His gift of commonsense screams: "That is fabricated emotion by the hands of man. That is only a manikin; that is not of God."

But the voice of common sense cannot be heard over the Never-Available-Before-Volumes-of-Music. And in time, as man continues to seek new and improved ways; the continual testing of new and improved inventions designed to dominate the airways with greater and greater decibels, convinces even good men that the power of beyond-common-sense emotion that he feels in his flesh is the power of God.

Automatically he is drafted into the 21st Century ranks of Decibel Discipleship, and pledges his allegiance to the **Decibel Doctrine.** His brotherly rebuttal to the boring followers-of-the-Old-Paths who try to warn him against the New Thing and the New Way will become the forever common retort: "Whatever... **it works**! Whatever... **now I can make it happen**!"

189

The good-man-turned-Decibel-Disciple will be stuck-like-chuck to the new "whatever," never to recover. There appears to me that no remedy-for-release exists in this childish analogy of Tar Baby.

And in my small world, real life experiences testify that attachment to the **Decibel Doctrine** is **irreversible**. The Decibel Disciples that I know are totally captivated, sold out, and helplessly ensnared by "whatever" because "**it works.**" Conveniently, even instantly, with the simple flip of a switch and a silent slide of lever, "it" or "whatever" "**makes it happen.**" I know not a man, even among good men, able to let go. The unnatural affinity between a Decibel Disciple and his Sound System is too great. The attachment is even greater than sticky tar.

Herein is deception pronounced upon the good-man-turned-Decibel-Disciple. He feels in control of the power that "makes it happen" in his **Decibel Doctrine** church service. But he is powerless of any effort to remove himself from its addiction. And he is duped into thinking he is controlling power from God above.

This New Thing and New Way current among us Pentecostals is not invincible. It does have an "Achilles' heel." Its power of life relies upon a constant supply of man-made electricity.

Should an electrical failure cause the sound system volumes to be reduced to less-than-rock-n-roll-volumes in a **Decibel Doctrine** church service, the resulting vacuum would suck the life out of the assembly and the spirit of the Sanctuary would be diagnosed as DEAD.

And no Pastor wants this diagnosis from his peers.

A wreath is placed upon the church entrance door for all the New-Agers to mourn.

Cause of spiritual death? - Mechanical Failure.

****

In closing.

Totally consumed by beyond-common-sense emotion, they forget that the assembling of the Redeemed was a setting invented by the Ancient of Days, a long, long, time ago.

And requested by Him, a long, long, time ago, for His pleasure.

No matter, "whatever."

David Clark
4-7-07

Serendipity

Serendipity - Definition

1. *The faculty of happening upon fortunate discoveries when not in search of them.*

2. *The ability of finding valuable things unexpectedly.*

The word "serendipity" was coined by Horace Walpole. It came about from a fairy tale, The Three Princes of Serendipity, the heroes of which were continually finding articles by chance.

This article reviews the Serendipity of a few commonly known inventions.

Innumerable are the inventions discovered by accident that have forever affected mankind's existence upon this earth. Most of them are documented with a date and a name of the discoverer. And most inventions are for the good of mankind. But not so for the **Decibel Doctrine.** Rather to the contrary. Serendipity that discovered the **Decibel Doctrine** was most unfortunate for the relationship between man and his Creator.

The Microwave - Percy L. Spencer

Percy Spencer, an engineer at Raytheon after his WWI stint in the Navy, was known as an electronics genius. In 1945, Spencer was fiddling with a microwave-emitting magnetron — used in the guts of radar arrays — when he felt a strange sizzling sensation in his pants pocket. Spencer paused and found that a chocolate bar in his pocket had started to melt. Figuring that the microwave radiation of the magnetron was the cause, Spencer immediately set out to realize the culinary potential at work. The end result was the microwave oven.

Super Glue - Harry Coover

In what might have been a very messy moment of discovery in 1942, Dr. Harry Coover of Eastman-Kodak Laboratories found that a substance he created — cyanoacrylate — was a miserable failure. It was not, to his dismay, at all suited for a new precision gun sight as he had hoped — it infuriatingly stuck to everything it touched. So, it was forgotten. Six years later, while overseeing an experimental new design for airplane canopies, Coover found himself stuck in the same gooey mess with a familiar foe — cyanacrylate was proving useless as ever. But this time, Coover

191

observed that the stuff formed an incredibly strong bond without needing heat. Coover and his team tinkered with sticking various objects in their lab together, and realized they had finally stumbled upon a use for the maddening goop. Coover filed a patent on his discovery, and in 1958, a full 16 years after he first got stuck, cyanoacrylate was being sold on shelves as Super Glue.

Penicillin

In 1928, a scientist, Sir Alexander Fleming was searching for a "wonder drug" that could cure diseases. However, it wasn't until Fleming threw away his experiments that he found what he was looking for; today it is called Penicillin. Fleming noticed that a contaminated Petri dish he had discarded contained a mold that was dissolving all the bacteria around it. When he grew the mold by itself, he learned that it contained a powerful antibiotic, penicillin.

Gun Powder

Ninth-century Chinese alchemists made an explosive discovery in their quest to find an elixir for eternal life. They found out the hard way that mixing salt peter, sulfur, and charcoal is not a recipe for immortality; it makes gunpowder.

Continent of America

Columbus was looking for a route to Asia and as poets say: "Columbus stubbed his toe on America."

Telephone

Alexander Graham Bell was trying to improve the telegraph and failed, but he came up with a telephone.

Rubber Tires

Charles Goodyear, a self-taught chemist, had been trying to remove the stickiness out of rubber. He put a piece of rubber that was smeared with sulfur near the fire. The next morning it was non-sticky and vulcanized. The Goodyear Tire and Rubber Company was named after him.

****

Decibel Doctrine Discovery

The older I get, the more answers I realize I don't know for sure. An interesting fact concerning the **Decibel Doctrine** that I have never discovered; **when was its power and special effects discovered?**

Surely no human was seeking to discover such a repugnant theory, especially to be used in the Sanctuary of the One True God. There is no biblical validity to even hint that the **Decibel Doctrine** was a missing element in worship that needed discovering. Therefore, all common sense birthed in the light, has to confess that discovery of the **Decibel Doctrine** had to have happened serendipitously.

A Possible Scenario of Serendipity in History

It could be that one day in the 21st century, a church sound-man went to church with a common cold. His head was congested, and his hearing was dulled. Sitting at his position of duty in the sound booth, he began to do his job. The volume lever on the sound board for which he was responsible, had to be moved up to position 8 in order for him to hear the same intensity of sound that was normally produced at position 5. Unknowingly to him, the sound system was working properly and position 8 produced 60% greater decibels than the normally used position 5.

His congestion-impaired hearing had caused him to misjudge what the audience was hearing.

The usual choruses were sung that day, and the same singer led congregational songs. But this day, the reaction of most of the saints was different. Some grimaced and searched for cotton to plug their ears; but others, especially the younger people and the saints known to be lukewarm, seemed to gravitate toward the over-amplified speakers, as though they were drawn to the source of power that they felt. As a whole, physical motion of the audience became more than exuberant, as though the PRAISERS were doubly excited about their God and what He had done for them. This day even the lukewarm and the sinner turned into ACTIVE PRAISERS.

But right in the middle of the church service, the sound man's ears suddenly popped as the pressure caused by his head cold rebalanced back to normal. The impairment to his hearing now gone, he realized his overcorrection of volume. Now realizing that his sound system was working with normal accuracy, he began to re-adjust for his error.

Magically it seemed, the exuberant motion of praise diminished proportionally with the diminishing volume of music. The preacher preached, and souls responded in repentance, and lives were changed as the Word of God spoke to hearts, and the presence of God stirred and healed.

The sound man laid awake for a long time that night in his home, pondering the phenomenon of which only he was fully aware. Falling asleep he wondered, "what if ….?"

When the music started for the next church service, the sound man checked the sound settings that he had meticulously and methodically established over the years as he sought first class quality for God's sanctuary. All of his life as a sound man for his church, he had diligently sought to accomplish the simple goal and purpose for which sound systems were invented; to make sound, whether voices or music, audible to the congregation. "That was first grade commonsense stuff," he had always said.

But then that unanswered question from the previous church service kept nagging at his mind, "What if….? Could it be….?" And he could not resist the test.

He slowly slid the main volume lever beyond the normal and adequate position 5, (the same position of volume control that had been sufficient for over 20 years), toward the much louder position 8, and again, almost instantly, the spirit of the service seemed to change. The atmosphere seemed to become "charged," and livelier.

An increase in physical display of motion began to manifest, exuberance seemed to multiply exponentially, even the lukewarm and the sinner again appeared to get involved.

The sound man thought to himself, "Wow!" "Could what I'm thinking really be so….?" And a hypothesis formed in his mind. *"Is it possible, that I can control the spirit of the church service with this power at my fingertips?"*

He tested this hypothesis again the next time the servants of God assembled in the Sanctuary. And to his amazement, it worked again.

This night after church service, the sound man laid awake all night, mesmerized by the power that he had tapped into. His late-night questions developed from a hypothesis into a theory that he felt compelled to prove. He verbalized to himself, "The proof is in the pudding. If it works, it works."

It worked the next service and the next service and the next. He remembered being taught in college, "It is not true science or true physics unless it can be repeated." And he had discovered that this controlling power could be repeated at his will, therefore he knew that his hypothesis and theory was scientifically valid.

The power at his fingertips seemed endless, and soon he learned that his manipulations of the spirit with volume could create "fire" in the sanctuary that would "take-over" the service, especially on Sunday nights, and consume the time allotted to preaching the Word.

The Pastor soon began to pat him on the back, and the young sheep seemed excited. He learned to ignore the mature old-path lovers-of-God as they stood in the way, asking him for a little mercy with tears in their eyes. Per his pastor's instructions, he wrote this group off as elder has-beens and wet blankets. Nudniks that know not God.

Initially he was disheartened to separate himself from the much-respected Elders of the Old Paths who thought the power of God should be prayed down, or preached down, or praised down, or sent down by God Himself.

But he must please his pastor, and besides, his normally-unnoticed talent now placed him above that of just a servant. His discovery had lifted him up to an elevated position of control. He alone had discovered this power, and he had the right to use this power in the Sanctuary.

He alone, in his little cubicle in the back of the Sanctuary, had become the REAL WORHSIP LEADER. He knew it, his Pastor knew it, the New Age audience knew it, and the Spirit of Serpent Seed Music knew it.

Time and chance allowed the discovery, the discovery formed a hypothesis, this hypothesis developed into a theory, and this theory (metamorphosed) into a doctrine. The elevated twenty first century **Decibel Doctrine**. The **Decibel Doctrine**; discovered, tested, proven, and forever with us.

The Dark Depths of Serendipity.

When and where and by whom was it discovered? I know not.

Neither do I know the end.

I do know very well that the Dark Appetite of The Spirit of Serpent Seed Music is insatiable, especially in the form of the **Decibel Doctrine**.

What can I say but, "Come quickly Lord Jesus"?

David Clark

Natural Enemies

Thou art worthy, O Lord, to receive glory and honour and power:
for thou hast created all things, and for thy pleasure they are and were created.
Revelation 4:11

Allow me to amplify the above verse with country-boy simplicity. This is what the four and twenty elders meant as they spoke these recorded words and bowed before the throne in heaven: All things were created by the Lord for His own pleasure, and all things that **were** created for His pleasure still **are** (exist now) for His pleasure.

Again, in country-boy simplicity: **When God created man, that creation called man had the ability to bring pleasure to his Creator. And still does**.

Because I believe this precept, I have **Natural Enemies** in the religious world.

I believe that the creation called man was created with an inherent ability to bring pleasure to God.

Disciples of the **Decibel Doctrine** do not. They believe rather that God had to wait six thousand years for His creation called man to discover the power of electricity, and develop today's technology of transducers and amplifiers to fulfill man's ability to please their Creator.

Naturally I do not.

Decibel Disciples and I are **Natural Enemies**.

I still contend that before sin, Adam and Eve brought pleasure to God as they communed with Him in the Garden of Eden. If I am correct, then Decibel Disciples are critically wrong, and vice versa.

Either way, I am a **Natural Enemy** to Decibel Disciples and vice versa.

Decibel Disciples believe that God is impressed by, or finds pleasure in, their extreme volumes of electronic sound created by manipulating physics. In addition, they believe that their Creator is impressed by, or finds pleasure in, the physical demonstration of movement manifested when the God-created creation called man is subjected to the special effects of the **Decibel Doctrine**.

I do not. I am their **Natural Enemy**.

Decibel Disciples believe that when the Psalmist wrote, *play skilfully with a loud noise* and *make a loud noise*, that God-inspired Holy Scripture was referring to today's manmade technology and electric manipulation of physics. And God had to wait a long time for this 21ˢᵗ century technology to be discovered and brought into His Sanctuary.

<u>I do not.</u>

I consider this belief to be spiritually repugnant at best, so in defense of the pleasure of God my Creator, I am a **Natural Enemy** of Disciples of the **Decibel Doctrine**.

On October 16th, 2016, a lifetime friend named Dale, reminded me of the time he told the soundman in his home church that he (the soundman) needed hearing aids. We chuckled at the insanity of the scenario, but really, it is not funny to God nor to those who are forced to suffer the **Decibel Doctrine** in the Sanctuary.

I reminded Dale of the time that I told my soundman-friend named Craig in my home church that he must be deaf and in need of hearing aids. (At this time the **Decibel Doctrine** was freshly being established in my home church.) In an instant, I witnessed a total transformation of a friend-turned-foe, as violent anger defended the **Decibel Doctrine**.

I naturally understood then that Craig and I had become **Natural Enemies;** as he embraced the **Decibel Doctrine** holding it dear, as I simultaneously abhorred it.

Decibel Disciples believe that the **Decibel Doctrine** can save souls if the decibels of music are excessively loud enough.

<u>I do not.</u>

It is only **Natural** to the Holy Spirit within me to acknowledge myself as an enemy of Decibel Disciples.

A cat fuzzes up and extends his claws when a strange dog approaches nearby because they are **Natural Enemies.** – And a chicken hen hides when a hawk soars overhead because the hawk is a **Natural Enemy** of chickens. – Rabbits scamper into a hole in the ground for safety when their **Natural Enemy,** the coyote creeps close.

Modern medical technology has determined poor diets, lack of exercise, high stress, heavy metals, "free radicals," etc. to be a **Natural Enemy** of our health. The

Holy Scripture declares sins and weights to be **Natural Enemies** to the soul that seeks eternal life.

It appears to me that most all things have **Natural Enemies**.

As the "father of lies," the devil is a **Natural Enemy** of Truth. And the devil is a **Natural Enemy** of all righteousness. Like as Holiness is a **Natural Enemy** of all unrighteousness.

So, it is only natural to declare the spirit of the **Decibel Doctrine** to be a **Natural Enemy** of God-given Common Sense and Biblical Compliance.

It is the spirit of the **Decibel Doctrine** that is a **Natural Enemy** of any Holy Ghost filled saint who does not believe that the electronically amplified volume of music assimilates the power of God.

I believe that the words written by John in Revelation were ALL God-inspired and accurate.

*And I saw as it were a sea of glass mingled with fire: and them that had gotten the victory over the beast, and over his image, and over his mark, and over the number of his name, stand on the sea of glass, having **the harps** of God. 3 And they sing the song of Moses the servant of God, and the song of the Lamb, saying, Great and marvellous are thy works, Lord God Almighty; just and true are thy ways, thou King of saints.*
Revelation 15:2-3

Decibel Disciples consider these written words that describe the pleasantly soft music of harps and old ancient songs that John witnessed in Heaven as *Surely Fake News*.

I do not.

They question: How can we rock the house with a harp?? How can we get God's attention with only a harp?? How can we bring pleasure to God with just a harp??

Decibel Disciples believe that Christian "victors" in heaven will chant in unison: "Got the devil under my feet" one hundred and one times in staccato succession, to please God. AND/OR, their favorite Sunday Night chant: "I'm gonna dance, dance, dance-dance-dance, all night, all night, Ditto-Ditto-Ditto…." All to the accelerated beat of their amplified drums.

I do not.

I believe their beliefs are false. And my belief makes me their **Natural Enemy**.

The two courses of song described above are twin catalysts to what Decibel Disciples tout as a "run-away-service." A "run-away-service" is often a Premeditated-Sunday-Night-Specialty where the **Decibel Doctrine** is practiced in full force. When the volume and beat are properly applied, Decibel Disciples believe that God steps in and disallows time for His Word to speak.

I do not.

Rather I believe the term "run-away-service," more often than not, means that the **Decibel Doctrine** Pastor "ran-away-from" the Word of God, in effect, silencing the Lord.

Decibel Disciples think that the phrase "harps of God" is just a prophetic typology of music in heaven that indicates permission to bring their sacred sound equipment onto that sea of glass and enhance the atmosphere of praise with artificial volume and beat.

I do not.

With God-inspired accuracy, John wrote of seeing Altars in heaven. Eight times John pens the word "Altar" in the Book of Revelation as he describes scenes in Heaven.

Decibel Disciples believe that the word "Altar" is used symbolically as a type and shadow of personal altars only in men's hearts.

I do not.

Decibel Disciples believe that if Altars really are in heaven, they will be a hindrance to worship just as they propose to be so in Sanctuaries on earth.

I do not.

I am NATURALLY a **Natural Enemy** of the **Decibel Doctrine** and all Disciples of that Doctrine.

Disciples of the **Decibel Doctrine** confess to believe that the Upper Room in Jerusalem, referred to in Acts 1:12-15, was filled with loud invigorating music on the Day of Pentecost when about 120 were filled with the Holy Ghost. Decibel Disciples also believe that the false accusations of drunkenness described that day in Acts 2:13-15, stemmed from manifestations caused by ten days of intoxicating music.

<u>I do not.</u>

The Spirit lurking within the **Decibel Doctrine** is a supplanter of the Biblical Worship that rightly offers homage of worth to God.

That Spirit, often referred to as The Spirit of Serpent Seed Music, seeds and propagates *Not-Right* worship. And that fact naturally justifies my position as a **Natural Enemy** of the **Decibel Doctrine**.

False interpretation of the following scripture is only one of many that make me a **Natural Enemy** of religious nonsense: *Mark 5:6 - But when he saw Jesus afar off, he ran and worshipped him.*

Decibel Disciples believe that this man, possessed by a legion of devils, worshipped Jesus by running. And received his deliverance.

<u>I do not.</u>

I believe rather that the possessed man ran in desperation to Jesus, and then fell on his knees in humble worship at the feet of Jesus; and at that instant, the devils knew their time was short.

I just naturally believe that the word "worship" means exactly what both Hebrew and Greek claim it to mean.

Therefore, as a defender of Biblical Worship, I am a **Natural Enemy** to that perverted belief system called the **Decibel Doctrine**.

The poor soundman who is pastored by a Decibel Disciple finds himself in a predicament. He discovers the essence of the words of Jesus as he told his Disciples:

No man can serve two masters: for either he will hate the one and love the other; or else he will hold to the one and despise the other. Ye cannot serve God and mammon.
Matthew 6:24

This terminology used by the Creator of the Universe, "<u>hate and despise</u>," and "<u>love and hold to</u>," are nowhere near passive in intent. Rather, they indicate aggression. Aggressive Emotions and Aggressive Embracing.

Servants to the spirit of the **Decibel Doctrine** aggressively serve and love their master. Proponents and servants of the **Decibel Doctrine** will aggressively defend and cling to and embrace and hold to its agenda. Anyone who dares to question biblical authenticity for the **Decibel Doctrine** is a **Natural Enemy** of that Spirit and shall be treated so.

Likewise, servants of the Creator of the Universe have a covenant to aggressively serve and love their Master. They are compelled by scripture to aggressively defend and hold to the desires of their Master.

When two servants aggressively serve, and aggressively love, and aggressively defend, and aggressively hold to opposing masters, it is only **Natural** that they become **Natural Enemies.**

When a sincere, God-fearing, God-serving, God-loving, God-seeking, common-sense saint, dares to question any biblical certification of the **Decibel Doctrine**, he will be aggressively treated as a **Natural Enemy**. And such ascribed qualities in a True Christian make him irrevocably and undeniably, a **Natural Enemy** of all Decibel Disciples; **NATURALLY.**

So, in summation, Decibel Disciples think that they impress the God of Creation with their artificial volumes of their man-created sound systems.... AND I DO NOT.

In fact, I find myself allergic to such a shallow opinion of The Creator.

I daily discover the absoluteness of **Natural Enemies** within the spiritual realm.

I possibly spoke such a destiny into my life the day I declared the following words as I sat in the office of the author of *The Spirit of Serpent Seed Music* and *The Music of the Golden Calves* and *Strange Fire*: "Pastor (M.E. Burr), I want to be a viable enemy of this Spirit."

Alas, the longer it takes me to print this Collection of Articles titled **The Decibel Doctrine**, the more enemies I will naturally have; for the recruiting of men into the ranks of the **Decibel Doctrine Defenders** is aggressively successful in numbers. As Decibel Discipleship increases daily, my targeted audience that I hope to help proportionally decreases likewise daily.

I highly esteem the Word of my Lord and seriously regard its value. This irrevocable position of my spirit, naturally makes all men that do violence to the Word of God, my **Natural Enemy.**

Yet that same Word that judges my enemies, still commands me:

But I say unto you, Love your enemies, bless them that curse you, do good to them
that hate you, and pray for them which despitefully use you, and persecute you;
Matthew 5:44

<u>So, I try to do so, with a smile.</u>

David Clark
10-31-16

Just a thought, a paralyzing thought:

Surely commonsense Thinkers Think: Why do Decibel Disciples limit the decibels of "worship" that they offer unto their God????

Technology has made almost-unlimited decibels of music available with just the turn of a knob, or with just the slide of a lever. If more "worthy worship" is so easily available in the Sanctuary; why not increase their offering of "worship" up to a higher, more "worthy" level of value?

I mean, Max-Out the capable volume limits of your instrument of worship!

Why withhold more-worthy-worship from God in the Sanctuary??

Why withhold something from God that He finds pleasure in??

To the Decibel Disciple, I say: Is your God not worthy of your best??

Is your Creator not worthy of the LOUDEST??

As one searches for logic within the **Decibel Doctrine**, he will discover that there are many unasked questions and many avoided answers.

Selah.

The Hound Dog Tenacity of Truth

My neighbor across the rural road that I live on is a fox hunter. His name is Toby. A more than wonderful Christian neighbor. His hobby is fox hunting. He raises and trains black and tan hound dogs to hunt and chase foxes. Obviously, his knowledge in training fox hounds is excellent, for I have seen multiple rooms in his home full of trophies that were won at fox hunting competitions.

I have many times observed the tenacity of his fox hounds in action. The most obvious and prominent spectacle is that these hound dogs never stop hunting and tracking the fox. Surmising what I have witnessed with my neighbor as he trains many fox hounds, **I have learned that the hound dog pursues relentlessly.**

The tenacity of a trailing hound dog is relentless. There is no rest for the quarry. There is no hope of escape for a target sought by a relentlessly pursuing hound dog, even at the end of the trail. Tenacious in his agenda, the hound dog seeks until the quarry is subdued.

One of the most clever and elusive targets of any hound dog is the wily fox. In calculated efforts to elude a tenaciously tracking hound dog, foxes have been known to wade up streams or back-track and then leap upon a rock or leaning tree. Some foxes are cunning enough to circle back and make false trails in attempts to confuse their tracker.

And sometimes the confusion is successful, but only temporarily. For it is just a matter of time before the relentless tenacity of the ever-snuffling hound dog finds again the trail of his elusive target. Ultimately, hound dog and fox meet face to face.

And, so it is with TRUTH. TRUTH never goes away. TRUTH may seem to disappear momentarily or may even be mistakenly thought to be successfully avoided. But it will inevitably appear on the trail behind, for TRUTH is tenacious. It relentlessly tracks its target. The hound dog tenacity of TRUTH will not allow it to cease seeking. Ultimately, TRUTH discovers its target, and face-to-face, it judges as only TRUTH can do.

The TRUTHS revealed in this collection of articles concerning the **Decibel Doctrine** will never go away. In elusive moves, the exposed targets, (men, not foxes) will color these TRUTHS with multiple shades of camouflage, in subtle efforts to elude their accuracy.

Most of the Decibel Disciples that I know are very cunning, but the hound dog tenacity of TRUTH will forever track them. The meeting is inevitable. One day, as sure as a true arrow sent to its mark, promoters of the **Decibel Doctrine** will concede to TRUTH face-to-face. The hound dog tenacity of TRUTH is unrelenting and inescapable and absolute.

The "New Paths" traveled by Decibel Disciples leave very vivid signs that follow. TRUTH finds the Decibel Disciple easy-to-follow, but hard to capture and coerce into confession. Meanwhile, the spiritually blind, AND those light on discernment, AND the unlearned, AND the carnal, AND the pleasers of self, all blindly bask in the explosive decibels of the **Decibel Doctrine.** Meanwhile, the Decibel Pastor convinces them that the power they feel is the condoning power of God.

But one day, every Decibel Disciple will be confronted with TRUTH, and the reality of TRUTH must be reckoned with.

I say that the decibels orchestrated by a Decibel Disciple in a church service IS NOT really the life changing power of God. I say that the physical fruit of the **Decibel Doctrine** created in the Sanctuary IS NOT Biblical worship. I say that the **Decibel Doctrine** is a false doctrine. I say that its manmade works are only superficial and self-serving.

Decibel Disciples say that I am wrong, and that the old paths are dead and boring. They say and believe that the **Decibel Doctrine** is of God and that it is not just another manmade doctrine.

Comparing the principles taught to me by Elders like Murray E. Burr to the principles taught by the **Decibel Doctrine**, I am blessed to find myself at the opposite end of the spectrum from the proponents of the **Decibel Doctrine**.

There is a great gulf fixed between the old paths that I continue to embrace and the new paths created by Decibel Disciples. Both I and they claim to practice Biblical TRUTH, but both cannot be TRUTH, for they are too diverse. The two beliefs, mine and theirs, are diametrical to each other.

One day TRUTH will announce and proclaim only one of these paths as the True Apostolic Doctrine that the church continued in from the Day of Pentecost. Surely, that "Great and Notable Day of the Lord" is the day that the elusive quarry that thought to have escaped the Hound Dog Tenacity of Truth will be subdued at bay and forced to confess TRUTH. On their knees.

TRUTH never goes away. It never tires. It never falters.

One day, that day of reckoning, when TRUTH faces its foe, TRUTH shall speak for herself, and flinch not.

David Clark
5-22-2012

SECTION FOUR

Finale

Coming-Out-of-the-Closet with Boldness

The Act of Being Honestly Open with Formerly Hidden Feelings

Twenty-seven years ago, under the direction of God Himself, I became self-employed. The business that God helped me build burned down on December 31st, 2018. Mine and my wife's lives were changed dramatically. In fact, today, six months after this incident, our world has been transformed into scenarios that we never even imagined that we could survive. God's mercy has kept us. In fact, God did a most notable miracle for us in the midst of this dark calamity, of which we testify often.

I had hoped to finish this collection of articles titled *The Decibel Doctrine* before the summer of 2019. Needless to say, my time and energy and focus was demanded by an effort to survive for the last six months.

Sadly, the stock pile of information relating to today's **Decibel Doctrine** that I have collected for almost twenty years, has lain idle on my desk; where it is unable to help anybody struggling with today's new paths of church "worship."

However, on Monday, June 10th, 2019, I heard words that again stirred me to quicken my pen to reveal the delusion I find so prevalent in today's "worship" scene. On this Monday, a fellow-Christian told me of an experience with his Pastor that was allowing the practice of the **Decibel Doctrine** in church services. He had humbly questioned the Pastor: "Why is the music so loud in our church?" The Pastor's honest reply was: **"It has been proven that loud music makes people "worship" more actively"**!!!

(And the Thinkers Think: *How does one bow or kneel or humble himself more actively?*) (Obviously Decibel Doctrine Pastors don't think.)

For twenty plus years I have heard Decibel Disciples avoid telling saints the TRUTH in response to the question: "Why is the music becoming louder and louder in our church?" For years Pastors have responded to this frequently asked question with erroneous evasive explanations that are commonly known as "cop-outs," or "little white lies."

But now with a seared conscience, they are **coming-out-of-the-closet with boldness**. They now confess the Truth without shame. Now, they and their peers have proven, and will continue to prove, that extreme volumes of music make **all people** "worship" more actively. By **Decibel Doctrine Definition**.

Interestingly - **ALL** "worship" more actively - believer/non-believer, good/evil, honest/dishonest, sincere/hypocrite, zealous/lukewarm, real/not-real, humble/proud, repented/un-repented, and of course, submissive/rebellious.

God spews this manmade illegitimate noxious substitute for worthy worship out of His mouth, yet He continues to fill the thirsty and sincere with His Spirit wherever He finds them; knowing that He will be falsely accused of honoring the ever-present **Decibel Doctrine**.

David Clark
June 10, 2019

The mass exodus of Pastors coming-out-of-the-closet in these Last Days, qualified this article to be in **The Finale Section.**

Few There Be That Find It

*Enter ye in at the strait gate: for wide is the gate, and broad is the way, that leadeth to destruction, and many there be which go in thereat: **14** Because strait is the gate, and narrow is the way, which leadeth unto life, and **few there be that find it.***
Matthew 7:13-14

Plainly, the wide gate and the broad way are diametrically opposed to the strait gate and the narrow way. And likewise, the "worship" that New Age Pentecostals now offer God is diametrically opposed to Biblical absolutes pertaining to worship in definition and demonstration.

The 21st century demonstrations deemed as "worship" in some church settings are alien to Biblical demonstrations of worship described by the inspiration of God Himself from Genesis to Revelation.

These are **New Ways** established by **New Paths**, and the **Decibel Doctrine** is the **New Mother** that has given birth to this **New Worship**.

Thus saith the LORD, Stand ye in the ways, and see, and ask for the old paths, where is the good way, and walk therein, and ye shall find rest for your souls. But they said, We will not walk therein.
Jeremiah 6:16

The understanding and mental grasp that the old paths and old weapons found in the Bible are truly best for the Apostolic Church, is a revelation that crosses swords with the carnality of Pseudo-Pentecostals of today. The Old Paths are absolutely a narrow way. And our culture, our carnality, our superfluity, our Pied-Piper syndrome, our contemporary peer pressure, are all obstructions that make the Old Paths appear even more narrow and the price to walk therein even greater. These same obstructions cause the End-Time-Laodicean-Christian to stupidly stare at the antique gate called Strait and its narrow path, as they fulfill words of Jesus Christ: *"few there be that find it."*

The Old Paths, the Old Ways, established long ago as God-pleasing, are only a vague memory, less than a faintly lingering fragrance among many modern church leaderships today. Many sanctuaries of God are void of Scripture-Ordained worship, **leaving the now-generation no memory of the Old Paths to reflect upon.**

The demand for physical motion by the **Decibel Doctrine** in our day has replaced Biblical Worship in various religions, often referred to as New Age

Religions. This causes the New Age Christians to scoff at the worship found in the Old Testament (pronounced-**shâchâh** in Hebrew) and the New Testament (pronounced-**proskynéō** in Greek). The New Paths, the New Ways, are more invigorating, more exciting to the flesh, and create a wide gate, a wide path, through which many there be who go therein.

In Jeremiah 6:16, the Lord speaks absolutes of "old paths" that are good for the soul, and the response of "they" who received the instructions was, *We will not.*

"They," to whom the Lord spoke through Jeremiah's pen, had a choice to obey the Lord or to follow their own desires. God had given them a good choice:

> *ask for the old paths, where is the good way, and walk therein,*
> *and ye shall find rest for your souls.*

> But they said, **We will not walk therein.**

Today's end-time now-generation, does not have that same good-way choice. Yes, I said **today's end-time now -generation, does not have that same good-way choice**. Today's generation has not been taught or exposed to Old Paths of Biblical Absolutes because the Elders, who had a choice in past generations said, *"We will not,"* and accordingly, they quit teaching and practicing Old Biblical Paths. Thus, **unfairly leaving the now-generation without knowledge of a comparative option from which to choose the good way.**

They have been taught all their young life (the youthful formative years) that the volume of the music attracts the presence of God. And having been taught by example, this now-generation is convinced that what they feel in the euphoric atmosphere of extreme volumes of music and dominating beat is God's presence. "They" now believe that the physical display of motion forced by those extreme volumes and beat is Biblical Worship that should be offered unto God in the Sanctuary to show His worth.

They do not know any other option of Worship; therefore, they do not have the same Good-Way choice that God gave their Forefathers.

They have been robbed of a choice to say "We will" or "We will not."

So, they do as they have been taught by example, completely unaware that there is an Old Path and a Good Way that promises rest for their soul.

They are not offered that same Old Narrow Path as an option to choose and walk therein when it comes to worship that God seeks.

Just thinking with my pen…if Jeremiah walked into one of our Special-Effects-Pentecostal-Sunday-Night-Jubilee-Services, and the usher said, "Welcome to the party," would the "Weeping-Prophet" of God weep?

And all the sane say in unison,…**Surely So!**

David Clark
2-3-2018

Voracious is the Root

This month is May. The year is 2017. My wife and I have added a room and bath onto my deceased father's cabin in Jena, Louisiana. I hired a Pentecostal veteran from Natchitoches, Louisiana to chip down and grind some acreage of thick woods that was between the cabin and a creek that ran East to West. The far side of the creek, which is now visible and accessible, is bordered by a very dense thicket of bamboo.

To a nature lover, the bamboo thicket is an attractive background to the creek. I am a lover of nature and consider a bamboo thicket beautiful as long as it stays on the other side of the creek, away from my residence. But alas, the bamboo seed somehow spread to the camp side of the creek. Bamboo sprouts began to aggressively grow out of the ground in many places, threatening to take over the grounds around our cabin and consume our open space. The roots would run underground for up to 20 feet and then shoot up out of the ground seemingly overnight, quickly maturing into a tall stalk that never quit growing.

In attempts to eradicate this intrusive bamboo; I began to chop it, cut it, dig it, and poison it with strong herbicides. Still yet, the accelerated growth rate and aggressiveness of the bamboo was very hard to control. I would kill a root here and overnight, a root would appear over there. It took about a year to eradicate the bamboo roots that were encroaching near our cabin. It required consistent efforts and much work to protect our cabin, yard, and open space from the very nature of bamboo.

I finally had to deposit granules of a special herbicide next to the roots of the largest active bamboo to stop their aggressive propagation. It is hard to fathom that such a voracious attempt to consume our camp grounds started with only a rooted seed.

The **Decibel Doctrine** prevalent in Church Sanctuaries today has roots that are equally aggressive and equally resistant to any efforts to uproot it. The roots of the **Decibel Doctrine** are eagerly voracious in their efforts to take dominion of the Sanctuary. And of course, it starts with a seemingly small harmless seed.

The strength of the **Decibel Doctrine** is in its roots, and its roots are seeded by "The Spirit of Serpent Seed Music." Just a seeds-worth of *Not-Right* music producing a seeds-worth of *Not-Right* worship begins the supplanting of Worthy Biblical Worship in the Sanctuary. Like its parallel in the nature of bamboo, the **Decibel Doctrine** seeks to overtake every square inch of God's space, especially His Sanctuary. And of course, the sacrifice of praise (the fruit of the lips) and

Biblical Worship offered by the Redeemed is smothered and covered in the Sanctuary.

The **Decibel Doctrine** demands space and preeminence. It starts as a seemingly harmless seed, but when the seed becomes a root, the intrusion is voracious.

A Decibel Disciple, + a lukewarm soundman, + a powerful electronic sound system EQUALS the "Miracle Grow Seed Bed" that allows the **Decibel Doctrine** to flourish and take over. Consuming and Devouring Biblical Worship with voracity.

Seldom, *in fact never,* have I known of a minister who was able to change his mind and uproot this seed of perversion after he had embraced the **Decibel Doctrine** as Biblical and viewed it as the beautiful presence of God. The only remedy and hope for the congregation is just as spiritual and supernatural as the roots of the **Decibel Doctrine** itself, but on the side of Godliness and Light.

THE SUPERNATURAL SPIRITUAL REMEDY IS TO PREACH AGAINST THE **DECIBEL DOCTRINE**.

But no Decibel Disciple can bring himself to preach against his only source of power.

Who can "have church" without power?

And the **Decibel Doctrine** is their source of power.

I am not convinced that even Copper Sulfate, an extremely effective chemical that kills encroaching roots in the natural, has the power to eradicate the entrenched Roots of the **Decibel Doctrine** from God's Sanctuary.

In my opinion, which is formed by my experiences, **there is no remedy for a Decibel Disciple Pastor, to rescue and preserve a Church Sanctuary that has welcomed the seed of the Decibel Doctrine**.

****

<u>**Voracious**</u> – Adjective – Fitting Definitions by Webster

1. Eating with greediness; ravenous.
2. Greedy; rapacious.
3. Ready to swallow up or engulf.
4. Insatiable; immoderate.

****

Every Christian has read Apostle Peter's warning:

> *Be sober, be vigilant; because your adversary the devil, as a roaring lion, walketh about, seeking whom he may devour:*
>
> **1 Peter 5:8**

Every man's soul is sought by a voracious enemy.

The non-sober and non-vigilant see only beauty in the **Decibel Doctrine.**

David Clark
May 2017

Run For Your Life

Leaving your home church is not an easy thing. It involves the painful departing from your church family and precious memories. It is a very serious decision and should be supported with much prayer and consideration.

Such a serious decision should not be prompted by frivolous issues nor personal idiosyncrasies. The reason for making such a serious and weighty decision should be equal in its seriousness.

The intrusion of the **Decibel Doctrine** with its perverted fruit into a church assembly, which is always ushered in by the Pastor of that church, is sufficiently serious to justify the more-than-serious decision to protect yourself and your family.

The **Decibel Doctrine** is a Double-Deadly Delusive Doctrine that deceives even the most-sincere.

The works and signs that follow the presence of the **Decibel Doctrine** are a more-than-valid reason to remove yourself and your family from any environment supporting the **Decibel Doctrine**.

It is a more-than-sufficient reason to run for your life; to escape with your soul.

Departure from that Sanctuary for the safety of your soul is demanded by the definition of common sense.

A saint can hide his head in a hole in the ground as folklore insinuates of the ostrich, and pretend he does not know what is going on, but that is an irresponsible decision when the souls of your family are at stake.

The **Decibel Doctrine** and the spirit of a true child of God just do not belong together. Even Jesus Christ, should He walk in flesh on this earth again and enter the assembly of a twenty-first century **Decibel Doctrine** Church during the worship service, would exit in search of peace, though He is the Prince of Peace.

Ironic - Jesus is the Prince of Peace, and the Sanctuary is His and for Him. The Sanctuary is not a place of assembling that belongs to the Decibel Disciple. Why is it that Jesus is the one who has to leave, and not the **Decibel Doctrine** Pastor?

So, I say to the sincere saint who is miserable sitting on a pew where a Decibel Disciple pastors: "**Run for Your Life.**" Run for your eternal soul's sake. Run for the sake of your family.

Overcome fear of man and RUN!

And take your precious family with you to safety.

David Clark
10/20

Feeble Justification of the Decibel Doctrine

The pastor screams into his over-amplified microphone:

"David liked loud music."

A feeble effort to justify the **Decibel Doctrine** and quench the RESISTERS.

By "LOUD," they imply the rock concert volumes of music that they have recently forced upon the poor sheep in the Sanctuary.

It is a ploy to mask common sense. A ploy to sidetrack the thinkers.

A little white lie to preserve the magic that the Pastor has discovered in the **Decibel Doctrine**.

A question to the sheep, a question to the saints of the Most-High God, a question to the common-sense thinkers: *"How loud do you think David got with a harp and a ten-stringed instrument?"* *"Without an electronic amplifier to plug into to make his music HOT!"*

When the word "loud" was penned 3,500 years ago in the Psalms, the God-inspired Word was not referring to today's rock-concert-electronic-volumes that are now available at the flip of a switch.

Decibel Doctrine Pastors say "David liked loud music," falsely implying that David, a man after God's own heart, would covet their powerful Sound Systems of today's technology.

I say "that statement proves their son-ship," for they are unashamedly lying to the sheep.

David Clark

The End

It is most unfortunate that this collection of articles has no end. The subject **Decibel Doctrine** is a living organism that thrives and propagates through self-justification. And justification of the **Decibel Doctrine** is fabricated daily.

I sought a closing, but found none.

At first, I considered closing with a recap that began with my initiation to the **Decibel Doctrine** which occurred at my home church, Faith Tabernacle, in the East Texas town called Port Arthur. This church was at that time under the temporary leadership of a Decibel Disciple that was substituted for Elder Burr. This substitute for Elder Burr was not all bad, but rather to the contrary. He was just a victim. A Victim of the Fear of Failure, grasping onto what worked among his Pastor-Peers. Spiritually sodomized by the invisible Spirit of Serpent-Seed music.

Reflecting back, I now know that a recap, or synopsis of the last half of my life as plagued with the **Decibel Doctrine** should begin with God's plan to prepare me to endure this journey. The saga of "David Clark and the **Decibel Doctrine**" really began as I received years of teaching from a Man of God named Murry E. Burr in this East Texas town of Port Arthur, Texas.

Solid Years of Solid Teaching vaccinated my soul to resist the foundational principles of the **Decibel Doctrine**.

Therefore, in attempted closing of this collection of articles that exposes the **Decibel Doctrine,** which has no end, I leave with the audience excerpts from the pastor who began a long time ago, unknowingly, to prepare me for a Christian path that was contrary to the **Decibel Doctrine.**

****

Excerpts from subject lessons taught in Faith Tabernacle by Pastor Murray E. Burr

Subject Lesson – *The Spirit of Serpent Seed Music*

Quotes from my Teacher:

The Cult of the Beat – *"From the deepest recesses of the pit. From the diabolical mind and lips of the arch-friend himself - uncensored, unfiltered, unrestrained, unabridged, a Satanic hybrid music; a perverted anti-culture tidal wave has engulfed the Pentecostal movement. A music that dominates, permeates and pollutes every aspect of true Apostolic worship."*

"Occult music will never possess spiritually elevating rhythm, melody, dignity, good taste, good sense, audible discernible words, bearing a wholesome message. The hellish core or hub around which occult music (if one can call it music) revolves is the "BEAT," the repetitive beat, the hypnotic beat, the mesmerizing beat, the narcotic beat, whose ultimate objective is a crashing, ear-splitting, crescendo of fractured sound and physical, bodily animal frenzy."

****

Subject Lesson – *The Music of the Golden Calves/The Bride and the Beat*

Quotes from my Teacher:

Mechanical, worked-up shouting bores me as a meaningless display of animal emotion. I have always taught "Spontaneous Worship," free, unfettered, without physical prompting, jungle rhythms, and artificial workup. I cannot see that God needs any help, neither is He deaf.

Ladies and Gentlemen, the mongrelizing of the Pentecostal Music and Worship is appalling. It leaves me sickened, shocked, and horrified! – No, rather let me say, "It leaves me STIRRED AND ANGRY."

Like Paul on Mars-Hill, his spirit was stirred when he beheld the wholesale Idolatry. I am nauseated when I behold the wholesale worship of the "Rock Beat." Even a superficial study will show that "Rock Music" draws its strength from the "Occult or Witchcraft" and is a product of "Shamanism." The "BEAT" is the "Core" or "Centerpiece," the "Eucharist" of "ROCK WORSHIP," and is exalted to the Pedestal of "IDOLATRY."

****

Subject Lesson – *Strange Fire*

Quotes from my Teacher:

If truly "Strange Fire" in the sight of Almighty God consists of the use of carnal – physical means to kindle praise and worship, then as a Movement, we are a people in deep trouble, for never is the "Cart" too ridiculous, nor the "Innovation" so rabid but what a Naïve, Beat-Crazed Priesthood will clutch it all the tighter to their bosom, "ESPECIALLY IF IT WILL DRAW A CROWD OR CREATE EXCITEMENT."

Viewing the twenty-first century Neo Pentecostal Movement – I am frightened when I behold the almost insane craze for Charismatic New-Carts – Innovations, and especially the "IDOLATRY OF THE BEAT." We are beset by a cadre of Entrepreneurs of the Occult – and that among us.

Oh, why can't you see – "MY OBSESSED BRETHREN" that your Charismatic "INNOVATIONS" can lead to "TOTAL APOSTASY AND THE GREAT VOMITING OUT"?

****

Even today as I discussed laying my pen at rest, a report found me by phone that dictated to my conscience: "*Not-Right* Worship continues to grow like a cancer, with the spiritual agenda to metastasize to the soul of this present generation. "

The subject report by phone came from an Apostolic Pastor while attending the 2021 Peak Conference in Tulsa, Oklahoma. It was his words that alerted me to accept the fact that *Not-Right* Worship continues to grow like an unmonitored plague. His words were: "*the worship at Peak this year was wilder than ever.*"

I say again: **The spiritual agenda of *Not-Right* Worship via the Decibel Doctrine, is to metastasize to the soul of this present generation with such completeness that it cannot be removed without the death of the host.**

I have no faith that "this too shall pass" before the Second Advent.

David Clark

SECTION FIVE

Drumming

Things That I Did Not Know About Drums

And Prefer to Have Not Known

The Drum

Introduction

My experiences concerning The Drum come from my circle of friends in America.

My world of drum experiences is small. In my small world of drum experiences, most of the times past, when a Pastor has told me of trouble in his church, the source of trouble was in the church music department and commonly the drummer.

In my small world, the Drum is the only instrument that I have witnessed to be defended with a lie from the pulpit. (As written in the article detailing experiences in my home church concerning signs that follow the **Decibel Doctrine**.)

Planting a home mission church without music has been enlightening to me. Our home mission church has been blessed with one guitar musician, and we are presently blessed with a self-taught piano player. We still often purposely sing a capella in the Sanctuary because the human voice excels in value to God. (It is interesting that *Unger's Bible Dictionary* describes Hebrew Music as "mostly vocal.") The value of sound from man-made instruments surely pales in the presence of God-made human voices.

Through the past years, I have turned down numerous offers of drummers to beat their drums for us in the Sanctuary. It seems to be in my small world that everybody wants to be a drummer, even when there is a shortage of biblically preferred music such as stringed instruments, reed instruments, trumpets, organs, cymbals, harps, and above all else - the breath of humans praising with their voices.

Meeting so many men in my small world, with such a vehement passion to beat drums for our church has made me suspicious of the manmade priority put on drums.

I never liked the phrase "drums lead the music," as if drums are crucial to praise in the Sanctuary - AND - as if singing to the Lord was non-existent for thousands of years of Pre-Drum Praise.

I never trusted the phrase "drums keep the church service going," which found me, though my world be small. Even my younger sister surprised me by saying, "It is impossible to play the keyboard without drums leading." (At that time, she was attending a **Decibel Doctrine** Church.)

If these beliefs are numerous in my small world, beliefs that accredit undue priority to the drum must be prolific in the larger world of religion.

It bugs me that the drum is always the loudest instrument, always overriding the meaning of a song's words, causing God to hear a drummer assisted by voices of praise instead of hearing voices of praise assisted by a drummer.

And it bugs me that the drum has become the premiere man-made instrument in most all types of music, and yet it is incapable of making any music at all; it can only make a beat.

The drum set seeks preeminence over the airways in God's Sanctuary; and the drum set always takes preeminence in platform space, occupying more space than any other single instrument used in music. It bugs me that these are acceptable norms in my small world.

It bugs me that the term "Holy Ghost Fit" is a popular meme for Sanctuary Worship recorded on You Tube; always depicting a drummer beating wildly or a human in the midst of an ecstatic physical demonstration driven by the Drum Beat.

Yep, I'm bugged.

My very soul is bugged when I realize why Vodou and Pagan practices of worship to their deities pour out libations before the Drum, only before the Drum. They consider no other inanimate object worthy of libations.

Webster's Definition of **Libations** – *a liquid ceremonially poured out, as in honor of a deity.*

That really bugs me. And it should bug any thinkers.

This Collection of Articles would not be complete without at least some reference to The Drum.

There are reasons that The Drum rules where the **Decibel Doctrine** is practiced. The Drum with its beat is a core asset to the spirit of the Decibel Doctrine. Without a drum to beat, no matter how much power is demonstrated by volume, the magic seems to be missing adequate catalyst to "make it happen."

A Decibel Disciple shudders at the thought of trying to "worship" in the presence of God Almighty without a Drum. "No Drums? - No Drummer? - No Drumming? - GAG! Who will kick-start the service? – GAG! What will keep the church service going?"

Therefore, all references to music in this collection of articles named The **Decibel Doctrine** encompass the art of drumming. Without drumming, "LOUD" cannot complete the special effects predetermined by Decibel Disciples.

This Article on **DRUMMING** furnishes the reader with information that I have recently discovered for myself in study.

I have always struggled with the common thread of acceptance among the semi-learned that our drums are found in the Bible. In my research on The Drum, I was surprised to discover how many educated men believe as I that our revered drums are not found in the Bible.

I have doubted for a long time that the "tabrets" prepared in Lucifer legalize worship with drum-sets as taught today by Decibel Disciples.

Decibel Disciples also teach that the "pipes" prepared in Lucifer were musical pipes, and together with drums, Lucifer was a musical band and a "walking sound system" (an illogical phrase that I have heard from the pulpit). I find this teaching erroneous; plainly a wresting of Holy Scripture to please the flesh of man.

Study for yourself the Hebrew word used for "pipes." In study you will find the word "bezel." A bezel is the receptacle that holds a precious stone in place.

Logically NOT for music. Logically to hold precious stones in place.

*Thou hast been in Eden the garden of God; **every precious stone was thy covering**, the sardius, topaz, and the diamond, the beryl, the onyx, and the jasper, the sapphire, the emerald, and the carbuncle, and gold: the workmanship of thy **tabrets** and of thy **pipes** was prepared in thee in the day that thou wast created.*
Ezekiel 28:13

Discrediting the validity of calling Lucifer a "walking sound system" is Simple Simon Stuff and certainly non-challenging.

Common sense bonds me with ministry that will not accept today's drums as a justified substitute for the tabrets prepared in Lucifer.

My seeking for accurate information to discover the source and the beginning of THE DRUM, has led me to an in-depth study of the history of THE DRUM. Researching with sincerity has also required a thought process that circumvents the popular trending practices in today's religions.

While studying for this **Drumming** Section, I discovered that there was much about THE DRUM I have never learned. The origin of drums and the historical use of drums in some forms of religion has been an interesting study. I include some information on drums that is easily discovered in Public Domain.

I do not think that THE DRUM is perpetually only evil.

I do not think that THE DRUM always summons evil spirits.

As confessed, I am just now learning about THE DRUM.

I do know that THE DRUM seeks preeminence of the airways, whether in a Rock N Roll Concert or in a Church Sanctuary controlled by a Decibel Disciple. I am suspicious of the reason.

I do know that THE DRUM is credited for bringing life to the New Age Pentecostal Sanctuary. I am concerned as to why my Pentecostal peers believe this.

I do know that THE DRUM is the manmade item used to create the dancing beat that the world gravitates toward.

THE DRUM is the instrument effectively used to stimulate people to move, but I am unable to associate that movement with Biblical Worship.

I do see and understand the physiology of the flesh, but I struggle to associate the dance-beat with the Spirit of God.

I do know and agree with peers that THE DRUM is the instrument that best mesmerizes and hypnotizes the brain. But I cannot comprehend such as being God-Pleasing in His Sanctuary.

Therefore, this Section on <u>Drumming</u> contains very little of my own words.

Reader, please allow reality to stir your mind for a moment: -

Why do the practices of Idolatry and Witchcraft and Voodoo and Paganism use the drum as the specifically preferred avenue of healing and peace and spiritual power?

David Clark

Drumming Connects Christians

Source – Public Domain

This article contains repeated highlights as expressed in Public Domain. I understand that Public Domain information is not always certified as truth. However, it is always an accurate synopsis of educated public opinion. Therefore, in this article I expose their opinion of **Drumming for Purpose-and-Effect.**

If you the reader can tolerate or agree with the principles implied in this Public Domain information on Drumming; you are of another spirit than I.

There is a World of the Drum associated with Christianity that I know not of. So, Public Domain opinion dominates this article.

THE FOLLOWING STATEMENTS AND BELIEFS ARE NOT MINE.

David Clark

Public Domain Opinion speaks..........

Drumming Connects Christians – "Drumming during worship makes Christians around the world feel connected. Using drums in worship reminds them that they're a part of the universal body of Christ. It reminds them that the God they believe in and worship isn't of a certain ethnic group or culture, but He loves His creation regardless of the nation or tradition they belong to."

Drumming Encourages Participation in Worship

"If we look at Western worship traditions, most of them have congregational participation only limited to verbal expression. Now, this poses a challenge for people who can't read.

In addition to coming in the way of participation in worship, it also restricts the range of human expressions in worship. *Drumming encourages participation in worship, which aligns with what the scripture says.*

It allows Christians to come together and praise the One, no matter which social status, culture, or health category they belong to. *It's especially beneficial for people who worship best through music or kinesthetic (active movement) styles.*

Drummers require little to no training and thus, even children and senior citizens can easily play the drum in a way that produces good sound."

Drumming Supports Bodyliness

"The whole idea of *reformed worship* was that Christians should be able to read and understand the Bible and worship God on their own. This led to an increased emphasis on the ability to study biblical words, implying that perhaps it's the intellect of a believer that God really loves.

However, if we believe that God wants us to bring a cultural transformation, **we should perhaps focus on our actions and body movements.**

The catchy beats of drums invite us to sway our bodies, bob our heads, and move our feet as God-inspired bodily responses.

People who can't dance to what they believe in probably don't have a strong belief. The reformed worship concept asks Christians to learn how to drum and dance in God's praise."

Living Out the Summary of the Law

"When Jesus asked a young ruler about the Law of God, he answered:

> *"Love the Lord your God with all your heart and with all your soul and with all your strength and with all your mind'; and, 'Love your neighbor as yourself."*
> **Luke 10:27**

Essentially, our belief should be put into action – and drumming is a great way to do it.

We can only participate *in drum circle worship* **when we're mentally connected to God, when our emotions are invested in the Christian belief** *and our muscles engage as the drums are played*, **and when we feel we're a member of a large community.**"

Spiritual Formation

"**Drumming encourages many of the behaviors mentioned in the scriptures.** God invites us to come to Him "like a little child," (Luke 18:17) and drumming encourages us to be spontaneous, playful, and genuine while worshipping Him.

In essence, there's a special mention of **drums in the Bible**. The sounds of drums distract us from our otherwise noisy routines and invite us to praise and worship God.

The **reformed worship is all about being in rhythm with God** and always finding our way back to Him when we feel lost in this world."

228

My added words:

This "Reformed Worship" referred to in Public Domain is not futuristic worship to come. It is with us and among us today. And "Reformed Worship" will stay where drums stay.

Drum Circles

This Article contains Public Domain information from a Drum Circle Invitation.

Nine Reasons to Come to a Community Drum Circle

Makes you Happy - Induces Deep Relaxation - Helps Control Chronic Pain

Helps your Immune System - Creates a Sense of Connectedness

Aligns your Body and Mind with the Natural World – Releases Negative Emotions

Provides a way to Access a Higher Power - Allows for Personal Transformation

Community Drum Circles are becoming the coolest thing to do on a Friday night! In a safe, welcoming and playful environment, people gather for recreation, healing and celebration.

Physical Health Benefits - Mental Health Benefits - Good Clean FUN!

Drum Circles are becoming the NEW YOGA!

At **Circles of Rhythm,** we are committed to providing this weekly event to give people from all walks of life the opportunity to attend a circle on a regular basis. Just like good nutrition, sunshine and regular exercise, it is apparent that drumming is best when taken in regular doses! Come get your weekly or monthly dose of Vitamin "D" - DRUM!

End of Drum Circle Brochure.

The author's comments on the Drum Circle Brochure

The mindless Christian yells AMEN to the Drum Circle Brochure! – While the thinking Christian thinks: **Why not give Honor, Praise, and Credit to a circle of guitars, or pianos, or saxophones, or trumpets, or flutes???** And no real Christian likes the answer to this common question.

The correct answer:

Because Somebody or Something believes that ONLY ONE INSTRUMENT can do these magical wonders for humans without God. The Drum!

The hands of man have made many instruments for many purposes, BUT NONE can equal the preeminent power of **The Drum**. Whether used goodly or evilly, nothing that ever came from man's imagination can equal **The Drum**.

David Clark

Shamanic Drumming Circles

Statements from Experienced Shamanic Drummers

Indigenous shamanic peoples of diverse cultures have gathered in community drumming circles for thousands of years. Although most of us did not grow up in an indigenous shamanic tradition, we can still tap into the healing power of shamanic drumming.

A shamanic drumming circle is a place for practitioners to get together for learning, healing, and the direct revelation of spiritual guidance. A drumming circle provides an opportunity to connect with your own spirit at a deeper level, and also to connect with a group of other like-minded people.

Shamanic drumming circles serve many functions. Foremost among them are:
•**Deepening the participants' relationships with their helping spirits through shamanic practice;**

•**Providing help, healing and support for individuals and for the community;**

•**Acquiring shamanic knowledge through collaborative sharing and from helping spirits through direct revelation.**

End of Quoted Statements

****

Moral of the Drum Circle Story

If you need spiritual help, join a Drum Circle and start drumming, and it will do more for you than a prayer meeting.

No other MANMADE instrument will work.

****

Chilling Thought – *If your Pastor is a Disciple of the **Decibel Doctrine**, He already knows all this.*

David Clark

Rhythm Healing

Personal Testimony and Advice of a Proponent of Rhythm Healing

Rhythm healing is an ancient approach that uses therapeutic rhythm techniques to promote health and well-being. **Rhythm healing** employs specialized rhythmic drumming patterns designed to influence the internal rhythmic patterns of the individual and harmonize those which are thought to be causing the illness or imbalance. When administered correctly, specific rhythms may be used to accelerate physical healing, stimulate the release of emotional trauma, and produce deeper self-awareness. This technique has been used for thousands of years by indigenous cultures around the planet to treat a variety of conditions.

Rhythm healing relies on the natural law of resonance to restore the vibrational integrity of body, mind, and spirit. Resonance is the ability of a sound wave to impart its energy to a substance such as wood, metal, or the human body, making it vibrate in sympathy. When we drum, our living flesh, brainwaves, and spiritual energy centers begin to vibrate in response. The drum pattern projects onto the body a supportive resonance or sound pattern to which the body can attune. This sympathetic resonance forms new harmonic alignments, opens the body's various energy meridians and charkas, releases blocked emotional patterns, promotes healing, and helps reconnect us to our core, enhancing our sense of empowerment and stimulating our creative expression.

Though the **rhythm healer** may have a repertory of established rhythms, every situation is unique. Determining the right rhythm in each case is a highly individual matter. No predetermined formulas are given. The rhythmist needs to create a dialogue between the sounds he/she produces and the responses of the person being treated. Tuvan shamans, for example, often improvise sounds, rhythms, and chants in order to converse with both the spirit world and the patient.

The sounds produced by the shaman and the drum go out, and certain frequencies and overtones are then reflected back. Information is generally received as subtle vibrations, which the shaman then interprets as sounds, pictures, or as rhythms. Through trained observation, the shaman discovers the right rhythm for their patient. It may be a new rhythm, uniquely indicated for the situation.

This means that one must learn to listen very carefully to the sound of the drum. **The drum, like all our relations, is alive, and it is trying to tell you something.**

Listen with more than just your ears. **To hear the voice of the drum, you must listen with your entire being. Ask your drum and your helping spirits to help you. State your intention in a clear and concise manner, and then open yourself to the help that comes.**

You must open the heart and empty the mind. Become like a *"hollow bone"* and allow the power of the spirits to fill you. Give up the need for control. This requires an attitude of surrender and trust.

I learned that when I trust my spirit helpers to play the appropriate rhythm, which I don't know in advance, I can't go wrong. I know only that what I play is what I experience, and **it is a way to honor my helping spirits.**

I also feel a profound connection with everything around me. The key is to let spirit work through you for the purpose of healing -- to become an instrument of healing.

To learn more, research *Shamanic Drumming: Calling the Spirits*.

End of Personal Testimonies and Instructions from Proponents of Rhythm Healing.

****

The implied public acceptance of sorcery in America frightens me for my loved ones.

And the only instrument trusted by Shamans for a spiritual medium is:

THE DRUM.

David Clark

A Call to Worship

This article is a short-form story of a Pentecostal Pastor who personally witnessed a "Christian" **Circle of Drums**. The short-form story below is sourced out of the *Indiana Bible College PERSPECTIVES volume 18, NO 3*.

While sitting in a coffee shop, he heard the pounding of drums in the distance and questioned the waiter, "What is that?"

The waiter, who was familiar with the sound answered, "**It's a Call to Worship**."

Going to the scene of the sound, this Pentecostal Pastor found forty-plus instruments pounding out the **Call to Worship**. The beating of the drums drew a crowd of hundreds. Some would move into the circle and start dancing and staggering. Nothing appeared to be off-limits or unacceptable.

As the incessant ritual continued, more and more were drawn into the circle. Shouts of "**Get Free**" and "*Let Your Mind Go*" were heard. Some would step out of the circle, fall, and cry. Others became trance-like zombies.

This highly respected Pastor warns: "**The CIRCLE OF DRUMS is a dangerous regression into darkness. Don't be lulled into thinking it can't happen at a church near you**."

He asked this sensible question to anyone who reads about his first-time experience as a witness to worship in a CIRCLE OF DRUMS. "**On what Biblical example could someone justify a revival of Godless rituals that induce altered states of consciousness?**"

He wisely concludes: "**As I see it, the use of beat, music, dance, chanting, and repetitive phrases as a tool to emotionalism or spiritual experience is an effort to avoid repentance, the authoritative Word, and the cleansing pure move of the Holy Spirit.**"

End of short-form story.

It is interesting to see what a Holy Ghost filled minister senses in a Drum Circle.

Thank God for Godly Men with discernment to warn us.

A Call to Worship

Summoned by the Drum

Has become a Common Call

In New Age Pentecostal Sanctuaries

May God have mercy on us all!
David Clark

Bible Scholar Quotes About the Drum

Professional Bible Scholars Appeal to Common Sense

This article contains quotes of wisdom and knowledge concerning DRUMS.[2]

<u>Quotes From Bible Scholars</u>

Because of the potential volume of which drums are capable, it is easy for them to overpower the voices, particularly in smaller auditoriums. There is a danger of abuse, and this writer has experienced it a number of times. Without great care, the beat can overwhelm the singers.

I have been in services where the volume of the drums and amplified guitars was so deafening I could not hear those singing next to me. This smacks of a return to the Dark Ages, when the joy of fellowship in song was taken from the congregation and replaced with a performance by the "professionals." Lost is the wonderful experience of the harmonious singing of God's praises, in which we are able to appreciate the contribution of all.

Further--and this is a critical point; it could be argued that a constant drumming-- or drumming that seems to compete with the singing--tends to turn a spiritual ministry (through the message of the words) into a more sensual experience (through the rhythm of the music).

Are we losing a sense of the distinction between fleshly excitement and spiritual joy? Let the exhilaration of our congregational singing arise primarily from an appreciation of the truth--and of God Himself (Psalm 28:7), and not simply a physiological and psychological response to the music.

The latter may, in fact, distract worshippers from a true worship.

More than a century ago, Charles Haddon Spurgeon criticized some of the church music of his day with words that still ring true: "Is it not a sin to be tickling men's ears with sounds when we profess to be adoring the Lord?...Do not men mistake physical effects for spiritual impulses? Do they not often offer to God strains more calculated for human amusement than for divine acceptance?" (from *Psalms*, by Spurgeon).

Percussion instruments have a long history, and are mentioned in the Word of God (though for some reason drums never are). They have been used to mark time, to send a signal, and, in the case of symphonic bands and symphony

---

[2] Source of Quotes - WORDWISE-BIBLE-STUDIES.COM.

orchestras, to add accent and emphasis at certain points in a musical work. Historically, and for many years, drum sets (traps) have been used predominantly in dance bands, and secular rock bands. There they provide a driving beat which stirs rhythmic response and adds excitement for dancing.

As noted previously, due to their intrusiveness and tendency to dominate, drum sets do tend to draw attention to the individual. In the services of the church, and in congregational singing, this is surely contrary to our purpose, where *"He must increase, but I must decrease,"* (John 3:30).

The music of the world intrudes on our lives at every turn, on radio and television, in restaurants and doctors' offices, in malls and elevators, and even as we walk down the street. Should there not be some haven free from it? Perhaps there ought to be, in the house of God, a music that is distinctly His, and not simply a copy of what the world is doing.

Sometimes music that is called "Christian" is superficial, and even downright unbiblical. We are to be in the world, but not of the world (II Corinthians 6:15-17).

Some congregations are prepared to "endure" the drums as a kind of compromise, in hopes of keeping teen-agers in the church. But at what cost? It is demonstrable that for at least some young people, music with a dominating rhythm is a passion--one would almost say an addiction-- that has robbed them of a fuller appreciation of other kinds of music. We may do these individuals a disservice by accommodating them without careful thought.

Further, in my experience, this attempt to keep young people interested in church by copying what they enjoy in the world has had very limited success.

Bottom line: Neither drums nor any instrument should intrude a platform "performance" into the fellowship of singing. Better to have no instruments than that! The volume need never be deafening. In fact, it should never prevent worshippers from hearing and blending with voices around them.

End of Quotes of Professional Bible Scholars.

****

I emphatically agree with the above Bible Scholars.

My non-professional quote: **Believing that timbrels as mentioned in the Bible are equivalent to our 21st Century drums – is like believing that the thimbles used by Grandma while sewing-by-hand are no different from 200-pound brass Tower Bells.**

David Clark

Drumming to Worship Deities

Historical Excerpts on Haitian Drumming[3]

As the author of the collection of articles titled, **The Decibel Doctrine**, I am fully aware that the entity Wikipedia does not guarantee their free information as absolute and irrefutable History. However, the information enclosed in this article aligns itself with reputable historians.

My purpose for including Wikipedia's statements concerning Haitian Drumming is to expose how "Drumming to Deities" for religious practices is viewed by the public scholars.

The information within this article is hard for American Christians to follow due to its foreign cultural content, but I ask the reader to focus on a serious single question: **Why is the drum valued as the preponderant primal instrument in worship of deity?**

AND WHY, Pray-tell, is the "**Drumming to Deity**" a MUST-HAVE, a CANNOT-WORSHIP WITHOUT-IT, in our Modern Pentecostal Sanctuary Practices today?

Just when did this practice evolve?

I see no evil in beating a bucket with a stick if the musicians need help keeping rhythm. But how did this beat-producer become a Must-Have that dominates our platforms and airways in God's Sanctuary, even though many Bible scholars agree that drums are not even found in the Bible?

Decibel Disciples smile and compare their drum-sets to biblical timbrels and tabrets on steroids.

Surely, we have "fallen off the wagon" of Biblical paths and joined the Pied-Piper entourage of *Not-Right* worship.

Wikipedia's Synopsis of Drumming to Worship Deities as found in Haiti.[4]

Vodou drumming is widely practiced in urban centers in Haiti and some cities in North America (especially New Orleans, Louisiana). Vodou is a ritualistic faith system that involves ceremonies consisting of singing, drumming, and dancing.

---

[3] Source: Wikipedia.
[4] Source of Information – Public Domain.

Voodoo is almost always spelled "Vodou" by Anthropologists, religion scholars, and practitioners themselves.

Religious and Cultural History and Context

While drumming does exist in other contexts in the country, by far the richest traditions come from this distinctly Haitian religion. As such, before one can come to play, appreciate, and understand this music one should view it in its religious context. Haitian Vodou is a henotheistic religion.

Due to religious discrimination, Haitian vodou practitioners had to find ways to disguise their beliefs by assigning their deities Catholic saint names. Similar process occurred with the slaves of Cuba who created the religion of Santeria. In fact, Candomble in Brazil, Obeayisne in Jamaica, and Shango in Trinidad were all examples of this religious transformation. Even though Haiti became independent during a slave uprising in 1804, (the only successful slave revolt in modern history), Vodou continued to be practiced in different ways by different communities around the country. It remains the most prominent religion in the country to this day.

Loas and Nanchons

Vodou rites are done to call upon spirits, called **Loas** (or Lwas), for their aid, instruction, special powers and strengths. **Loas** are ancestral spirits who have become abstracted through the generations to become embodiments of certain principles or characteristics.

A great feast is often prepared to entice the **Loas** to attend. Practitioners of the religion wear white clothes and are assisted by Ougan and Manbo (male and female Vodou priests, respectively) **to become "possessed" by the loas**.

Through singing, dancing, and **particularly the music of the drums**, spirits come to "ride" their mortal hosts. The analogy of someone riding, and thereby controlling, a horse is given as an explanation of this phenomenon.

The **loas** are divided up into several **nanchons** (from the French *nations*), families of spirits from the same ethnic group and/or serving a similar function. The most prominent **nanchons** are Rada, Nago, Djouba, Petwo (also written Petro), Kongo, Ibo, and Gède. Traditionally each one of these **nanchons** would have had particular rites, rhythms and adherents. They even would have had their own drums that were unique to that **nanchon** to call upon its **loas**.

Below is an overview of a common **nanchon, Rada**.

Rada - The **loas** of this **nanchon** are strong, but benevolent, balanced in their treatment of their servants. These are the most revered spirits, and many Vodou rituals begin with adulations for them.

They originate from the Fon people of Dahomey (present day Benin). In fact, the word Vodou comes from the Fon word for "God."

There are many **loas** in this group. To name a few: Papa Legba – Guardian of the Crossroads; Marassa – twin spirits who represent childhood; Dambala – the serpent spirit who represents energy and life; Ezili Freda – spirit of love and femininity; Lasirèn – mistress of the sea and music. Rhythm and dance styles played for the Rada **nanchon** include: Yanvalou, Parigol, Zepol, Mahi, Fla Voudou and Daomé.

Aspects of the Music

An extremely important aspect of the performance of this music is the Kasé (from the French Casser, to break). The kasé is a break from the main cycle of the rhythm into a kind of alter-ego rhythm, usually instigated by the maman drum. Dancers also change their steps to follow the kasé.

The kasé is typically played to assist with aspects of the Vodou ritual, such as **pouring libations before the drums**. Sometimes these are cued by the officiating priests, sometimes by the maman player himself.

However, the most dramatic use of the kasé is to facilitate spiritual possession. If the maman player recognizes the physical signs at the inception of a possession of one of the servants or dancers, he will play a heated kasé to entice the loa and may keep up the intense drumming of the kasé until the chwal in question is fully possessed.[5]

****

As the author of this collection of articles called **The Decibel Doctrine**, I close this article with the moral-of-the-story within the above Historical information about Vodou Religious Practices.

Moral of the Story – Vodou servants practice beating drums in worship to their Deities, until servants/dancers show signs of "inception" of possession. Then they "heat-up" the pace of beat until that servant/dancer is fully possessed.

<u>Chilling Thought</u> – If your Pastor is a Disciple of the **Decibel Doctrine**, he already knows all this.

---

[5] End of Historical Information - furnished by Wikipedia through Public Domain.

I really don't want to say that I have witnessed this same premeditated procedure of manipulating-the-beat orchestrated many times in my latter years of attending **Decibel Doctrine** Churches, but I am thinking….

David Clark

Drum Preeminence

On Monday, February 21, 2011, my friend Caleb from Colorado was working for me in Orange, Texas. He told me about a youth rally he attended that weekend in Moss Bluff, Louisiana. He described the young Pastor walking back and forth on the platform exhorting worship while beating a base drum that was strapped onto him. This Pastor testified of the great Pentecostal Church that his great-grandfather had built in North Little Rock, Arkansas with a drum. In his fervent exhortation, this Pastor declared: **"If you don't have a drum, get one; a drum can do things for you that a prayer meeting cannot."**

Caleb said the crowd went "WILD" in response to the words: "a drum can do things for you that a prayer meeting cannot." In essence, the crowd witnessed spiritual libation of worth and honor poured out before the drum as in Voodoo Worship. And it drove them wild.

In a New Age church setting, the word "WILD" means extreme physical motion or ecstatic commotion; that which they now call "worship." The phrase "Prayer meeting" refers to time set aside from our busy schedule to meet with God to commune and share our heart with Him, and to hear Him share the desires of His heart with us.

The Proverbial Principle that was taught to the sheep that night: **The beating of a drum, not the drum itself, but the beat, will accomplish things that a prayer meeting with the One True God cannot.**

This makes me suspicious of like-minded men and their drum.

THE DRUM TAKES PREEMINENCE!

Ostentatious at best. Surely, verging on blasphemy.

And God says, **"weep for their children**." And I say also, "**Poor God!**"

I find myself saying, "**Poor God"** more and more often as I witness the mockery of Biblical Worship accelerate to untold depths. Those two words, "Poor God," are simply my heart-felt sympathy for the one who died for me and seeks worthy worship.

Assuredly, I am beginning to feel so surely, that there is a time soon coming when our long-suffering God will cease to strive for His Word, and nausea will turn into judgement.

It would serve every Christian well to research the contemporary popularity of "Drumming for Spiritual Strength," "Drum Circles for Healing," "Drumming for

Inner Peace," and more.

Then ask God for yourself:

"Why do men give such unbalanced preeminence to drums?"

"Why not give preeminence to just any inanimate object other than drums?"

Any Christian with spiritual discernment will agree with the Pastor quoted above; "a drum **CAN DO SOMETHING** for you that a prayer meeting with the One True God cannot do."

David Clark
2011

Origin of Drums?

Researching for the origin of drums, I read multiple statements of information such as this: Drums have been used to set a marching beat for soldiers, as well as motivate soldiers, for thousands of years.

That is great and that is grand, and that is intriguing and that is wonderful. Such information appears to be verifiable.

But my question still remains unanswered…

Is there a certifiable origin of drums?

AND…

When did drums start being used for God's pleasure?

AND…

When did drumming become a preeminent priority to please God in His Sanctuary?

David Clark

SECTION SIX

Epilogue

Scenes Evolving in the Last Days

Considering the direction of the Christian Church Metamorphosis, no one was surprised that the following conversation became common IN TIME. And all nodded their heads with a chuckle.

Grandson: "Grandpa, what were those benches near the front of that old church we visited?"

Decibel Disciple Grandpa: "Those are called altars. We have been taught that they get in the way of worship. Their Pastor don't know how to have church yet."

Grandson: "Grandpa, I could hear the congregation singing and praying."

Decibel Disciple Grandpa: "Yes, quite different from normal church, they have so much to learn."

Grandson: "Grandpa, the music was beautiful and stirring, but I could not feel the thunder like in our church."

Decibel Disciple Grandpa: "Pray for them. They are good people. Their Pastor is one of the last to resist the **Decibel Doctrine**."

I can remember back when young boys "played church" in the yard. They would stand on a stump or on a bucket and pretend to preach. If you can remember those days, you better hold those memories dear, for they are quickly becoming extinct from our American Christian Culture.

The **Decibel Doctrine** continued to permanently taint the youth of the last-day generations. Young boys learned a new way to play church from their teachers.

IT SOON CAME TO PASS IN TIME when young boys were pretending to be in the Sanctuary; they would pick an imaginary electric guitar and beat an imaginary set of drums. Always with the bobbing of the head and the swaying of the hips. Finished products of the **Decibel Doctrine**.

This particular confession became more and more common among the youth: "I love church when I can feel the vibrations of the music." No longer did this New Age expression raise the eyebrows of mature Christians.

IN TIME - This exposing declaration of carnality by unsuspecting youth became the norm. Evidence of continued deception by the Dark Side. Predetermined fruit as Satan continued to use Decibel Disciples to mold the spirits of youth by tantalizing their flesh with the **Decibel Doctrine**. The former generation could see the spiritual deception exposed in this confession, but the next generation could no longer see. They were *Blinded* by the Master of Deception as was Laodicea.

IN TIME - **Ecumenical Worship** became the worldwide agenda of religion. The flavor of doctrine and beliefs, whether God-Made or Man-Made, no longer inhibited Decibel Disciples from "worshipping" together.

And just what caused this dramatic worldwide evolution, birthing a One World Worship?

What magnetic force had the power to draw such a mixed multitude together in worship?

ANSWER- Discovery of the **Decibel Doctrine** by all religions.

IN TIME – All religions discovered the magic in extreme volumes of music created by their sound system. Music that was felt, PHYSICALLY; did finally completely UNIFY them.

IN TIME - The addictive adrenaline rush of spasmodic repetitive rhythm could not remain hidden. All religions learned to worship THE SOURCE of vigorous incitement of emotion that follows a musical crescendo. They found a higher SPIRITUAL LEVEL that is synonymous with an upward change in key to a higher octave. The Secret was in the special effects of volume all along.

What they all unanimously sought and found was in the volume of music – it was in the volume of music all along. And they all discovered the magic therein.

As time passed on, all religions discovered the **Decibel Doctrine,** and then all embraced the **Ecumenical "Worship"** that requires no sacrifice.

IN TIME - All believers in a Higher Power, Biblical or Non-Biblical, could now feel their god while in the presence of the **Decibel Doctrine**. **Decibel Doctrine** worship **united them**.

The Biblical sacrifice of praise, the fruit of our lips giving thanks to His name; was forced to submit to the preeminent power of the **Decibel Doctrine** in ALL Sanctuaries.

> *By him therefore let us offer the sacrifice of praise to God continually,*
> *that is, the fruit of our lips giving thanks to his name.*
> **Hebrews 13:15**

This scripture and the Biblical principle therein were blotted out of their Bibles, and permanently blotted out of their heart, and vanished from the collective sounds of the Sanctuary.

The mouths of Apostolic Elders who continually warned: "be careful what you offer as worship to God in the Sanctuary, keep it Biblical," were silenced one by one, as they passed away. And there remained no man to stand in the gap.

And IN TIME, church became a party.

The Sanctuary became designed to support Party Time.

The precious Word of God got misplaced in the Party.

And of course, the **Decibel Doctrine** flourished all over the world during Sanctuary Party Time.

IN TIME - The word "worship" became reduced to a lightly esteemed common catch-phrase, totally unconscious of any intent of sacred depth.

The word "worship" became a popular word to use on Church signage: The House of Worship, The Place of Worship, Love and Compassion Worship Center, Love Fellowship Worship Center, Freedom Worship Center, Come Worship with Us, Sunday Worship, Morning Worship, Evening Worship, etc. All religions began to exploit the word "worship" on Church websites, on Church media, and on any narrative that described their Church. Yet Sanctuaries remained void of Biblical Worship.

IN TIME - The quantity of **few** who would consider practicing Biblical Worship in the Sanctuary was reduced to **none**.

Pulpits began to use the word "worship" repetitively as preachers led the congregation. Everything and anything began to be referred to as "worship." Even the "clapping of hands" was eventually rendered as "worship."

IN TIME - The protocol in all types of church services continued to evolve; the word "worship" started being used multiple times more frequently than "praise" or "love" or "prayer" or even the name "Jesus."

As the world was reduced to a lawless society, Criminal Trespass of Sacred Intents of Biblical Words as "worship" were no longer even noticed.

IN TIME - Men invented Church Names that were even more intriguing than "The Cowboy Church" or "The Outlaw Church."

IN TIME - **Decibel Doctrine** pastors chose to name their church <u>The Loud House Church</u> to draw a crowd and to entice the youth.

<u>The Loud House Church</u> became the fastest growing church in America. It was exciting to the youth.

<u>The Loud House Church</u> **ROCKED**.

<u>The Loud House Church</u> was a **PARTY**.

The younger generation filled THE LOUD HOUSE CHURCH and THE LOUD HOUSE CHURCH filled them.

IN TIME – New Age Pentecostal PARTY CHURCHES experienced the numbing of spiritual discernment.

For a long time, the "Party" churches resisted song lyrics that blatantly blasphemed the honor and worth of our Holy and Sacred God.

BUT IN TIME - Excessive volumes and aggressive beat afforded by the **Decibel Doctrine** progressively paralyzed spiritual sensitivity of even the more sincere Christians.

Sanctuary Songs continued to digress and descend to depths revealed by worship songs with disrespectful lyrics such as the ones listed below.

Holy Ghost Hop – by Carman

Everybody used to do the twist

The mashed potato and it goes like this

The funky chicken, monkey too

There was nothing they would not do

But there's a new dance no one can stop

A leap for joy we call the Holy Ghost Hop.

Now get ready, hold steady

Don't deny it, just try it

Be bold now, let it go now

Give the Holy Ghost control now.

AND IN TIME, these lyrics became "FUN" in the Sanctuary of the One who died for them.

Eccentric Comments from Loud Music Lovers

Evolved into Cultural Protocol

as History was Erased.

IN TIME – These popular quotes referring to loud music became the acceptable-norm.

These exclamations and accolades that praise excessive volumes of music, whether it be secular music entertaining pagans or Sanctuary music offered to God, no longer raised suspicion even among mature Christians.

Biblical normality that was once used for comparison, was erased along with History.

Listed below are a few current Public Domain quotes from loud-music-lovers that slowly became a norm; even entertainingly cute.

Mesmerizes me --- I like to feel it in my bones.

A pure adrenaline rush and excitement.

It gives me a rush to get out there and jam.

Exaltation.

At loud volumes, the music seems to pulse and move through you. It is a very invigorating experience.

Loud makes me feel the music and get into it more.

The music has more energy when it is loud.

Loud music gets deeper in my body and feeds me the rhythm.

So far in my life, I have witnessed no remedy of hope for a Christian who becomes deceptively seduced by the **Decibel Doctrine.** No repentance, *no turning around* from the collective clutches of the **Decibel Doctrine**. The flesh literally LOVES it.

It matters not whether the "Fatal Attraction" was in ignorance or in submission to a Pastor; God's response to *Not-Right* Worship is FOREVER established in the Fourth Chapter of Genesis.

> *But unto Cain and to his offering* **he had not respect.** *And Cain was very wroth, and his countenance fell.*
> **Genesis 4:5**

AND IN TIME – All Cains walked out of the presence of God, FOREVER.

David Clark

Trust Me

I Am Your Watchman on the Wall

****

IN THE PROCESS OF TIME

The Watchman-on-the-Wall received another spirit.

(As Paul feared in II Corinthians 11:4)

AND

Now Embellished with a More Exciting Spirit

The Watchman Continued to Watch

It took a while, but strong words repeated through powerful sound systems eventually remolded all Christians.

Chill out all you old-path-saints; **TRUST ME** *– I Am Your Watchman-on-the-Wall. I fulfill a God-Ordained position to watch for your soul. Don't be Ancient of Days. Don't get left behind while walking old worn-out paths of worship.*

The **Decibel Doctrine** is exhilarating and brings excitement into the Sanctuary. The fruit of the **Decibel Doctrine** is cutting-edge worship that shows God's worth.

The **Decibel Doctrine** will "keep" the youth and save souls. Quit resisting the New-Age-Paths of Pentecost and embrace the **Decibel Doctrine**; "Thou shalt not surely die." **TRUST ME.**

TRUST ME. When the Holy Ghost inspired writer of Psalms 98 wrote, "make a **loud** noise," he was referring to the technology that would only now be available. When God inspired the words "**loud** cymbals" in Psalms 150, He was referring to electronically enhanced volumes that are now ours. We are THE NOW GENERATION. THE CHOSEN GENERATION.

TRUST ME; these scriptures were written of things to come. "**Loud**" was prophetic, prophesying of the future NOW GENERATION.

TRUST ME; The "**loud**" referred to by these God-inspired scriptures was not for God's people who served him B.C., but for us, the NOW GENERATION True Worshippers.

I've told you over and over, God has waited a long time for man to discover the technology necessary to bring Him pleasure. Our NOW GENERATION has been given the honorable ability to bless God with the "**loud**" that He requested several thousand years ago.

The core value of the **Decibel Doctrine** is the privilege of offering the "**loud**" that God seeks in the Sanctuary. **TRUST ME**; I understand True Worship.

As your Watchman-On-The-Wall, I am anointed with spiritual understanding.

TRUST ME; We cannot please everyone with the volume of music, BUT WE CAN please our God. Pleasing God is what matters. It is His Sanctuary. And He likes it loud and hot!

Your ear pain from the sound system will go away…. in time. Is there any sacrifice too great for our Redeemer? Accept the ear pain and headaches from the sound system to be a sacrifice. That pain will go away….in time.

The number of resisters to the **Decibel Doctrine** is diminishing; we are winning. But pray for these nudniks; it is the Christian thing to do. Regardless, we must please the One that "seeketh such to worship him" John 4:23.

TRUST ME. Now that TRULY "**loud**" is available through electronically amplified sound systems, we must fulfill God's pleasure.

*You must forget the boring "old paths" that bind and hold you captive. You must let the "**loud**" decibels of music move you.*

*The extreme decibels of music will "keep" you and your children. **TRUST ME.***

*Our **loud** music entertains our God. **TRUST ME.***

*You will be endued with power from on high after that the extreme decibels of music have come upon you. **TRUST ME**. I am your Pastor, and I Watch for your soul.*

*Open your heart to the beat. Quit resisting the urge to move to the beat in the Sanctuary. Allow the rhythm to guide you into true worship. **TRUST ME**.*

***TRUST ME**. As your Watchman-on-The-Wall, I make you this promise: If you will only yield to the power that forces the extreme decibels of rhythm and beat into the Sanctuary, the ancient antique teachings of the Elders and Prophets will diminish and wane away to a dim and vague memory, and that undesirable feeling of conviction will go away.*

*I encourage you to abandon all doubts and questions in your mind and blindly trust the power of "**loud**" in extreme decibels of music to wash away the stains of old-path-teaching from your memory.*

Dare to be Born Again. Enjoy a New-Path life.

***TRUST ME**. There is an exciting New Path to follow.*

***TRUST ME**. Let this New-Age-Power mold you and rebuild your foundation.*

***TRUST ME** to pastor you to safety. "Thou shalt not surely die."*

Sincerely,

Your New Age Watchman-on-the-Wall

IN TIME

God's Tolerance Level Never Changed

Disobedience - VERSUS - *Not-Right* Worship

The following Bible scenarios continued to be played out IN TIME

As men continued to be men.

*But Jonah rose up to flee unto Tarshish **from the presence of the LORD**, and went down to Joppa; and he found a ship going to Tarshish: so he paid the fare thereof, and went down into it, to go with them unto Tarshish **from the presence of the LORD**.*
Jonah 1:3

*And Cain **went out from the presence of the LORD**, and dwelt in the land of Nod, on the east of Eden.*
Genesis 4:16

Both Jonah and Cain voluntarily went out from the Presence of God.

Jonah **fled from the presence of God in disobedience**. Disobedient to the calling of God to preach to Nineveh. AND GOD CHASED HIM. God chased him to Joppa, then into a ship, and then into the belly of a great fish, where **God coerced Jonah to repent and return**.

Cain went out from the presence of God in rebellion. Rebellion against God's personal preference of offerings of "worship" from man. GOD DID NOT CHASE HIM. **Cain never repented or returned**!!

IN TIME – God's Tolerance Level to *Not-Right* worship Never Changed. The embracing of *Not-Right* worship continued to usher souls out of the presence of God; FOREVER.

Embracing the **Decibel Doctrine** as Biblical appears to be a FOREVER decision; for which there seems to be no remedy.

Just maybe God is serious about what is offered unto Him as worship. God does have that prerogative.

I close this Bible Principle with another Scripture Setting that depicts God as being particularly obsessed with the quality of offerings to His Name.

6 A son honoureth his father, and a servant his master: if then I be a father, where is mine honour? and if I be a master, where is my fear? saith the LORD of hosts unto you, O

priests, that despise my name. And ye say, Wherein have we despised thy name?
7 Ye offer polluted bread upon mine altar; and ye say, Wherein have we polluted thee? In that ye say, The table of the LORD is contemptible.
*8 And if ye offer the blind for sacrifice, **is it not evil?** and if ye offer the lame and sick, **is it not evil?** offer it now unto thy governor; will he be pleased with thee, or accept thy person? saith the LORD of hosts.*
9 And now, I pray you, beseech God that he will be gracious unto us: this hath been by your means: will he regard your persons? saith the LORD of hosts.
*10 Who is there even among you that would shut the doors for nought? neither do ye kindle fire on mine altar for nought. **I have no pleasure in you**, saith the LORD of hosts, neither will I accept an offering at your hand.*
Malachi 1:6-10

Plainly, God expects and deserves the quality of offerings of worship that He requests in His Word.

TWICE, God said through the pen of Malachi; **it is evil** to offer Me less than I ask for in My Word.

If God calls such worship and offerings "EVIL," then *Not-Right* Worship is EVIL and surely a SIN.

Offerings that are *less than* or *other than* what God demands through His Word – are irrevocably *Not-Right* Worship. God calls it EVIL, and I am logically calling it SIN.

And the remedy for SIN is repentance.

But unfortunately, one of the Tell-Tale signs established in Genesis that follow *Not-Right* Worship is the inability to Repent.

IN TIME - disobedience by man continued - AND - Rebellion against Biblical Worship continued to escalate to bizarre extremes until the New Testament Covenant came to a close.

A small portion of those living sinful lives were fortunate to find repentance, which wrought mercy. Thank God.

But, of the numerous group that continued to rebel against God's Word concerning Worship, and continued to rebel against the WORTH that is to be offered unto the Lord, **none were able to find that precious place of repentance.**

David Clark

The Power and Effect of Rhythm and Volume

Upon the Human Mind and Body

Never Changed

The Power of Rhythm and the Power of Volume as documented by Professional Research is **timeless** and **perpetual**.

The past-discovered POWER and EFFECTS of Volume and Rhythm upon the human brain were not limited to only a season or a dispensation; they are also **timeless** and **perpetual**.

IN TIME - The absolutes of this invisible realm never weakened nor did they wane away.

IN TIME - The effects of Loud Music and Aggressive Rhythm Never Changed. It continued to exist for generations until Jesus returned and destroyed all carnality. No human was exempt.

IN TIME - The Special Effects of Music Volume and Rhythm continued to dominate Christian Sanctuaries until Jesus came back.

The Power of Rhythm and Volume continued to be forced upon the brains of Christians until their Creator returned to rescue them.

May God help us all!

David Clark

A Never-Ending Epilogue

The **Decibel Doctrine** continued manifesting fruit among God's people until that day The Lord returned to Earth.

History continued to repeat herself.

> *In those days there was no king in Israel: every man did that which was right in his own eyes.*
> **Judges 21:25**

The "worship" meme for New Age Pentecost became "How You Worship God is Your Personal Prerogative". (…*every man did that which was right in his own eyes*)

> **17** *And when Joshua heard the noise of the people as they shouted, he said unto Moses, There is a **noise of war** in the camp.*
> **18** *And he said, It is not the voice of them that shout for mastery, neither is it the voice of them that cry for being overcome: but the noise of them that sing do I hear.*
> **Exodus 32:17-18**

Music, as called Sanctuary Worship, continued to digress in the direction led by the **Decibel Doctrine** – Replicating the music and dance and noise that Israel offered to the golden calf idol that they had requested on their way to The Promise Land.

IN TIME - Without any guidelines of moderation, Worship-in-the-Sanctuary began to reflect the *noise of war*.

But Farther IN TIME -Even **Decibel Doctrine** Pastors became double minded about what **THEY** preferred; should **THEIR** Sanctuary Worship sound like a War or like a Party? The Ancient, long-forgotten, Biblical answer to their dilemma lay dormant.

The absolute, forever settled Word-of-God answer is: **Biblical Worship that displays WORTH should sound like neither.**

IN TIME – The prophesied day of God's Wrath came to pass. Decibel Disciples were seen mournfully bowing before piles of smoldering ashes that only yesterday were highly esteemed sound systems of great power. Being so totally consumed and encapsulated by the deception of the **Decibel Doctrine**, they knew not that the Lord had come; habitually rejecting the very thought that God would destroy something so sacred as their Man-Made power.

IN TIME – All Christian Sanctuaries were retrofitted to accommodate the **Decibel Doctrine** with this agenda: **Crank It Up HOT Without Distortion.**

IN TIME - When **loud** music had attained complete preeminence in all Christian Sanctuary Services, from the beginning to the ending; that same spirit began to dominate the space and time of everyday life everywhere.

Music met people everywhere they went. Music became inescapable in every facet of Society. Music established a fixed position attached to every part of human activity.

Restaurants began to force constant music of all types upon their customers, for effect. Management of public restaurants began to laugh at the common request of customers: "Please turn the music down so we can visit."

Department stores and Supermarkets of all designs began to inundate their customers with un-wholesome music while they were trying to purchase supplies. When shoppers complained to the local store manager; they received a cop-out such as "we are just obeying higher powers."

IN TIME – Medical facilities, offices, elevators, etc., were no longer safe places to hide from the world's choice of music. Even the outside parking lot entrances were included as a place of uninvited music that is obnoxious to Christians.

IN TIME – The subconscious mind could find no space to escape the subtle influence of loud music. The music became a twenty-four-hours-a-day assault ordered by Higher Powers for subliminal control of the human brain.

AND - of course, the omnipresent music got louder and louder to enhance the effects intended by Higher Powers.

IN TIME - Technology that was developed for hands-free communication facilitated a constant flow of media entertainment into the brain; Completely Circumventing the ability to *Think on These Things:*

> [8]*Finally, brethren, whatsoever things are true, whatsoever things are honest, whatsoever things are just, whatsoever things are pure, whatsoever things are lovely, whatsoever things are of good report; if there be any virtue, and if there be any praise,*
> ***think on these things****.*
> **Philippians 4:8**

IN TIME – The minds of Mankind became so inundated with manmade media; they could no longer *retain God in their knowledge.*

*28 And even as they did not like to **retain God in their knowledge**, God gave them over to a reprobate mind, to do those things which are not convenient;*

Romans 1:28

IN TIME – "Social media" and entertainment through earbuds replaced individual social communication in most everyday activities within families and friends.

The prophetic Last-Days words, "Without Natural Affection," became a common manifestation.

IN TIME - The whole world became filled with worldly music. Worldly music became a must-be at all social functions.

Even personal properties in peaceful neighborhoods became soiled by loud music with obnoxious intent.

Booming music in vehicles became louder and louder to infiltrate the peaceful, private space of the non-boomers.

IN TIME – God's creation became a world of loud music.

The previous church generation had begged for louder music to help *save the youth*.

IN TIME - The next church generation asked for even louder music to help *save their youth*.

IN TIME - The next church generation and the next and next church generations, each asked for even louder music to help *save their youth*.

And music got louder and louder in churches as well as in every facet of life, **because the Higher Powers of this World know the Invisible Power in Loud Music.**

INTERESTINGLY - **Neuroscientists and their learned counterparts wisely continued to avoid loud music!**

David Clark

Revelations That John Saw in Heaven

John has often been referred to as John-the-Revelator simply because he reveals the revelations that God allowed him to see.

The Book of Revelation in our Bible is often logically called The Revelation of St. John and/or The Revelation to John.

In this Book of Revelation at the end of our Bible, we find John revealing prophetic events that are to come to pass in the "Last Days." And just as importantly for us, he revealed the present activities that he witnessed as current in Heaven.

This article will bring focus to only the current events that John experienced. And I will refer to only two of John's descriptions of current events for purpose and effect as an antithesis for the principles of the New Age **Decibel Doctrine**.

The subject principles conveyed within this article are swiftly coming to completion; given time and the direction of Sanctuary practices. Since the deception of the **Decibel Doctrine** has not incorporated all us, as of yet, I have placed this "revelation" in the Epilogue section of this Collection of Articles.

What John Witnessed

And after these things I heard a great voice of much people in heaven, saying, Alleluia; Salvation, and glory, and honour, and power, unto the Lord our God:
Revelation 19:1

And I heard as it were the voice of a great multitude, and as the voice of many waters, and as the voice of mighty thunderings, saying, Alleluia: for the Lord God omnipotent reigneth.
Revelation 19:6

The sound of many human voices was heard by John as he was allowed to view scenes in Heaven. This experience was recorded in the Book of Life, Our Bible, as though it was important to the Author.

John revealed to us that the sounds of human voices praising God were heard in Heaven, where God has preeminence, and **Decibel Doctrine** soundmen were nonexistent.

IN TIME - ON EARTH - It became a precedent to fire the soundman for failure-to-follow-orders if these current heavenly sounds of the redeemed were to become audible in a New Age Sanctuary Worship Service.

The spirit of the **Decibel Doctrine** abhors the sounds that flow from the heart and mouth of God's redeemed. That spirit DEMANDS that the voice of the redeemed be covered and annihilated by not-so-lovely, harsher electronic sounds with emphasis on the beat and not on the words.

And only the right soundman can fulfill this demand. The soundman's master will nod his head in approval – only when the airways are dominated by the metallic roar of over-amplified special-effects music. And this earthly-current scenario is accomplished by the one in control; the Obedient Sound-Man.

When the fruit-of-the-lips of the redeemed can be heard in the Sanctuary, it is a SICKENING reminder to the Master-of-Deception about current scenes in Heaven. He once dwelt there. He knows John's account to be true.

The Prince of the Power of the Air can tolerate the sound of a few redeemed, if and only if, their voices are amplified sufficiently harsh to lose the caress of love and worth for the One True God. But Lucifer refuses to tolerate the sound of MANY redeemed as in an assembled congregation. Too much like Heaven for him. Too much like his "first estate."

---

*And the four and twenty elders and the four beasts **fell down and worshipped God** that sat on the throne, saying, Amen; Alleluia.*
Revelation 19:4

8And I John saw these things, and heard them. And when I had heard and seen, ***I fell down to worship before the feet of the angel** which shewed me these things.*
*9Then saith he unto me, **See thou do it not**: for I am thy fellowservant, and of thy brethren the prophets, and of them which keep the sayings of this book:* ***worship God.***
Revelation 22:8-9

John revealed to us the current worship of God taking place in Heaven.

I am sure that John was careful to accurately describe what he saw as he witnessed the sacred act of Worship-before-God as He sat on His throne.

What John saw in Heaven became foreign to "worship" witnessed on Earth during Worship Services in New Age Christian Sanctuaries. Meanwhile, the **None-New-Age Churches** endured persecution from their peers and continued to practice Biblical Worship.

IN TIME – The worship that John witnessed as current in Heaven became Oh-Too-Foreign to fit into New-Age Sanctuary Worship.

We all know stubborn people who will "argue with a fence post" when they think that they are right. And there are adamant personal opinions equally stubborn concerning the question: JUST WHAT IS BIBLICAL WORSHIP?

What John Saw and Heard as current activity in Heaven, continued in process FOREVER IN ETERNITY and man was unable to change it..., in Heaven.

IN TIME - Most of my Apostolic Brethren soon became persuaded by their teachers that jumping, leaping, running, jigging to the beat, or any other form of physical activity is Biblical Worship - Worthy to be offered unto The One True God in His Sanctuary to show forth His Worth.

IN TIME - My suggestion to friends became: if you don't trust John to write the Truth, then question the honesty of the Angel that John saw in Revelation 22:8. This unnamed Angel recognized the act of John "falling down at his feet" as worship and quickly told John, don't do that to me, "for I am thy fellow servant": **"worship God."**

****

My Two Personal Comments Please...

On What John Described as Current in Heaven.

Comment One - In case of a power failure of the sound-system-for-worship in your church; prepare to hear the voice of much people from the congregation of the redeemed, AND don't be surprised if someone yells out: "This sounds like Heaven!"

Comment Two – We have become a generation of New Age Pentecostal Christians who have perfected compliance to the FIRST and SECOND of the TEN COMMANDMENTS.

First Commandment:

Thou shalt have none other gods before me.
Deuteronomy 5:7

We have this First Commandment "down pat," mastered and understood perfectly. We could never accept two or three or four or more gods.

We never flinch from the Truth found in **Deuteronomy 6:4:**

Hear, O Israel: The LORD our God is one LORD:

Second Commandment:

*[8]Thou shalt not make thee any graven image, or any likeness of any thing that is in heaven above, or that is in the earth beneath, or that is in the waters beneath the earth: [9]****Thou shalt not bow down thyself unto them****, nor serve them: for I the LORD thy God am a jealous God…*

Deuteronomy 5:8-9

IN TIME - We New Age Pentecostal Christians will have perfected compliance to the Second Commandment to such a degree that we do not bow down to any gods in worship, not even the One True God.

<u>Until that Day:</u>

For it is written, As I live, saith the Lord, every knee shall bow to me,…

Romans 14:11

So help me God!

David Clark

SECTION SEVEN

Conclusion

Great Massive Unprecedented End-Time Revival in the Last Days

I am writing before daylight on March 23, 2018. I have struggled for over 15 years to finalize and conclude this collection of articles concerning the **Decibel Doctrine**. It seems to be that there is not a more fitting conclusion than to credit the **Decibel Doctrine** for a Great Massive Unprecedented End-Time Revival, IF IT WERE TRUE.

The preaching of an imminent "end-time revival of unprecedented proportions in the last days" has become a popular crowd-pleaser behind our Pentecostal pulpits. This man-made doctrine has accelerated in fervency in the last few years and continues its acceleration in 2018. I deem it man-made simply because I find no scriptural support for "**massive unprecedented end-time revival**."

Neither do I find any Apostolic Certification of this doctrine in the scriptures. Therefore, though I wish it to be true, I cannot preach this doctrine.

I do find the Apostles certifying the outpouring of the Holy Ghost on the Day of Pentecost as the beginning of the fulfillment of the Prophet Joel's God-inspired prophecy concerning the "last days."

*14But Peter, standing up with the eleven, lifted up his voice, and said unto them, Ye men of Judaea, and all ye that dwell at Jerusalem, be this known unto you, and hearken to my words: 15For these are not drunken, as ye suppose, seeing it is but the third hour of the day. 16But **this is that which was spoken by the prophet Joel**; 17And it shall come to pass **in the last days**, saith God, I will pour out of my Spirit upon all flesh: and your sons and your daughters shall prophesy, and your young men shall see visions, and your old men shall dream dreams*:
Acts 2:14-17

So, the Apostles who were chosen and trained by Jesus, declared that the "last days" started two thousand years ago. And this "Upper Room" experience continues today because it is a PROMISE from God.

*37Now when they heard this, they were pricked in their heart, and said unto Peter and to the rest of the apostles, Men and brethren, what shall we do? 38Then Peter said unto them, Repent, and be baptized every one of you in the name of Jesus Christ for the remission of sins, and ye shall receive the gift of the Holy Ghost. 39For **the promise** is unto you, and to your children, and to all that are afar off, even as many as the Lord our God shall call.*
Acts 2:37-39

Do I believe that the promise of this experience is available from God in our day and will continue to be available from God until the end??

Ten thousand times YES!

Do I wish that there was scriptural support that promised a "**Great Massive Unprecedented End-Time Revival in The Last Days**"? Ten thousand times Yes!

But unfortunately, I am unable to discover God-inspired scripture promising such a wonderful thought.

However, I do find scripture that warns us all concerning the "last days."

*Let no man deceive you by any means: for that day shall not come, **except there come a falling away first**, and that man of sin be revealed, the son of perdition;*
2 Thessalonians 2:3

*Now the Spirit speaketh expressly, that **in the latter times some shall depart from the faith**, giving heed to seducing spirits, and doctrines of devils;*
1 Timothy 4:1

The "Falling Away" is often misunderstood by Christians.

First and foremost, because it is prophesied, the "Falling Away" is an absolute that must come to pass, even while there are deceivers trying to convince men differently.

The "Falling Away" refers to men "falling away" from a precious status or position. They will "fall away" from something good. It is not referring to rebellious evil doers that will "fall away" from their dark deeds. Children of Darkness that serve not Jesus will not "fall away".

But rather Paul is speaking of Christian men "falling away" from their Faith in the Gospel of Christ that they once embraced and held dear. And it is prophesied to happen before that notable Day of the Lord.

To continue the warning of this prophesied absolute, Paul writes a similar warning to Timothy; (my verbiage for summary purpose) "The Holy Ghost declares explicitly, irrevocably: in the latter times some will be spiritually deceived by Demonic Doctrines of Darkness created by the Spirit of Anti-Christ, and depart from the light of the Gospel of Christ embellished in the Apostles Doctrine."

I do wish it was not true, for God's sake. I cannot stop Prophecy. I cannot preach a different message.

As one reads prophetic scripture concerning the "last days," it is disheartening to realize that carnal men will wax worse and worse, becoming more and more ungodly in their hearts and deeds as they are seduced by the present *spirit of antichrist*.

And every spirit that confesseth not that Jesus Christ is come in the flesh is not of God: and this is that spirit of antichrist, whereof ye have heard that it should come; and even now already is it in the world.
1 John 4:3

*¹This know also, that **in the last days** perilous times shall come.*
²For men shall be lovers of their own selves, covetous, boasters, proud, blasphemers, disobedient to parents, unthankful, unholy,
³Without natural affection, trucebreakers, false accusers, incontinent, fierce, despisers of those that are good,
⁴Traitors, heady, highminded, lovers of pleasures more than lovers of God;
*⁵**Having a form of godliness, but denying the power thereof***: *from such turn away.*
2 Timothy 3:1-5

Here we find Paul warning his fellow disciple Timothy that in the "last days," "religious society" will have a "form of godliness" while yet continuing in their numerous transgressions against God's Word. They will claim to be religious with their mouth, but their deeds will oppose every biblical principle. Their "form of godliness" will be similar to "just believe and keep sinning" – no repentance, no water baptism in the Name of Jesus, no born-again experience of the Holy Ghost, and no desire to seek a God-pleasing life of holiness.

The synopsis of that society or people is that they will have **Non-Biblical Revival**. Meaning revival will come in paths other than the pricking of hearts as God leads men to repentance and being born again of the water and of the Spirit.

And such revival is powerless. Such revival is false revival. It is externally physical and superficially shallow revival that is powerless to convert a soul.

Both the Spirit of God and the spirit of godly men view this depth of revival as fake revival. It is a conscience-soothing deceptive substitute, empty of life-changing power. It is a new path, appalling to a true born-again Christian. At the very best; it is **Great Massive Unprecedented End-Time PSEUDO Revival.**

*³For **the time will come** when they will not endure sound doctrine; but after their own lusts shall they heap to themselves teachers, having itching ears;*
⁴And they shall turn away their ears from the truth, and shall be turned unto fables.
2 Timothy 4:3-4

Paul seems to declare: The so called "End-time revival" of unprecedented numbers of multitudes expected by some will exist without Truth or Sound Doctrine.

...but after their own lusts shall they heap to themselves teachers

"Heap." Greek word Episōreúō - meaning – (to accumulate further, or seek additionally.)

In the "last days" the "religious society" will "Accumulate/Heap" and seek to add teachers to their religion.

The teachers whom they will seek and add to their religion will appease and justify *their own lusts.*

And then they will be satisfied with what they hear with ears that itch for something other than Wholesome Truth within the Apostolic Doctrine.

And they continued stedfastly in the apostles' doctrine and fellowship, and in breaking of bread, and in prayers.
Acts 2:42

Albeit technically, there may be a "Great Massive Unprecedented End-Time Revival in The Last Days" that numerically exceeds any revival period in History. But it appears per scripture to be a powerless revival taught by teachers of religion who have been "Accumulated/Heaped" and are willing to justify acts of carnal lusts while avoiding the converting Power of Truth.

Such pseudo revival WILL NOT come forth from "continuing steadfastly in the Apostle's Doctrine."

This pseudo revival will be driven by a diabolic spirit of deception, causing those without the Power of Truth to "FEEL SAVED" in their transgressions. And the **Decibel Doctrine** is the perfect man-made covering for such a mutation of Biblical Revival.

I have witnessed, you have witnessed, we all have witnessed, and God has witnessed the false approval that humans feel when overwhelmed with the power of rock concert volumes of "New Age Worship Music." They mistake the physiological ecstasy they feel to be God condoning their lifestyle without repentance. And the teachers of the **Decibel Doctrine** who have been "Accumulated/Heaped" and added to religion encourage the carnal to accept the VICTORY dance as God's forgiveness and approval of their lifestyle. (a manifestation described in the article *Saved From The African Siguco*)

The **Decibel Doctrine** and its "Accumulated/Heaped" teachers are dangerously deceptive. The **Decibel Doctrine** is a lure that attracts the simple-minded man who trusts anything that any Teacher Teaches or any Preacher Preaches, even without Biblical validation. The volume of music presented by the **Decibel Doctrine** appeases (and damages) itching ears, while the electronically-induced power of the ever-throbbing beat, beats-lively-life into the church attender in our day.

But the power of that lively-life is without power from above, and ebbs away at the flipping of a switch to the off position. This manner of "reviving" irrevocably edifies Paul's prophecy and warning concerning the fallacy of "**Great Massive Unprecedented End-Time Revival in The Last Days.**"

However, there is a new emerging sign that follows *Not-Right* Worship, and it could be the precursor to "**Great Massive Unprecedented End-Time Revival in The Last Days.**"

There has recently been a NEWER New-Age trend birthed in churches. This NEWER New-Age trend is to greet everyone as they enter the Sanctuary with these words: "**Welcome to the Party**."

This greeting is of course more exciting to the flesh than "Praise the Lord" or "God Bless You" or "Welcome to the House of the Lord," and most certainly satisfies the flesh of itching ears more so than words of the Psalmist:

> *O come, let us worship and bow down: let us kneel before the LORD our maker...*
> **Psalm 95:6**

Peter repeated the foundational formula to revival as he was taught by his Lord Jesus:

> *Then Peter said unto them, Repent, and be baptized every one of you in the name of Jesus Christ for the remission of sins, and ye shall receive the gift of the Holy Ghost.*
> **Acts 2:38**

But this Acts 2:38 doctrine is too demanding and oppressive on the flesh to compete with the carnal words: "**Welcome to the Party**."

"**Welcome to the Party**" is much more pleasing to itching ears than morbid self-sacrificing words like "*I die daily*" as Apostle Paul wrote of himself.

The enticing words - "**Welcome to the Party**" - **attracts a different crowd** than these words of Jesus:

"…If any man will come after me, let him deny himself, and take up his cross daily, and follow me."

Luke 9:23

The words - "**Welcome to the Party**" - are words of promise to the visitor, Boy Scout honor promise to the visitor, a sworn hand-on-the-Bible promise to the visitor, that the sanctuary into which he is entering is *void of altars,* and there is plenty of room to respond to the beat of the music. And everybody knows that *"Party Music"* is excessively loud and hypnotic and motion-demanding.

The inference intended by the words; "**Welcome to the Party**"[6] is unshaded instruction to pay homage to the creation rather than the Creator, and then call it Biblical Worship.

So, in a party atmosphere, the lukewarm and transgressor "worship" with the saints until all are wet with sweat. And they anxiously return again next week with itching ears because they want to be a part of the Party that produces **Great Massive Unprecedented End-Time Revival in The Last Days.**

Come to think of it, the WHOLE WORLD likes to party.

The WHOLE WORLD is a massive number of people. And the invitation to PARTY may very well be the key to **"Great Massive Unprecedented End-Time Revival"** as promised by Decibel Disciples.

I presume that if the "whole world" enters the Sanctuary for Party Time, and the **Decibel Doctrine** saves them in-their-sins, some ministries will declare it: "**Great Massive Unprecedented End-Time Revival in The Last Days.**"

IN TIME - This attractive man-made religion will fit nicely into the ONE WORLD ORDER, better than a missing piece to a puzzle.

The "ORDER" of the ONE WORLD RELIGION:

"Religious Practices that *glorify the One called JESUS! Is No Longer Allowed.*"

So, New-Age Party Churches and their unmatched numbers will continue to fit-in nicely until the end.

And God weeps … for now.

But in the midst of it all, my God is still Worthy of Worth.

David Clark
March 23, 2018

---

[6] The Party Church Theme Song – *We Like to Party* by Krazy Frog.
https://www.youtube.com/watch?v=5QjlVZgVDTQ

Just Thinking

Just Thinking

Grimace Upon My Face

The Catastrophic Clash

The Decibel Doctrine Finds Place

Inside The Pearly Gates

Twenty years of experiencing and conveying siren warnings about **The Decibel Doctrine** has been heavily sobering to my person. I am beginning to feel the weight lifting.

So now, I shall sign off with humor, David Clark style.

Gabriel was seen permanently planting this sign in front of the Pearly Gates as a deterrent to Lovers of The Decibel Doctrine.

To Order Additional Copies of David's books:

THE MUSIC OF THE GOLDEN CALVES by Murray E Burr

DECIBEL DOCTRINE

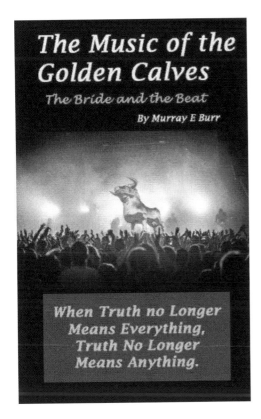

EMAIL him at:

Decibeldoctrine@gmail.com

Or write him at:

Decibel Doctrine
P. O. Box 374
Hillister, TX 77624

Books are also available on amazon.com

Made in the USA
Columbia, SC
24 July 2024

39240096R00152